I0015446

Learning Embedded Linux Using the Yocto Project

Develop powerful embedded Linux systems with the Yocto Project components

Alexandru Vaduva

[PACKT] open source
PUBLISHING
community experience distilled

BIRMINGHAM - MUMBAI

Learning Embedded Linux Using the Yocto Project

First published: June 2015

Production reference: 1240615

Published by Packt Publishing Ltd.
Livery Place
35 Livery Street
Birmingham B3 2PB, UK.

ISBN 978-1-78439-739-5

www.packtpub.com

Credits

Author
Alexandru Vaduva

Reviewers
Peter Ducai
Alex Tereschenko

Commissioning Editor
Nadeem N. Bagban

Acquisition Editor
Harsha Bharwani

Content Development Editor
Vaibhav Pawar

Technical Editor
Shivani Kiran Mistry

Copy Editor
Sonia Michelle Cheema

Project Coordinator
Nidhi J. Joshi

Proofreader
Safis Editing

Indexer
Mariammal Chettiyar

Graphics
Sheetal Aute
Disha Haria
Jason Monteiro
Abhinash Sahu

Production Coordinator
Conidon Miranda

Cover Work
Conidon Miranda

About the Author

Alexandru Vaduva is an embedded Linux software engineer whoes main focus lies in the field of open source software. He has an inquiring mind and also believes that actions speak louder than words. He is a strong supporter of the idea that there is no need to reinvent the wheel, but there is always room for improvement. He has knowledge of C, Yocto, Linux, Bash, and Python, but he is also open to trying new things and testing new technologies.

Alexandru Vaduva has been a reviewer of the book *Embedded Linux Development with Yocto Project, Packt Publishing*, which is a great asset to the Yocto Project community.

About the Reviewer

Peter Ducai has 15 years of experience in the IT industry, including the fields of programming and OS administration. Currently, he works at HP as an automation engineer.

Alex Tereschenko is an avid Maker. He believes that computers can do a lot of good when they are interfaced with real-world objects (as opposed to just crunching data in a dusty corner). This drives him in his projects and is also the reason why embedded systems and the Internet of Things are the topics he enjoys the most.

www.PacktPub.com

Support files, eBooks, discount offers, and more

For support files and downloads related to your book, please visit www.PacktPub.com.

Did you know that Packt offers eBook versions of every book published, with PDF and ePub files available? You can upgrade to the eBook version at www.PacktPub.com and as a print book customer, you are entitled to a discount on the eBook copy. Get in touch with us at service@packtpub.com for more details.

At www.PacktPub.com, you can also read a collection of free technical articles, sign up for a range of free newsletters and receive exclusive discounts and offers on Packt books and eBooks.

PACKT™

https://www2.packtpub.com/books/subscription/packtlib

Do you need instant solutions to your IT questions? PacktLib is Packt's online digital book library. Here, you can search, access, and read Packt's entire library of books.

Why subscribe?

- Fully searchable across every book published by Packt
- Copy and paste, print, and bookmark content
- On demand and accessible via a web browser

Free access for Packt account holders

If you have an account with Packt at www.PacktPub.com, you can use this to access PacktLib today and view 9 entirely free books. Simply use your login credentials for immediate access.

Table of Contents

Preface

With regard to the Linux environment today, most of the topics explained in this book are already available and are covered in a fair bit of detail, This book also covers a large variety of information and help in creating many viewpoints. Of course, there are some very good books written on various subjects also presented in this book, and here, you will find references to them. The scope of this book, however, is not to present this information all over again, but instead to make a parallel between the traditional methods of interaction with the embedded development process and the methods used by the Yocto Project.

This book also presents the various challenges that you might encounter in embedded Linux and suggests solutions for them. Although this book is intended for developers who are pretty confident of their basic Yocto and Linux skills and are trying to improve them, I am confident that that those of you who have no real experience in this area, could also find some useful information here.

This book has been built around various big subjects, which you will encounter in your embedded Linux journey. Besides this, technical information and a number of exercises are also given to you to ensure that as much information as possible is passed on to you. At the end of this book, you should have a clear picture of the Linux ecosystem.

What this book covers

Chapter 1, Introduction, tries to offer a picture of how an embedded Linux software and hardware architecture looks. It also presents you information on the benefits of Linux and Yocto along with examples. It explains the architecture of the Yocto Project and how it is integrated inside the Linux environment.

Chapter 2, Cross-compiling, offers you the definition of a toolchain, its components, and the way in which it can be obtained. After this, information on the Poky repository is given to you and a comparison is made with the components.

Chapter 3, Bootloaders, gives you information on a boot sequence, U-Boot bootloader, and how it can be built for a specific board. After this, it gives access to the U-Boot recipe from Poky and shows how it is used.

Chapter 4, Linux Kernel, explains the features of the Linux kernel and source code. It gives you information on how to build a kernel source and modules and then moves on to explain the recipes of the Yocto kernel and presents how the same things happen there after that the kernel is booted.

Chapter 5, The Linux Root Filesystem, gives you information on the organization of root file system directories and device drivers. It explains the various filesystems, BusyBox, and what a minimal filesystem should contain. It will show you how BusyBox is compiled inside and outside the Yocto Project and how a root filesystem is obtained using Poky.

Chapter 6, Components of the Yocto Project, offers an overview of the available components of the Yocto Project, most of which are outside Poky. It provides an introduction and a brief presentation of each component. After this chapter, a bunch of these components are explained in more detail.

Chapter 7, ADT Eclipse Plug-ins, shows how to set up the Yocto Project Eclipse IDE, setting it up for cross development and debugging using Qemu, and customizing an image and interacting with different tools.

Chapter 8, Hob, Toaster, and Autobuilder, goes through each one of these tools and explain how each one of them can be used, mentioning their benefits as well.

Chapter 9, Wic and Other Tools, explains how to use another set of tools, very different form the ones mentioned in the previous chapter.

Chapter 10, Real-time, shows the real-time layers of the Yocto Project, their purposes, and added value. Documented information on Preempt-RT, NoHz, userspace RTOS, benchmarking, and other real-time related features are also mentioned.

Chapter 11, Security, explains the Yocto Project's security-related layers, their purposes, and the ways in which they could add value to Poky. Here, you will also be given information about SELinux and other applications, such as bastille, buck-security, nmap and so on.

Chapter 12, Virtualization, explains the virtualization layers of the Yocto Project, their purposes and the ways in which they could add value to Poky. You will also be given information about virtualization-related packages and initiatives.

Chapter 13, CGL and LSB, gives you information on the Carrier Graded Linux (CGL) specifications and requirements as well as the specifications, requirements, and tests of Linux Standard Base (LSB). In the end, a parallel will be made with the support provided by the Yocto Project.

What you need for this book

Before reading this book, prior knowledge of embedded Linux and Yocto would be helpful, though not mandatory. In this book, a number of exercises are available, and to do them, a basic understanding of the GNU/Linux environment would be useful. Also, some of the exercises are for a specific development board and others involve using Qemu. Owning such a board and previous knowledge of Qemu is a plus, but is not mandatory.

Throughout the book, there are chapters with various exercises that require you to already have knowledge of C language, Python, and Shell Script. It would be useful if the reader has experience in these areas, because they are the core technologies used in most Linux projects available today. I hope this information does not discourage you while reading the content of this book content, and that you enjoy it.

Who this book is for

The book is targeted at Yocto and Linux enthusiasts who want to build embedded Linux systems and maybe contribute to the community. Background knowledge should include C programming skills, experience with Linux as a development platform, basic understanding of the software development process. If you've previously read *Embedded Linux Development with Yocto Project, Packt Publishing*, it would be a plus as well.

Taking a look at technology trends, Linux is the next big thing. It offers access to cutting-edge open source products and more embedded systems are introduced to mankind every day. The Yocto Project is the best choice for any project that involves interaction with embedded devices due to the fact that it provides a rich set of tools to help you to use most of your energy and resources in your product development, instead of reinventing.

Conventions

In this book, you will find a number of text styles that distinguish between different kinds of information. Here are some examples of these styles and an explanation of their meaning.

Code words in text, database table names, folder names, filenames, file extensions, pathnames, dummy URLs, user input, and Twitter handles are shown as follows: "A `maintainers` file offers a list of contributors to a particular board support."

A block of code is set as follows:

```
sudo add-apt-repository "deb http://archive.ubuntu.com/ubuntu $(lsb_
release -sc) universe"
sudo apt-get update
sudo add-apt-repository "deb http://people.linaro.org/~neil.williams/
lava jessie main"
sudo apt-get update

sudo apt-get install postgresql
sudo apt-get install lava
sudo a2dissite 000-default
sudo a2ensite lava-server.conf
sudo service apache2 restart
```

When we wish to draw your attention to a particular part of a code block, the relevant lines or items are set in bold:

```
sudo add-apt-repository "deb http://archive.ubuntu.com/ubuntu $(lsb_
release -sc) universe"
sudo apt-get update
sudo add-apt-repository "deb http://people.linaro.org/~neil.williams/
lava jessie main"
sudo apt-get update

sudo apt-get install postgresql
sudo apt-get install lava
sudo a2dissite 000-default
sudo a2ensite lava-server.conf
sudo service apache2 restart
```

Any command-line input or output is written as follows:

```
DISTRIB_ID=Ubuntu
DISTRIB_RELEASE=14.04
DISTRIB_CODENAME=trusty
DISTRIB_DESCRIPTION="Ubuntu 14.04.1 LTS"
```

New terms and **important words** are shown in bold. Words that you see on the screen, for example, in menus or dialog boxes, appear in the text like this: " If this warning message appears, press **OK** and move further "

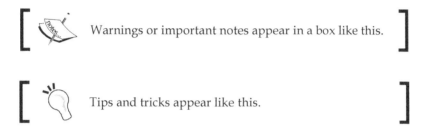

> Warnings or important notes appear in a box like this.

> Tips and tricks appear like this.

Reader feedback

Feedback from our readers is always welcome. Let us know what you think about this book—what you liked or disliked. Reader feedback is important for us as it helps us develop titles that you will really get the most out of.

To send us general feedback, simply e-mail `feedback@packtpub.com`, and mention the book's title in the subject of your message.

If there is a topic that you have expertise in and you are interested in either writing or contributing to a book, see our author guide at `www.packtpub.com/authors`.

Customer support

Now that you are the proud owner of a Packt book, we have a number of things to help you to get the most from your purchase.

Errata

Although we have taken every care to ensure the accuracy of our content, mistakes do happen. If you find a mistake in one of our books—maybe a mistake in the text or the code—we would be grateful if you could report this to us. By doing so, you can save other readers from frustration and help us improve subsequent versions of this book. If you find any errata, please report them by visiting `http://www.packtpub.com/submit-errata`, selecting your book, clicking on the **Errata Submission Form** link, and entering the details of your errata. Once your errata are verified, your submission will be accepted and the errata will be uploaded to our website or added to any list of existing errata under the Errata section of that title.

To view the previously submitted errata, go to `https://www.packtpub.com/books/content/support` and enter the name of the book in the search field. The required information will appear under the **Errata** section.

Piracy

Piracy of copyrighted material on the Internet is an ongoing problem across all media. At Packt, we take the protection of our copyright and licenses very seriously. If you come across any illegal copies of our works in any form on the Internet, please provide us with the location address or website name immediately so that we can pursue a remedy.

Please contact us at `copyright@packtpub.com` with a link to the suspected pirated material.

We appreciate your help in protecting our authors and our ability to bring you valuable content.

Questions

If you have a problem with any aspect of this book, you can contact us at `questions@packtpub.com`, and we will do our best to address the problem.

1
Introduction

In this chapter, you will be presented with the advantages of Linux and open source development. There will be examples of systems running embedded Linux, which a vast number of embedded hardware platforms support. After this, you will be introduced to the architecture and development environment of an embedded Linux system, and, in the end, the Yocto Project, where its Poky build system's properties and purposes are summarized.

Advantages of Linux and open source systems

Most of the information available in this book, and the examples presented as exercises, have one thing in common: the fact that they are freely available for anyone to access. This book tries to offer guidance to you on how to interact with existing and freely available packages that could help an embedded engineer, such as you, and at the same time, also try to arouse your curiosity to learn more.

> More information on open source can be gathered from the **Open Source Initiative (OSI)** at `http://opensource.org/`.

The main advantage of open source is represented by the fact that it permits developers to concentrate more on their products and their added value. Having an open source product offers access to a variety of new possibilities and opportunities, such as reduced costs of licensing, increased skills, and knowledge of a company. The fact that a company uses an open source product that most people have access to, and can understand its working, implies budget savings. The money saved could be used in other departments, such as hardware or acquisitions.

Usually, there is a misconception about open source having little or no control over a product. However, the opposite is true. The open source system, in general, offers full control over software, and we are going to demonstrate this. For any software, your open source project resides on a repository that offers access for everyone to see. Since you're the person in charge of a project, and its administrator as well, you have all the right in the world to accept the contributions of others, which lends them the same right as you, and this basically gives you the freedom to do whatever you like. Of course, there could be someone who is inspired by your project and could do something that is more appreciated by the open source community. However, this is how progress is made, and, to be completely honest, if you are a company, this kind of scenario is almost invalid. Even in this case, this situation does not mean the death of your project, but an opportunity instead. Here, I would like to present the following quote:

> *"If you want to build an open source project, you can't let your ego stand in the way. You can't rewrite everybody's patches, you can't second-guess everybody, and you have to give people equal control."*
>
> *– Rasmus Lerdorf*

Allowing access to others, having external help, modifications, debugging, and optimizations performed on your open source software implies a longer life for the product and better quality achieved over time. At the same time, the open source environment offers access to a variety of components that could easily be integrated in your product if there's a requirement for them. This permits a quick development process, lower costs, and also shifts a great deal of the maintenance and development work from your product. Also, it offers the possibility to support a particular component to make sure that it continues to suit your needs. However, in most instances, you would need to take some time and build this component for your product from zero.

This brings us to the next benefit of open source, which involves testing and quality assurance for our product. Besides the lesser amount of work that is needed for testing, it is also possible to choose from a number of options before deciding which components fits best for our product. Also, it is cheaper to use open source software, than buying and evaluating proprietary products. This takes and gives back process, visible in the open source community, is the one that generates products of a higher quality and more mature ones. This quality is even greater than that of other proprietary or closed source similar products. Of course, this is not a generally valid affirmation and only happens for mature and widely used products, but here appears the term community and foundation into play.

In general, open source software is developed with the help of communities of developers and users. This system offers access to a greater support on interaction with the tools directly from developers - the sort of thing that does not happen when working with closed source tools. Also, there is no restriction when you're looking for an answer to your questions, no matter whether you work for a company or not. Being part of the open source community means more than bug fixing, bug reporting, or feature development. It is about the contribution added by the developers, but, at the same time, it offers the possibility for engineers to get recognition outside their working environment, by facing new challenges and trying out new things. It can also be seen as a great motivational factor and a source of inspiration for everyone involved in the process.

Instead of a conclusion, I would also like to present a quote from the person who forms the core of this process, the man who offered us Linux and kept it open source:

> *"I think, fundamentally, open source does tend to be more stable software. It's the right way to do things."*
>
> *- Linus Torvalds*

Embedded systems

Now that the benefits of open source have been introduced to you, I believe we can go through a number of examples of embedded systems, hardware, software, and their components. For starters, embedded devices are available anywhere around us: take a look at your smartphone, car infotainment system, microwave oven, or even your MP3 player. Of course, not all of them qualify to be Linux operating systems, but they all have embedded components that make it possible for them to fulfill their designed functions.

General description

For Linux to be run on any device hardware, you will require some hardware-dependent components that are able to abstract the work for hardware-independent ones. The boot loader, kernel, and toolchain contain hardware-dependent components that make the performance of work easier for all the other components. For example, a BusyBox developer will only concentrate on developing the required functionalities for his application, and will not concentrate on hardware compatibility. All these hardware-dependent components offer support for a large variety of hardware architectures for both 32 and 64 bits. For example, the U-Boot implementation is the easiest to take as an example when it comes to source code inspection. From this, we can easily visualize how support for a new device can be added.

We will now try to do some of the little exercises presented previously, but before moving further, I must present the computer configuration on which I will continue to do the exercises, to make sure that that you face as few problems as possible. I am working on an Ubuntu 14.04 and have downloaded the 64-bit image available on the Ubuntu website at `http://www.ubuntu.com/download/desktop`

Information relevant to the Linux operation running on your computer can be gathered using this command:

```
uname -srmpio
```

The preceding command generates this output:

```
Linux 3.13.0-36-generic x86_64 x86_64 x86_64 GNU/Linux
```

The next command to gather the information relevant to the Linux operation is as follows:

```
cat /etc/lsb-release
```

The preceding command generates this output:

```
DISTRIB_ID=Ubuntu
DISTRIB_RELEASE=14.04
DISTRIB_CODENAME=trusty
DISTRIB_DESCRIPTION="Ubuntu 14.04.1 LTS"
```

Examples

Now, moving on to exercises, the first one requires you fetch the `git` repository sources for the U-Boot package:

```
sudo apt-get install git-core
git clone http://git.denx.de/u-boot.git
```

After the sources are available on your machine, you can try to take a look inside the `board` directory; here, a number of development board manufacturers will be present. Let's take a look at `board/atmel/sama5d3_xplained`, `board/faraday/a320evb`, `board/freescale/imx`, and `board/freescale/b4860qds`. By observing each of these directories, a pattern can be visualized. Almost all of the boards contain a `Kconfig` file, inspired mainly from kernel sources because they present the configuration dependencies in a clearer manner. A `maintainers` file offers a list with the contributors to a particular board support. The base `Makefile` file takes from the higher-level makefiles the necessary object files, which are obtained after a board-specific support is built. The difference is with `board/freescale/imx` which only offers a list of configuration data that will be later used by the high-level makefiles.

At the kernel level, the hardware-dependent support is added inside the `arch` file. Here, for each specific architecture besides `Makefile` and `Kconfig`, various numbers of subdirectories could also be added. These offer support for different aspects of a kernel, such as the boot, kernel, memory management, or specific applications.

By cloning the kernel sources, the preceding information can be easily visualized by using this code:

```
git clone https://git.kernel.org/pub/scm/linux/kernel/git/torvalds/linux.
git
```

Some of the directories that can be visualized are `arch/arc` and `arch/metag`.

From the toolchain point of view, the hardware-dependent component is represented by the GNU C Library, which is, in turn, usually represented by `glibc`. This provides the system call interface that connects to the kernel architecture-dependent code and further provides the communication mechanism between these two entities to user applications. System calls are presented inside the `sysdeps` directory of the `glibc` sources if the `glibc` sources are cloned, as follows:

```
git clone http://sourceware.org/git/glibc.git
```

The preceding information can be verified using two methods: the first one involves opening the `sysdeps/arm` directory, for example, or by reading the `ChangeLog.old-ports-arm` library. Although it's old and has nonexistent links, such as ports directory, which disappeared from the newer versions of the repository, the latter can still be used as a reference point.

These packages are also very easily accessible using the Yocto Project's `poky` repository. As mentioned at `https://www.yoctoproject.org/about`:

> "*The Yocto Project is an open source collaboration project that provides templates, tools and methods to help you create custom Linux-based systems for embedded products regardless of the hardware architecture. It was founded in 2010 as a collaboration among many hardware manufacturers, open-source operating systems vendors, and electronics companies to bring some order to the chaos of embedded Linux development.*"

Most of the interaction anyone has with the Yocto Project is done through the Poky build system, which is one of its core components that offers the features and functionalities needed to generate fully customizable Linux software stacks. The first step needed to ensure interaction with the repository sources would be to clone them:

```
git clone -b dizzy http://git.yoctoproject.org/git/poky
```

After the sources are present on your computer, a set of recipes and configuration files need to be inspected. The first location that can be inspected is the U-Boot recipe, available at `meta/recipes-bsp/u-boot/u-boot_2013.07.bb`. It contains the instructions necessary to build the U-Boot package for the corresponding selected machine. The next place to inspect is in the recipes available in the kernel. Here, the work is sparse and more package versions are available. It also provides some `bbappends` for available recipes, such as meta`/recipes-kernel/linux/linux-yocto_3.14.bb` and `meta-yocto-bsp/recipes-kernel/linux/linux-yocto_3.10.bbappend`. This constitutes a good example for one of the kernel package versions available when starting a new build using BitBake.

Toolchain construction is a big and important step for host generated packages. To do this, a set of packages are necessary, such as `gcc`, `binutils`, `glibc library`, and `kernel headers`, which play an important role. The recipes corresponding to this package are available inside the `meta/recipes-devtools/gcc/`, `meta/recipes-devtools/binutils`, and `meta/recipes-core/glibc` paths. In all the available locations, a multitude of recipes can be found, each one with a specific purpose. This information will be detailed in the next chapter.

The configurations and options for the selection of one package version in favor of another is mainly added inside the machine configuration. One such example is the Freescale `MPC8315E-rdb` low-power model supported by Yocto 1.6, and its machine configuration is available inside the `meta-yocto-bsp/conf/machine/mpc8315e-rdb.conf` file.

> More information on this development board can be found at `http://www.freescale.com/webapp/sps/site/prod_summary.jsp?code=MPC8315E`.

Introducing GNU/Linux

GNU/Linux, or Linux as it's commonly known, represents a name that has a long line of tradition behind it, and is one of the most important unions of open source software. Shortly, you will be introduced to the history of what is offered to people around the world today and the choice available in terms of selecting personal computer operating systems. Most of all, we will look at what is offered to hardware developers and the common ground available for the development of platforms.

GNU/Linux consists of the Linux kernel and has a collection of user space applications that are put on top of GNU C Library; this acts as a computer operating system. It may be considered as one of the most prolific instances of open source and free software available, which is still in development. Its history started in 1983 when Richard Stallman founded the GNU Project with the goal of developing a complete Unix-like operating system, which could be put together only from free software. By the beginning of the 1990s, GNU already offered a collection of libraries, Unix-like shells, compilers, and text editors. However, it lacked a kernel. They started developing their own kernel, the Hurd, in 1990. The kernel was based on a Mach micro-kernel design, but it proved to be difficult to work with and had a slow development process.

Meanwhile, in 1991, a Finnish student started working on another kernel as a hobby while attending the University of Helsinki. He also got help from various programmers who contributed to the cause over the Internet. That student's name was Linus Torvalds and, in 1992, his kernel was combined with the GNU system. The result was a fully functional operating system called GNU/Linux that was free and open source. The most common form of the GNU system is usually referred to as a *GNU/Linux system*, or even a *Linux distribution*, and is the most popular variant of GNU. Today, there are a great number of distributions based on GNU and the Linux kernel, and the most widely used ones are: Debian, Ubuntu, Red Hat Linux, SuSE, Gentoo, Mandriva, and Slackware. This image shows us how the two components of Linux work together:

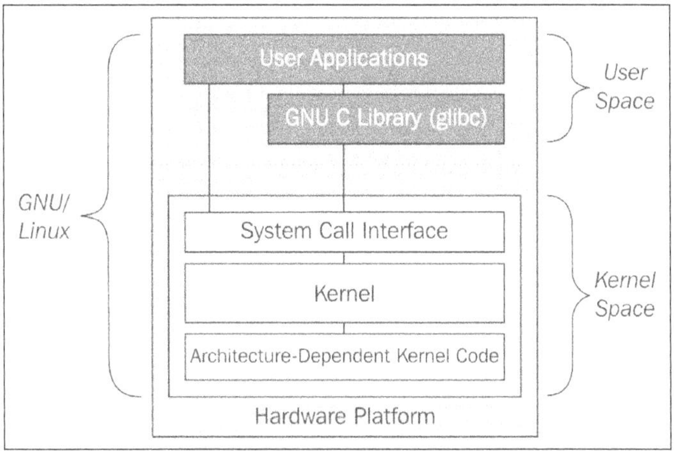

Although not originally envisioned to run on anything else then x86 PCs, today, the Linux operating system is the most widespread and portable operating system. It can be found on both embedded devices or supercomputers because it offers freedom to its users and developers. Having tools to generate customizable Linux systems is another huge step forward in the development of this tool. It offers access to the GNU/Linux ecosystem to new categories of people who, by using a tool, such as BitBake, end up learning more about Linux, its architecture differences, root filesystem construction and configuration, toolchains, and many other things present in the Linux world.

Linux is not designed to work on microcontrollers. It will not work properly if it has less then 32 MB of RAM, and it will need to have at least 4 MB of storage space. However, if you take a look at this requirement, you will notice that it is very permissive. Adding to this is the fact that it also offers support for a variety of communication peripherals and hardware platforms, which gives you a clear image of why it is so widely adopted.

> Well, it may work on 8MB of RAM, but that depends on the application's size as well.

Working with a Linux architecture in an embedded environment requires certain standards. This is an image that represents graphically an environment which was made available on one of free-electrons Linux courses:

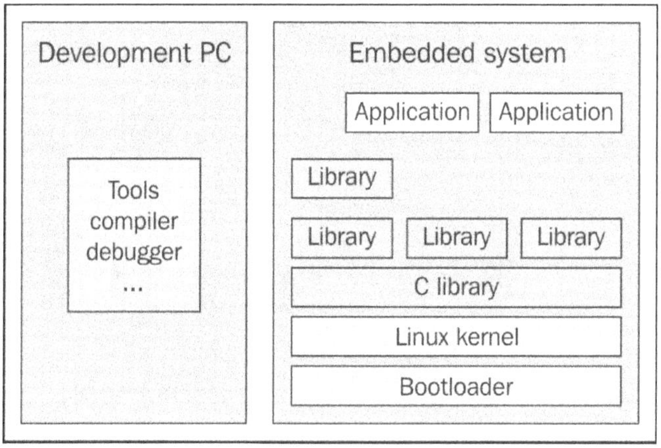

The preceding image presents the two main components that are involved in the development process when working with Linux in the embedded devices world:

- **Host machine**: This is the machine where all the development tools reside. Outside the Yocto world, these tools are represented by a corresponding toolchain cross-compiled for a specific target and its necessary applications sources and patches. However, for an Yocto user, all these packages, and the preparation work involved, is reduced to automatized tasks executed before the actual work is performed. This, of course, has to be prioritized adequately.
- **Target machine**: This is the embedded system on which the work is done and tested. All the software available on the target is usually cross-compiled on the host machine, which is a more powerful and more efficient environment. The components that are usually necessary for an embedded device to boot Linux and operate various application, involve using a bootloader for basic initiation and loading of the Linux kernel. This, in turn, initializes drivers and the memory, and offers services for applications to interact with through the functions of the available C libraries.

> There are also other methods of working with embedded devices, such as cross-canadian and native development, but the ones presented here are the most used and offer the best results for both developers and companies when it comes to software development for embedded devices.

To have a functional Linux operating system on an development board, a developer first needs to make sure that the kernel, bootloader, and board corresponding drives are working properly before starting to develop and integrate other applications and libraries.

Introduction to the Yocto Project

In the previous section, the benefits of having an open source environment were presented. Taking a look at how embedded development was done before the advent of the Yocto Project offers a complete picture of the benefits of this project. It also gives an answer as to why it was adopted so quickly and in such huge numbers.

Using the Yocto Project, the whole process gets a bit more automatic, mostly because the workflow permitted this. Doing things manually requires a number of steps to be taken by developers:

1. Select and download the necessary packages and components.
2. Configure the downloaded packages.
3. Compile the configured packages.
4. Install the generated binary, libraries, and so on, on `rootfs` available on development machine.
5. Generate the final deployable format.

All these steps tend to become more complex with the increase in the number of software packages that need to be introduced in the final deployable state. Taking this into consideration, it can clearly be stated that manual work is suitable only for a small number of components; automation tools are usually preferred for large and complex systems.

In the last ten years, a number of automation tools could be used to generate an embedded Linux distribution. All of them were based on the same strategy as the one described previously, but they also needed some extra information to solve dependency related problems. These tools are all built around an engine for the execution of tasks and contain metadata that describes actions, dependencies, exceptions, and rules.

The most notable solutions are Buildroot, Linux Target Image Builder (LTIB), Scratchbox, OpenEmbedded, Yocto, and Angstrom. However, Scratchbox doesn't seem to be active anymore, with the last commit being done in April 2012. LTIB was the preferred build tool for Freescale and it has lately moved more toward Yocto; in a short span of time, LTIB may become deprecated also.

Buildroot

Buildroot as a tool tries to simplify the ways in which a Linux system is generated using a cross-compiler. Buildroot is able to generate a bootloader, kernel image, root filesystem, and even a cross-compiler. It can generate each one of these components, although in an independent way, and because of this, its main usage has been restricted to a cross-compiled toolchain that generates a corresponding and custom root filesystem. It is mainly used in embedded devices and very rarely for x86 architectures; its main focus being architectures, such as ARM, PowerPC, or MIPS. As with every tool presented in this book, it is designed to run on Linux, and certain packages are expected to be present on the host system for their proper usage. There are a couple of mandatory packages and some optional ones as well.

There is a list of mandatory packages that contain the certain packages, and are described inside the Buildroot manual available at `http://buildroot.org/downloads/manual/manual.html`. These packages are as follows:

- `which`
- `sed`
- `make` (version 3.81 or any later ones)
- `binutils`
- `build-essential` (required for Debian-based systems only)
- `gcc` (version 2.95 or any later ones)
- `g++` (version 2.95 or any later ones)
- `bash`
- `patch`
- `gzip`
- `bzip2`
- `perl`(version 5.8.7 or any later ones)
- `tar`
- `cpio`
- `python`(version 2.6 or 2.7 ones)
- `unzip`
- `rsync`
- `wget`

Beside these mandatory packages, there are also a number of optional packages. They are very useful for the following:

- **Source fetching tools**: In an official tree, most of the package retrieval is done using `wget` from `http`, `https`, or even `ftp` links, but there are also a couple of links that need a version control system or another type of tool. To make sure that the user does not have a limitation to fetch a package, these tools can be used:
    - `bazaar`
    - `cvs`
    - `git`
    - `mercurial`
    - `rsync`

  - `scp`
  - `subversion`

- **Interface configuration dependencies**: They are represented by the packages that are needed to ensure that the tasks, such as kernel, BusyBox, and U-Boot configuration, are executed without problems:
  - `ncurses5` is used for the menuconfig interface
  - `qt4` is used for the `xconfig` interface
  - `glib2`, `gtk2`, and `glade2` are used for the `gconfig` interface
- **Java related package interaction**: This is used to make sure that when a user wants to interact with the Java Classpath component, that it will be done without any hiccups:
  - `javac`: this refers to the Java compiler
  - `jar`: This refers to the Java archive tool
- **Graph generation tools**: The following are the graph generation tools:
  - `graphviz` to use `graph-depends` and `<pkg>-graph-depends`
  - `python-matplotlib` to use `graph-build`
- **Documentation generation tools**: The following are the tools necessary for the documentation generation process:
  - `asciidoc`, version 8.6.3 or higher
  - `w3m`
  - `python` with the `argparse` module (which is automatically available in 2.7+ and 3.2+ versions)
  - `dblatex` (necessary for pdf manual generation only)

Buildroot releases are made available to the open source community at `http://buildroot.org/downloads/` every three months, specifically in February, May, August, and November, and the release name has the `buildroot-yyyy-mm` format. For people interested in giving Buildroot a try, the manual described in the previous section should be the starting point for installing and configuration. Developers interested in taking a look at the Buildroot source code can refer to `http://git.buildroot.net/buildroot/`.

> Before cloning the Buildroot source code, I suggest taking a quick look at `http://buildroot.org/download`. It could help out anyone who works with a proxy server.

Next, there will be presented a new set of tools that brought their contribution to this field and place on a lower support level the Buildroot project. I believe that a quick review of the strengths and weaknesses of these tools would be required. We will start with Scratchbox and, taking into consideration that it is already deprecated, there is not much to say about it; it's being mentioned purely for historical reasons. Next on the line is LTIB, which constituted the standard for Freescale hardware until the adoption of Yocto. It is well supported by Freescale in terms of **Board Support Packages** (**BSPs**) and contains a large database of components. On the other hand, it is quite old and it was switched with Yocto. It does not contain the support of new distributions, it is not used by many hardware providers, and, in a short period of time, it could very well become as deprecated as Scratchbox. Buildroot is the last of them and is easy to use, having a `Makefile` base format and an active community behind it. However, it is limited to smaller and simpler images or devices, and it is not aware of partial builds or packages.

OpenEmbedded

The next tools to be introduced are very closely related and, in fact, have the same inspiration and common ancestor, the OpenEmbedded project. All three projects are linked by the common engine called Bitbake and are inspired by the Gentoo Portage build tool. OpenEmbedded was first developed in 2001 when the Sharp Corporation launched the ARM-based PDA, and SL-5000 Zaurus, which run Lineo, an embedded Linux distribution. After the introduction of Sharp Zaurus, it did not take long for Chris Larson to initiate the OpenZaurus Project, which was meant to be a replacement for SharpROM, based on Buildroot. After this, people started to contribute many more software packages, and even the support of new devices, and, eventually, the system started to show its limitations. In 2003, discussions were initiated around a new build system that could offer a generic build environment and incorporate the usage models requested by the open source community; this was the system to be used for embedded Linux distributions. These discussions started showing results in 2003, and what has emerged today is the Openembedded project. It had packages ported from OpenZaurus by people, such as Chris Larson, Michael Lauer, and Holger Schurig, according to the capabilities of the new build system.

The Yocto Project is the next evolutionary stage of the same project and has the Poky build system as its core piece, which was created by Richard Purdie. The project started as a stabilized branch of the OpenEmbedded project and only included a subset of the numerous recipes available on OpenEmbedded; it also had a limited set of devices and support of architectures. Over time, it became much more than this: it changed into a software development platform that incorporated a fakeroot replacement, an Eclipse plug-in, and QEMU-based images. Both the Yocto Project and OpenEmbedded now coordinate around a core set of metadata called **OpenEmbedded-Core** (**OE-Core**).

The Yocto Project is sponsored by the Linux Foundation, and offers a starting point for developers of Linux embedded systems who are interested in developing a customized distribution for embedded products in a **hardware-agnostic environment**. The Poky build system represents one of its core components and is also quite complex. At the center of all this lies Bitbake, the engine that powers everything, the tool that processes metadata, downloads corresponding source codes, resolves dependencies, and stores all the necessary libraries and executables inside the build directory accordingly. Poky combines the best from OpenEmbedded with the idea of layering additional software components that could be added or removed from a build environment configuration, depending on the needs of the developer.

Poky is build system that is developed with the idea of keeping simplicity in mind. By default, the configuration for a test build requires very little interaction from the user. Based on the clone made in one of the previous exercises, we can do a new exercise to emphasize this idea:

```
cd poky
source oe-init-build-env ../build-test
bitbake core-image-minimal
```

As shown in this example, it is easy to obtain a Linux image that can be later used for testing inside a QEMU environment. There are a number of images footprints available that will vary from a shell-accessible minimal image to an LSB compliant image with GNOME Mobile user interface support. Of course, that these base images can be imported in new ones for added functionalities. The layered structure that Poky has is a great advantage because it adds the possibility to extend functionalities and to contain the impact of errors. Layers could be used for all sort of functionalities, from adding support for a new hardware platform to extending the support for tools, and from a new software stack to extended image features. The sky is the limit here because almost any recipe can be combined with another.

All this is possible because of the Bitbake engine, which, after the environment setup and the tests for minimal systems requirements are met, based on the configuration files and input received, identifies the interdependencies between tasks, the execution order of tasks, generates a fully functional cross-compilation environment, and starts building the necessary native and target-specific packages tasks exactly as they were defined by the developer. Here is an example with a list of the available tasks for a package:

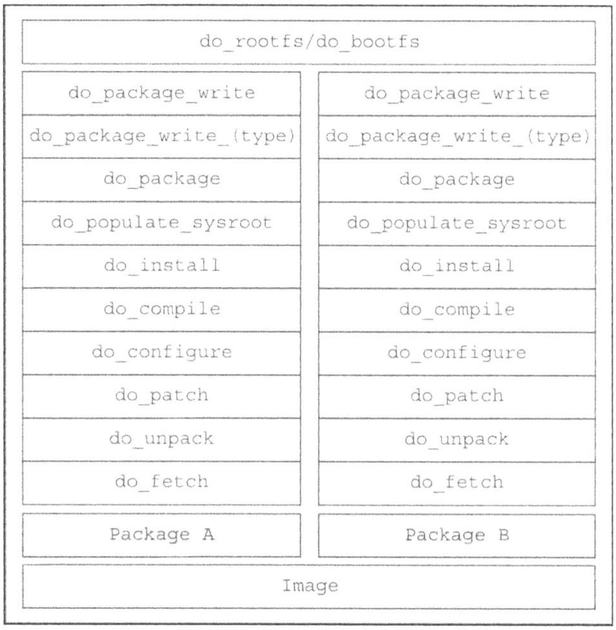

[More information about Bitbake and its baking process can be found in *Embedded Linux Development with Yocto Project*, by Otavio Salvador and Daiane Angolini.]

The metadata modularization is based on two ideas—the first one refers to the possibility of prioritizing the structure of layers, and the second refers to the possibility of not having the need for duplicate work when a recipe needs changes. The layers are overlapping. The most general layer is meta, and all the other layers are usually stacked over it, such as `meta-yocto` with Yocto-specific recipes, machine specific board support packages, and other optional layers, depending on the requirements and needs of developers. The customization of recipes should be done using `bbappend` situated in an upper layer. This method is preferred to ensure that the duplication of recipes does not happen, and it also helps to support newer and older versions of them.

An example of the organization of layers is found in the previous example that specified the list of the available tasks for a package. If a user is interested in identifying the layers used by the `test` build setup in the previous exercise that specified the list of the available tasks for a package, the `bblayers.conf` file is a good source of inspiration. If `cat` is done on this file, the following output will be visible:

```
# LAYER_CONF_VERSION is increased each time
build/conf/bblayers.conf
# changes incompatibly
LCONF_VERSION = "6"

BBPATH = "${TOPDIR}"
BBFILES ?= ""

BBLAYERS ?= " \
  /home/alex/workspace/book/poky/meta \
  /home/alex/workspace/book/poky/meta-yocto \
  /home/alex/workspace/book/poky/meta-yocto-bsp \
  "
BBLAYERS_NON_REMOVABLE ?= " \
  /home/alex/workspace/book/poky/meta \
  /home/alex/workspace/book/poky/meta-yocto \
  "
```

The complete command for doing this is:

cat build-test/conf/bblayers.conf

Here is a visual mode for the layered structure of a more generic build directory:

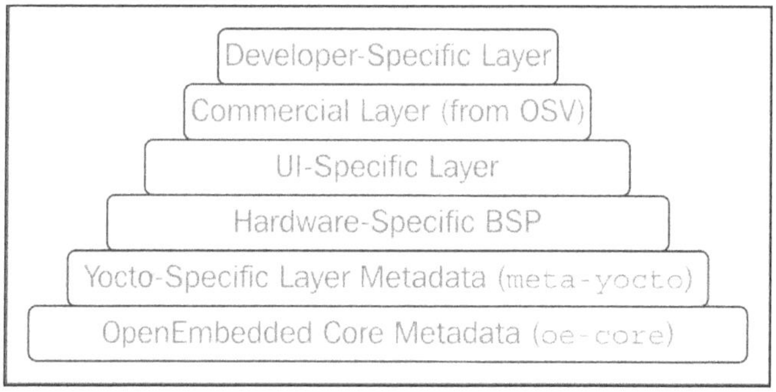

Yocto as a project offers another important feature: the possibility of having an image regenerated in the same way, no matter what factors change on your host machine. This is a very important feature, taking into consideration not only that, in the development process, changes to a number of tools, such as `autotools`, `cross-compiler`, `Makefile`, `perl`, `bison`, `pkgconfig`, and so on, could occur, but also the fact that parameters could change in the interaction process with regards to a repository. Simply cloning one of the repository branches and applying corresponding patches may not solve all the problems. The solution that the Yocto Project has to these problems is quite simple. By defining parameters prior to any of the steps of the installation as variables and configuration parameters inside recipes, and by making sure that the configuration process is also automated, will minimize the risks of manual interaction are minimized. This process makes sure that image generation is always done as it was the first time.

Since the development tools on the host machine are prone to change, Yocto usually compiles the necessary tools for the development process of packages and images, and only after their build process is finished, the Bitbake build engine starts building the requested packages. This isolation from the developer's machine helps the development process by guaranteeing the fact that updates from the host machine do not influence or affect the processes of generating the embedded Linux distribution.

Another critical point that was elegantly solved by the Yocto Project is represented by the way that the toolchain handles the inclusion of headers and libraries; because this could bring later on not only compilation but also execution errors that are very hard to predict. Yocto resolves these problems by moving all the headers and libraries inside the corresponding `sysroots` directory, and by using the `sysroot` option, the build process makes sure that no contamination is done with the native components. An example will emphasize this information better:

```
ls -l build-test/tmp/sysroots/
total 12K
drwxr-xr-x 8 alex alex 4,0K sep 28 04:17 qemux86/
drwxr-xr-x 5 alex alex 4,0K sep 28 00:48 qemux86-tcbootstrap/
drwxr-xr-x 9 alex alex 4,0K sep 28 04:21 x86_64-linux/
```

```
ls -l build-test/tmp/sysroots/qemux86/
total 24K
drwxr-xr-x 2 alex alex 4,0K sep 28 01:52 etc/
drwxr-xr-x 5 alex alex 4,0K sep 28 04:15 lib/
drwxr-xr-x 6 alex alex 4,0K sep 28 03:51 pkgdata/
drwxr-xr-x 2 alex alex 4,0K sep 28 04:17 sysroot-providers/
drwxr-xr-x 7 alex alex 4,0K sep 28 04:16 usr/
drwxr-xr-x 3 alex alex 4,0K sep 28 01:52 var/
```

The Yocto project contributes to making reliable embedded Linux development and because of its dimensions, it is used for lots of things, ranging from board support packages by hardware companies to new software solutions by software development companies. Yocto is not a perfect tool and it has certain drawbacks:

- Requirements for disk space and machine usage are quite high
- Documentation for advanced usage is lacking
- Tools, such as Autobuilder and Eclipse plug-ins, now have functionality problems

There are also other things that bother developers, such as `ptest` integration and SDK sysroot's lack of extensibility, but a part of them are solved by the big community behind the project, and until the project shows its limitations, a new one will still need to wait to take its place. Until this happens, Yocto is the framework to use to develop custom embedded Linux distribution or products based in Linux.

Summary

In this chapter, you were presented with the advantages of open source, and examples of how open source helped the Linux kernel, Yocto Project, OpenEmbedded, and Buildroot for the development and growth of projects, such as LTIB and Scratchbox; the lack of open source contribution meant the deprecation and disappearance of them over time. The information presented to you will be in the form of examples, which will give you a clearer idea of the concepts in this book.

In the next chapter, there will be more information on toolchains and its constituent components. Exercises that give you a better idea of toolchains will be generated using both the manual and automatic approach.

2

Cross-compiling

In this chapter, you will learn about toolchains, how to use and customize them, and how code standards apply to them. A toolchain contains a myriad of tools, such as compilers, linkers, assemblers, debuggers, and a variety of miscellaneous utilities that help to manipulate the resulting application binaries. In this chapter, you will learn how to use the GNU toolchain and become familiar with its features. You will be presented with examples that will involve manual configurations, and at the same time, these examples will be moved to the Yocto Project environment. At the end of the chapter, an analysis will be made to identify the similarities and differences between manual and automatic deployment of a toolchain, and the various usage scenarios available for it.

Introducing toolchains

A toolchain represents a compiler and its associated utilities that are used with the purpose of producing kernels, drivers, and applications necessary for a specific target. A toolchain usually contains a set of tools that are usually linked to each other. It consists of `gcc`, `glibc`, `binutils`, or other optional tools, such as a debugger optional compiler, which is used for specific programming languages, such as C++, Ada, Java, Fortran, or Objective-C.

Usually a toolchain, which is available on a traditional desktop or server, executes on these machines and produces executables and libraries that are available and can run on the same system. A toolchain that is normally used for an embedded development environment is called is a cross toolchain. In this case, programs, such as gcc, run on the host system for a specific target architecture, for which it produces a binary code. This whole process is referred to as cross-compilation, and it is the most common way to build sources for embedded development.

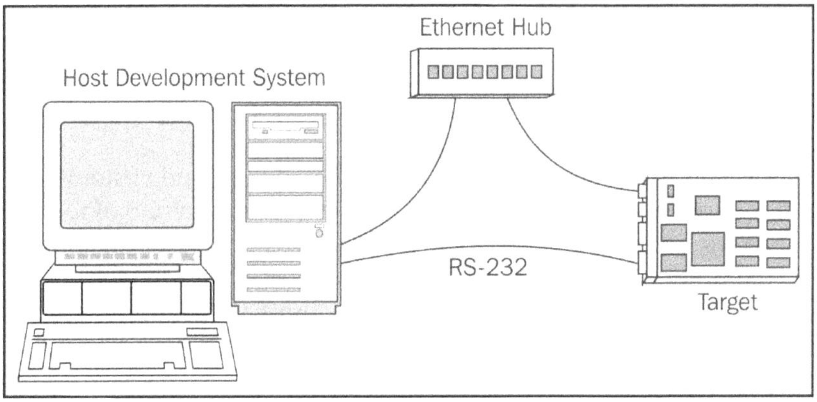

In a toolchain environment, three different machines are available:

- The build machine that represents the machine on which the toolchain was created
- The host machine that represents the machine on which the toolchain is executed
- The target machine that represents the machine that the toolchain produces a binary code for

These three machine are used to generate four different toolchain build procedures:

- **A native toolchain**: This is usually available on a normal Linux distribution or on your normal desktop system. This is usually compiled and run, and generates code for the same architecture.
- **A cross-native toolchain**: This represents a toolchain built on one system, though it runs and produces a binary code for the target system. A normal use case is when a native `gcc` is needed on the target system without building it on the target platform.
- **A cross-compilation toolchain**: This is the most widespread toolchain type used for embedded development. It is compiled and run on an architecture type, usually x86, and produces a binary code for the target architecture.

- **A cross-canadian build**: This represents a process that involves building a toolchain on system A. This toolchain is then run on another system, such as B, which produces a binary code for a third system, called C. This is one of the most underused build processes.

The three machines that generate four different toolchain build procedures is described in the following diagram:

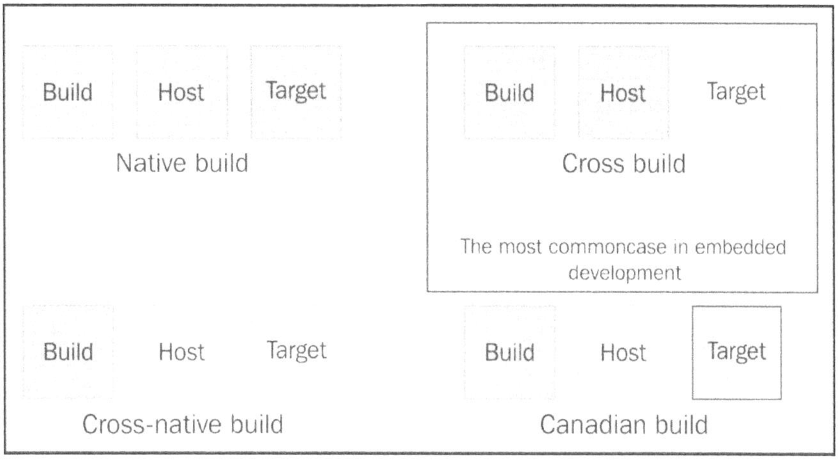

Toolchains represent a list of tools that make the existence of most of great projects available today possible. This includes open source projects as well. This diversity would not have been possible without the existence of a corresponding toolchain. This also happens in the embedded world where newly available hardware needs the components and support of a corresponding toolchain for its **Board Support Package** (**BSP**).

Toolchain configuration is no easy process. Before starting the search for a prebuilt toolchain, or even building one yourself, the best solution would be to check for a target specific BSP; each development platform usually offers one.

Components of toolchains

The GNU toolchain is a term used for a collection of programming tools under the **GNU Project umbrella**. This suite of tools is what is normally called a **toolchain**, and is used for the development of applications and operating systems. It plays an important role in the development of embedded systems and Linux systems, in particular.

The following projects are included in the GNU toolchain:

- **GNU make**: This represents an automation tool used for compilation and build
- **GNU Compiler Collection (GCC)**: This represents a compiler's suite that is used for a number of available programming languages
- **GNU Binutils**: This contains tools, such as linkers, assemblers, and so on - these tools are able to manipulate binaries
- **GNU Bison**: This is a parser generator
- **GNU Debugger (GDB)**: This is a code debugging tool
- **GNU m4**: This is an m4 macro processor
- **GNU build system (autotools)**: This consists of the following:
    - Autoconf
    - Autoheaders
    - Automake
    - Libtool

The projects included in the toolchain is described in the following diagram:

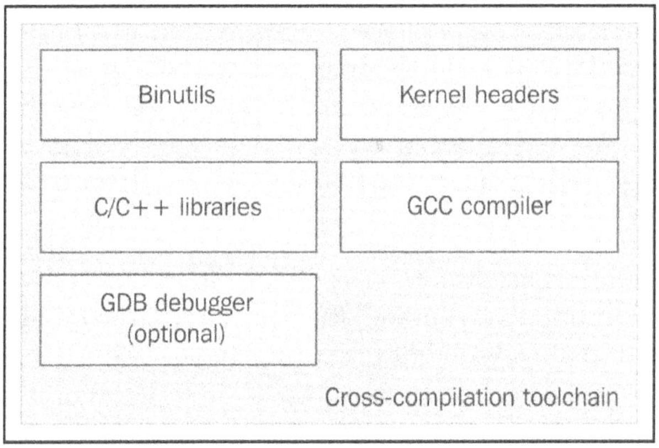

An embedded development environment needs more than a cross-compilation toolchain. It needs libraries and it should target system-specific packages, such as programs, libraries, and utilities, and host specific debuggers, editors, and utilities. In some cases, usually when talking about a company's environment, a number of servers host target devices, and an certain hardware probes are connected to the host through Ethernet or other methods. This emphasizes the fact that an embedded distribution includes a great number of tools, and, usually, a number of these tools require customization. Presenting each of these will take up more than a chapter in a book.

In this book, however, we will cover only the toolchain building components. These include the following:

- `binutils`
- `gcc`
- `glibc` (C libraries)
- kernel headers

I will start by the introducing the first item on this list, the **GNU Binutils package**. Developed under the GNU GPL license, it represents a set of tools that are used to create and manage binary files, object code, assembly files, and profile data for a given architecture. Here is a list with the functionalities and names of the available tools for GNU Binutils package:

- The GNU linker, that is `ld`
- The GNU assembler, that is `as`
- A utility that converts addresses into filenames and line numbers, that is `addr2line`
- A utility to create, extract, and modify archives, that is `ar`
- A tool used to listing the symbols available inside object files, that is `nm`
- Copying and translating object files, that is `objcopy`
- Displaying information from object files, that is `objdump`
- Generating an index to for the contents of an archive, that is `ranlib`
- Displaying information from any ELF format object file, that is `readelf`
- Listing the section sizes of an object or archive file, that is `size`
- Listing printable strings from files, that is `strings`
- Discarding the symbols utility that is `strip`
- Filtering or demangle encoded C++ symbols, that is `c++filt`
- Creating files that build use DLLs, that is `dlltool`
- A new, faster, ELF-only linker, which is still in beta testing, that is `gold`
- Displaying the profiling information tool, that is `gprof`
- Converting an object code into an NLM, that is `nlmconv`
- A Windows-compatible message compiler, that is `windmc`
- A compiler for Windows resource files, that is `windres`

The majority of these tools use the **Binary File Descriptor** (**BFD**) library for low-level data manipulation, and also, many of them use the `opcode` library to assemble and disassemble operations.

> Useful information about `binutils` can be found at `http://www.gnu.org/software/binutils/`.

In the toolchain generation process, the next item on the list is represented by kernel headers, and are needed by the C library for interaction with the kernel. Before compiling the corresponding C library, the kernel headers need to be supplied so that they can offer access to the available system calls, data structures, and constants definitions. Of course, any C library defines sets of specifications that are specific to each hardware architecture; here, I am referring to **application binary interface** (**ABI**).

An application binary interface (ABI) represents the interface between two modules. It gives information on how functions are called and the kind of information that should be passed between components or to the operating system. Referring to a book, such as *The Linux Kernel Primer*, will do you good, and in my opinion, is a complete guide for what the ABI offers. I will try to reproduce this definition for you.

An ABI can be seen as a set of rules similar to a protocol or an agreement that offers the possibility for a linker to put together compiled modules into one component without the need of recompilation. At the same time, an ABI describes the binary interface between these components. Having this sort of convention and conforming to an ABI offers the benefits of linking object files that could have been compiled with different compilers.

It can be easily seen from both of these definitions that an ABI is dependent on the type of platform, which can include physical hardware, some kind of virtual machine, and so on. It may also be dependent on the programming language that is used and the compiler, but most of it depends on the platform.

The ABI presents how the generated codes operate. The code generation process must also be aware of the ABI, but when coding in a high-level language, attention given to the ABI is rarely a problem. This information could be considered as necessary knowledge to specify some ABI related options.

As a general rule, ABI must be respected for its interaction with external components. However, with regard to interaction with its internal modules, the user is free to do whatever he or she wants. Basically, they are able to reinvent the ABI and form their own dependence on the limitations of the machine. The simple example here is related to various citizens who belong to their own country or region, because they learned and know the language of that region since they were born. Hence, they are able to understand one another and communicate without problems. For an external citizen to be able to communicate, he or she will need to know the language of a region, and being in this community seems natural, so it will not constitute a problem. Compilers are also able to design their own custom calling conventions where they know the limitations of functions that are called within a module. This exercise is typically done for optimization reasons. However, this can be considered an abuse of the ABI term.

The kernel in reference to a user space ABI is backward compatible, and it makes sure that binaries are generated using older kernel header versions, rather than the ones available on the running kernel, will work best. The disadvantages of this are represented by the fact that new system calls, data structures, and binaries generated with a toolchain that use newer kernel headers, might not work for newer features. The need for the latest kernel headers can be justified by the need to have access to the latest kernel features.

The GNU Compiler Collection, also known as GCC, represents a compiler system that constitutes the key component of the GNU toolchain. Although it was originally named the GNU C Compiler, due to the fact that it only handled the C programming language, it soon begun to represent a collection of languages, such as C, C++, Objective C, Fortran, Java, Ada, and Go, as well as the libraries for other languages (such as `libstdc++`, `libgcj`, and so on).

It was originally written as the compiler for the GNU operating system and developed as a 100 percent free software. It is distributed under the GNU GPL. This helped it extend to its functionalities across a wide variety of architectures, and it played an important role in the growth of open source software.

The development of GCC started with the effort put in by Richard Stallman to bootstrap the GNU operating system. This quest led Stallman to write his own compiler from scratch. It was released in 1987, with Stallman as the author and other as contributors to it. By 1991, it had already reached a stable phase, but it was unable to include improvements due to its architectural limitations. This meant that the starting point for work on GCC version 2 had begun, but it did not take long until the need for development of new language interfaces started to appear in it as well, and developers started doing their own forks of the compiler source code. This fork initiative proved to be very inefficient, and because of the difficulty of accepting the code procedure, working on it became really frustrating.

This changed in 1997, when a group of developers gathered as the **Experimental/Enhanced GNU Compiler System** (**EGCS**) workgroup started merging several forks in one project. They had so much success in this venture, and gathered so many features, that they made **Free Software Foundation** (**FSF**) halt their development of GCC version 2 and appointed EGCS the official GCC version and maintainers by April 1999. They united with each other with the release of GCC 2.95. More information on the history and release history of the GNU Compiler Collection can be found at `https://www.gnu.org/software/gcc/releases.html` and `http://en.wikipedia.org/wiki/GNU_Compiler_Collection#Revision_history`.

The GCC interface is similar to the Unix convention, where users call a language-specific driver, which interprets arguments and calls a compiler. It then runs an assembler on the resulting outputs and, if necessary, runs a linker to obtain the final executable. For each language compiler, there is a separate program that performs the source code read.

The process of obtaining an executable from source code has some execution steps. After the first step, an abstract syntax tree is generated and, in this stage, compiler optimization and static code analysis can be applied. The optimizations and static code analysis can be both applied on architecture-independent **GIMPLE** or its superset GENERIC representation, and also on architecture-dependent **Register Transfer Language** (**RTL**) representation, which is similar to the LISP language. The machine code is generated using pattern-matching algorithm, which was written by Jack Davidson and Christopher Fraser.

GCC was initially written almost entirely in C language, although the Ada frontend is written mostly in Ada language. However, in 2012, the GCC committee announced the use of C++ as an implementation language. The GCC library could not be considered finished as an implementation language, even though its main activities include adding new languages support, optimizations, improved runtime libraries, and increased speed for debugging applications.

Each available frontend generated a tree from the given source code. Using this abstract tree form, different languages can share the same backend. Initially, GCC used **Look-Ahead LR (LALR)** parsers, which were generated using Bison, but over time, it moved on to recursive-descendent parsers for C, C++, and Objective-C in 2006. Today, all available frontends use handwritten recursive-descendent parsers.

Until recently, the syntax tree abstraction of a program was not independent of a target processor, because the meaning of the tree was different from one language frontend to the other, and each provided its own tree syntax. All this changed with the introduction of GENERIC and GIMPLE architecture-independent representations, which were introduced with the GCC 4.0 version.

GENERIC is a more complex intermediate representation, while GIMPLE is a simplified GENERIC and targets all the frontends of GCC. Languages, such as C, C++ or Java frontends, directly produce GENERIC tree representations in the frontend. Others use different intermediate representations that are then parsed and converted to GENERIC representations.

The GIMPLE transformation represents complex expressions that are split into a three address code using temporary variables. The GIMPLE representation was inspired by the SIMPLE representation used on the McCAT compiler for simplifying the analysis and optimization of programs.

The middle stage representation of GCC involves code analysis and optimization, and works independently in terms of a compiled language and the target architecture. It starts from the GENERIC representation and continues to the **Register Transfer Language (RTL)** representation. The optimization mostly involves jump threading, instruction scheduling, loop optimization, sub expression elimination, and so on. The RTL optimizations are less important than the ones done through GIMPLE representations. However, they include dead code elimination, global value numbering, partial redundancy elimination, sparse conditional constant propagation, scalar replacement of aggregates, and even automatic vectorization or automatic parallelization.

The GCC backend is mainly represented by preprocessor macros and specific target architecture functions, such as endianness definitions, calling conventions, or word sizes. The initial stage of the backend uses these representations to generate the RTL; this suggests that although GCC's RTL representation is nominally processor-independent, the initial processing of abstract instructions is adapted for each specific target.

A machine-specific description file contains RTL patterns, also code snippets, or operand constraints that form a final assembly. In the process of RTL generation, the constraints of the target architecture are verified. To generate an RTL snippet, it must match one or a number RTL patterns from the machine description file, and at the same time also satisfy the limitations for these patterns. If this is not done, the process of conversion for the final RTL into machine code would be impossible. Toward the end of compilation, the RTL representation becomes a strict form. Its representation contains a real machine register correspondence and a template from the target's machine description file for each instruction reference.

As a result, the machine code is obtained by calling small snippets of code, which are associated with corresponding patterns. In this way, instructions are generated from target instruction sets. This process involves the usage of registers, offsets, and addresses from the reload phase.

> More information about a GCC compiler can be found at `http://gcc.gnu.org/` or `http://en.wikipedia.org/wiki/GNU_Compiler_Collection`.

The last element that needs to be introduced here is the C library. It represents the interface between a Linux kernel and applications used on a Linux system. At the same time, it offers aid for the easier development of applications. There are a couple of C libraries available in this community:

- `glibc`
- `eglibc`
- `Newlib`
- `bionic`
- `musl`
- `uClibc`
- `dietlibc`
- `Klibc`

The choice of the C library used by the GCC compiler will be executed in the toolchain generation phase, and it will be influenced not only by the size and application support offered by the libraries, but also by compliance of standards, completeness, and personal preference.

Delving into C libraries

The first library that we'll discuss here is the `glibc` library, which is designed for performance, compliance of standards, and portability. It was developed by the Free Software Foundation for the GNU/Linux operating system and is still present today on all GNU/Linux host systems that are actively maintained. It was released under the GNU Lesser General Public License.

The `glibc` library was initially written by Roland McGrath in the 1980s and it continued to grow until the 1990s when the Linux kernel forked `glibc`, calling it `Linux libc`. It was maintained separately until January 1997 when the Free Software Foundation released `glibc 2.0`. The `glibc 2.0` contained so many features that it did not make any sense to continue the development of `Linux libc`, so they discontinued their fork and returned to using `glibc`. There are changes that are made in `Linux libc` that were not merged into `glibc` because of problems with the authorship of the code.

The `glibc` library is quite large in terms of its dimensions and isn't a suitable fit for small embedded systems, but it provides the functionality required by the **Single UNIX Specification** (**SUS**), POSIX, ISO C11, ISO C99, Berkeley Unix interfaces, System V Interface Definition, and the X/Open Portability Guide, Issue 4.2, with all its extensions common with X/Open System Interface compliant systems along with X/Open UNIX extensions. In addition to this, GLIBC also provides extensions that have been deemed useful or necessary while developing GNU.

The next C library that I'm going to discuss here is the one that resides as the main C library used by the Yocto Project until version 1.7. Here, I'm referring to the `eglibc` library. This is a version of `glibc` optimized for the usage of embedded devices and is, at the same time, able to preserve the compatibility standards.

Since 2009, Debian and a number of its derivations chose to move from the GNU C Library to `eglibc`. This might be because there is a difference in licensing between GNU LGPL and `eglibc`, and this permits them to accept patches that `glibc` developers my reject. Since 2014, the official `eglibc` homepage states that the development of `eglibc` was discontinued because `glibc` had also moved to the same licensing, and also, the release of Debian Jessie meant that it had moved back to `glibc`. This also happened in the case of Yocto support when they also decided to make `glibc` their primary library support option.

The `newlib` library is another C library developed with the intention of being used in embedded systems. It is a conglomerate of library components under free software licenses. Developed by Cygnus Support and maintained by Red Hat, it is one of the preferred versions of the C library used for non-Linux embedded systems.

The `newlib` system calls describe the usage of the C library across multiple operation systems, and also on embedded systems that do not require an operating system. It is included in commercial GCC distributions, such as Red Hat, CodeSourcery, Attolic, KPIT and others. It also supported by architecture vendors that include ARM, Renesas, or Unix-like environments, such as Cygwin, and even proprietary operating systems of the Amiga personal computer.

By 2007, it also got support from the toolchain maintainers of Nintendo DS, PlayStation, portable SDK Game Boy Advance systems, Wii, and GameCube development platforms. Another addition was made to this list in 2013 when Google Native Client SDK included `newlib` as their primary C library.

Bionic is a derivate of the BSD C library developed by Google for Android based on the Linux kernel. Its development is independent of Android code development. It is licensed as 3-clause BSD license and its goals are publically available. These include the following:

- **Small size**: Bionic is smaller in size compared to `glibc`
- **Speed**: This has designed CPUs that work at low frequencies
- **BSD license**: Google wished to isolate Android apps from GPL and LGPL licenses, and this is the reason it moved to a non-copyleft license which are as follows:
    - Android is based on a Linux kernel which is based on a GPLv2 license
    - `glibc` is based on LGPL, which permits the linking of dynamic proprietary libraries but not with static linking

It also has a list of restrictions compared to `glibc`, as follows:

- It does not include C++ exception handling, mainly because most the code used for Android is written in Java.
- It does not have wide character support.
- It does not include a Standard Template library, although it can be included manually.
- It functions within Bionic POSIX and even system call headers are wrappers or stubs for Android -specific functions. This may lead to odd behavior sometimes.
- When Android 4.2 released, it included support for `glibc` `FORTIFY_SOURCE` features. These features are very often used in Yocto, and embedded systems in general, but are only present in the `gcc` version for Android devices with ARM processors.

The next C library that will be discussed is `musl`. It is a C library intended for use with Linux operating systems for embedded and mobile systems. It has a MIT license and was developed with the idea of having a clean, standard-compliant `libc`, which is time efficient, since it's been developed from scratch. As a C library, it is optimized for the linking of static libraries. It is compatible with C99 standard and POSIX 2008, and implements Linux, `glibc`, and BSD non-standard functions.

Next, we'll discuss `uClibc`, which is a C standard library designed for Linux embedded systems and mobile devices. Although initially developed for μClinux and designed for microcontrollers, it gathered track and became the weapon of choice for anyone who's has limited space on their device. This has become popular due to the following reasons:

- It focuses on size rather than performance
- It has a GNU Lesser General Public License (LGPL) free license
- It is much smaller the glibc and reduces compilation time
- It has high configurability due to the fact that many of its features can be enabled using a `menuconfig` interface similar to the one available on packages, such as Linux kernel, U-Boot, or even BusyBox

The `uClibc` library also has another quality that makes it quite useful. It introduces a new ideology and, because of this, the C library does not try to support as many standards as possible. However, it focuses on embedded Linux and consists of the features necessary for developers who face the limitation of available space. Due to this reason, this library was written from scratch, and even though it has its fair share of limitations, `uClibc` is an important alternative to `glibc`. If we take into consideration the fact that most of the features used from C libraries are present in it, the final size is four times smaller, and WindRiver, MontaVista, and TimeSys are active maintainers of it.

The `dietlibc` library is a standard C library that was developed by Felix von Leitner and released under the GNU GPL v2 license. Although it also contains some commercial licensed components, its design was based on the same idea as `uClibc`: the possibility of compiling and linking software while having the smallest size possible. It has another resemblance to `uClibc`; it was developed from scratch and has only implemented the most used and known standard functions. Its primary usage is mainly in the embedded devices market.

The last in the C libraries list is the `klibc` standard C library. It was developed by H. Peter Anvin and it was developed to be used as part of the early user space during the Linux startup process. It is used by the components that run the the kernel startup process but aren't used in the kernel mode and, hence, they do not have access to the standard C library.

The development of `klibc` started in 2002 as an initiative to remove the Linux initialization code outside a kernel. Its design makes it suitable for usage in embedded devices. It also has another advantage: it is optimized for small size and correctness of data. The `klibc` library is loaded during the Linux startup process from **initramfs** (a temporary Ram filesystem) and is incorporated by default into initramfs using the `mkinitramfs` script for Debian and Ubuntu-based filesystems. It also has access to a small set of utilities, such as `mount`, `mkdir`, `dash`, `mknod`, `fstype`, `nfsmount`, `run-init` and so on, which are very useful in the early init stage.

> More information on initramfs can be found using the kernel documentation at `https://www.kernel.org/doc/Documentation/filesystems/ramfs-rootfs-initramfs.txt`.

The `klibc` library is licensed under GNU GPL since it uses some components from the Linux kernel, so, as a whole, it is visible as a GPL licensed software, limiting its applicability in commercial embedded software. However, most of the source code of libraries is written under the BSD license.

Working with toolchains

When generating a toolchain, the first thing that needs to be done is the establishment of an ABI used to generate binaries. This means that the kernel needs to understand this ABI and, at the same time, all the binaries in the system need to be compiled with the same ABI.

When working with the GNU toolchain, a good source of gathering information and understanding the ways in which work is done with these tools is to consult the GNU coding standards. The coding standard's purposes are very simple: to make sure that the work with the GNU ecosystem is performed in a clean, easy, and consistent manner. This is a guideline that needs to be used by people interested in working with GNU tools to write reliable, solid, and portable software. The main focus of the GNU toolchain is represented by the C language, but the rules applied here are also very useful for any programming languages. The purpose of each rule is explained by making sure that the logic behind the given information is passed to the reader.

The main language that we will be focusing on will also be the C programming language. With regard to the GNU coding standard compatibility regarding libraries for GNU, exceptions or utilities and their compatibility should be very good when compared with standards, such as the ones from Berkeley Unix, Standard C, or POSIX. In case of conflicts in compatibility, it is very useful to have compatibility modes for that programming language.

Standards, such as POSIX and C, have a number of limitations regarding the support for extensions - however, these extensions could still be used by including a `-posix`, `-ansi`, or `-compatible` option to disable them. In case the extension offers a high probability of breaking a program or script by being incompatible, a redesign of its interface should be made to ensure compatibility.

A large number of GNU programs suppress the extensions that are known to cause conflict with POSIX if the `POSIXLY_CORRECT` environment variable is defined. The usage of user defined features offers the possibility for interchanging GNU features with other ones totally different, better, or even use a compatible feature. Additional useful features are always welcomed.

If we take a quick look at the GNU Standard documentation, some useful information can be learned from it:

It is better to use the `int` type, although you might consider defining a narrower data type. There are, of course, a number of special cases where this could be hard to use. One such example is the `dev_t` system type, because it is shorter than `int` on some machines and wider on others. The only way to offer support for non-standard C types involves checking the width of `dev_t` using `Autoconf` and, after this, choosing the argument type accordingly. However, it may not worth the trouble.

For the GNU Project, the implementation of an organization's standard specifications is optional, and this can be done only if it helps the system by making it better overall. In most situations, following published standards fits well within a users needs because their programs or scripts could be considered more portable. One such example is represented by the GCC, which implements almost all the features of Standard C, as the standard requires. This offers a great advantage for the developers of the C program. This also applies to GNU utilities that follow POSIX.2 specifications.

There are also specific points in the specifications that are not followed, but this happens with the sole reason of making the GNU system better for users. One such example would be the fact that the Standard C program does not permit extensions to C, but, GCC implements many of them, some being later embraced by the standard. For developers interested in outputting an error message as *required* by the standard, the `--pedantic` argument can be used. It is implemented with a view to making sure that GCC fully implements the standard.

The POSIX.2 standard mentions that commands, such as `du` and `df`, should output sizes in units of 512 bytes. However, users want units of 1KB and this default behavior is implemented. If someone is interested in having the behavior requested by POSIX standard, they would need to set the `POSIXLY_CORRECT` environment variable.

Another such example is represented by the GNU utilities, which don't always respect the POSIX.2 standard specifications when referring to support for long named command-line options or intermingling of options with arguments. This incompatibility with the POSIX standard is very useful in practice for developers. The main idea here is not to reject any new feature or remove an older one, although a certain standard mentions it as deprecated or forbidden.

> For more information regarding the GNU Coding Standards, refer to `https://www.gnu.org/prep/standards/html_node/`.

Advice on robust programming

To make sure that you write robust code, a number of guidelines should be mentioned. The first one refers to the fact that limitations should not be used for any data structure, including files, file names, lines, and symbols, and especially arbitrary limitations. All data structures should be dynamically allocated. One of the reasons for this is represented by the fact that most Unix utilities silently truncate long lines; GNU utilities do not do these kind of things.

Utilities that are used to read files should avoid dropping `null` characters or nonprinting characters. The exception here is when these utilities, that are intended for interfacing with certain types of printers or terminals, are unable to handle the previously mentioned characters. The advice that I'd give in this case would be to try and make programs work with a UTF-8 character set, or other sequences of bytes used to represent multibyte characters.

Make sure that you check system calls for error return values; the exception here is when a developer wishes to ignore the errors. It would be a good idea to include the system error text from `strerror`, `perror`, or equivalent error handling functions, in error messages that result from a crashed on system call, adding the name of the source code file, and also the name of the utility. This is done to make sure that the error message is easy to read and understand by anyone involved in the interaction with the source code or the program.

Check the return value for `malloc` or `realloc` to verify if they've returned zero. In case `realloc` is used in order to make a block smaller in systems that approximate block dimensions to powers of 2, `realloc` may have a different behavior and get a different block. In Unix, when `realloc` has a bug, it destroys the storage block for a zero return value. For GNU, this bug does not occur, and when it fails, the original block remains unchanged. If you want to run the same program on Unix and do not want to lose data, you could check if the bug was resolved on the Unix system or use the `malloc` GNU.

The content of the block that was freed is not accessible to alter or for any other interactions from the user. This can be done before calling free.

When a `malloc` command fails in a noninteractive program, we face a fatal error. In case the same situation is repeated, but, this time, an interactive program is involved, it would be better to abort the command and return to the read loop. This offers the possibility to free up virtual memory, kill other processes, and retry the command.

To decode arguments, the `getopt_long` option can be used.

When writing static storage during program execution, use C code for its initialization. However, for data that will not be changed, reserve C initialized declarations.

Try to keep away from low-level interfaces to unknown Unix data structures - this could happen when the data structure do not work in a compatible fashion. For example, to find all the files inside a directory, a developer could use the `readdir` function, or any high-level interface available function, since these do not have compatibility problems.

For signal handling, use the BSD variant of `signal` and the POSIX `sigaction` function. The USG `signal` interface is not the best alternative in this case. Using POSIX signal functions is nowadays considered the easiest way to develop a portable program. However, the use of one function over another is completely up to the developer.

For error checks that identify impossible situations, just abort the program, since there is no need to print any messages. These type of checks bear witness to the existence of bugs. To fix these bugs, a developer will have to inspect the available source code and even start a debugger. The best approach to solve this problem would be to describe the bugs and problems using comments inside the source code. The relevant information could be found inside variables after examining them accordingly with a debugger.

Do not use a count of the encountered errors in a program as an exit status. This practice is not the best, mostly because the values for an exit status are limited to 8 bits only, and an execution of the executable might have more than 255 errors. For example, if you try to return exit status 256 for a process, the parent process will see a status of zero and consider that the program finished successfully.

If temporary files are created, checking that the `TMPDIR` environment variable would be a good idea. If the variable is defined, it would be wise to use the `/tmp` directory instead. The use of temporary files should be done with caution because there is the possibility of security breaches occurring when creating them in world-writable directories. For C language, this can be avoided by creating temporary files in the following manner:

```
fd = open (filename, O_WRONLY | O_CREAT | O_EXCL, 0600);
```

This can also be done using the `mkstemps` function, which is made available by `Gnulib`.

For a bash environment, use the `noclobber` environment variable, or the `set -C` short version, to avoid the previously mentioned problem. Furthermore, the `mktemp` available utility is altogether a better solution for making a temporary file a shell environment; this utility is available in the GNU Coreutils package.

> More information about GNU C Standards can be found at `https://www.gnu.org/prep/standards/standards.html`.

Generating the toolchain

After the introduction of the packages that comprise a toolchain, this section will introduce the steps needed to obtain a custom toolchain. The toolchain that will be generated will contain the same sources as the ones available inside the Poky dizzy branch. Here, I am referring to the `gcc` version 4.9, `binutils` version 2.24, and `glibc` version 2.20. For Ubuntu systems, there are also shortcuts available. A generic toolchain can be installed using the available package manager, and there are also alternatives, such as downloading custom toolchains available inside Board Support Packages, or even from third parties, including CodeSourcery and Linaro. More information on toolchains can be found at `http://elinux.org/Toolchains`. The architecture that will be used as a demo is an ARM architecture.

The toolchain build process has eight steps. I will only outline the activities required for each one of them, but I must mention that they are all automatized inside the Yocto Project recipes. Inside the Yocto Project section, the toolchain is generated without notice. For interaction with the generated toolchain, the simplest task would be to call **meta-ide-support**, but this will be presented in the appropriate section as follows:

- **The setup**: This represents the step in which top-level build directories and source subdirectories are created. In this step, variables such as `TARGET`, `SYSROOT`, `ARCH`, `COMPILER`, `PATH`, and others are defined.
- **Geting the sources**: This represents the step in which packages, such as `binutils`, `gcc`, `glibc`, `linux kernel` headers, and various patches are made available for use in later steps.

- **GNU Binutils setup** - This represents the steps in which the interaction with the `binutils` package is done, as shown here:
    - Unzip the sources available from the corresponding release
    - Patch the sources accordingly, if this applies
    - Configur, the package accordingly
    - Compile the sources
    - Install the sources in the corresponding location
- **Linux kernel headers setup**: This represents the steps in which the interaction with the Linux kernel sources is presented, as shown here:
    - Unzip the kernel sources.
    - Patch the kernel sources, if this applies.
    - Configure the kernel for the selected architecture. In this step, the corresponding kernel config file is generated. More information about Linux kernel will be presented in *Chapter 4, Linux Kernel*.
    - Compile the Linux kernel headers and copy them in the corresponding location.
    - Install the headers in the corresponding locations.
- **Glibc headers setup**: This represents the steps used to setting the `glibc` build area and installation headers, as shown here:
    - Unzip the glibc archive and headers files
    - Patch the sources, if this applies
    - Configure the sources accordingly enabling the `-with-headers` variable to link the libraries to the corresponding Linux kernel headers
    - Compile the glibc headers files
    - Install the headers accordingly
- **GCC first stage setup**: This represents the step in which the C runtime files, such as `crti.o` and `crtn.o`, are generated:
    - Unzip the gcc archive
    - Patch the gcc sources if necessary
    - Configure the sources enabling the needed features
    - Compile the C runtime components
    - Install the sources accordingly

- **Build the glibc sources**: This represents the step in which the `glibc` sources are built and the necessary ABI setup is done, as shown here:
    - Configure the `glibc` library by setting the `mabi` and `march` variables accordingly
    - Compile the sources
    - Install the `glibc` accordingly
- **GCC second stage setup**: This represents the final setup phase in which the toolchain configuration is finished, as shown here:
    - Configure the `gcc` sources
    - Compile the sources
    - Install the binaries in the corresponding location

After these steps are performed, a toolchain will be available for the developer to use. The same strategy and build procedure steps is followed inside the Yocto Project.

The Yocto Project reference

As I have mentioned, the major advantage and available feature of the Yocto Project environment is represented by the fact that a Yocto Project build does not use the host available packages, but builds and uses its own packages. This is done to make sure that a change in the host environment does not influence its available packages and that builds are made to generate a custom Linux system. A toolchain is one of the components because almost all packages that are constituents of a Linux distribution need the usage of toolchain components.

The first step for the Yocto Project is to identify the exact sources and packages that will be combined to generate the toolchain that will be used by later built packages, such as U-Boot bootloader, kernel, BusyBox and others. In this book, the sources that will be discussed are the ones available inside the dizzy branch, the latest poky 12.0 version, and the Yocto Project version 1.7. The sources can be gathered using the following command:

```
git clone -b dizzy http://git.yoctoproject.org/git/poky
```

Gathering the sources and investigating the source code, we identified a part of the packages mentioned and presented in the preceding headings, as shown here:

```
cd poky
find ./ -name "gcc"
./meta/recipes-devtools/gcc
find ./ -name "binutils"
./meta/recipes-devtools/binutils
./meta/recipes-devtools/binutils/binutils
find ./ -name "glibc"
./meta/recipes-core/glibc
./meta/recipes-core/glibc/glibc
$ find ./ -name "uclibc"
./meta-yocto-bsp/recipes-core/uclibc
./meta-yocto-bsp/recipes-core/uclibc/uclibc
./meta/recipes-core/uclibc
```

The GNU CC and GCC C compiler package, which consists of all the preceding packages, is split into multiple fractions, each one with its purpose. This is mainly because each one has its purpose and is used with different scopes, such as `sdk` components. However, as I mentioned in the introduction of this chapter, there are multiple toolchain build procedures that need to be assured and automated with the same source code. The available support inside Yocto is for gcc 4.8 and 4.9 versions. A quick look at the `gcc` available recipes shows the available information:

```
meta/recipes-devtools/gcc/
├── gcc-4.8
├── gcc_4.8.bb
├── gcc-4.8.inc
├── gcc-4.9
├── gcc_4.9.bb
├── gcc-4.9.inc
├── gcc-common.inc
├── gcc-configure-common.inc
```

```
├── gcc-cross_4.8.bb
├── gcc-cross_4.9.bb
├── gcc-cross-canadian_4.8.bb
├── gcc-cross-canadian_4.9.bb
├── gcc-cross-canadian.inc
├── gcc-cross.inc
├── gcc-cross-initial_4.8.bb
├── gcc-cross-initial_4.9.bb
├── gcc-cross-initial.inc
├── gcc-crosssdk_4.8.bb
├── gcc-crosssdk_4.9.bb
├── gcc-crosssdk.inc
├── gcc-crosssdk-initial_4.8.bb
├── gcc-crosssdk-initial_4.9.bb
├── gcc-crosssdk-initial.inc
├── gcc-multilib-config.inc
├── gcc-runtime_4.8.bb
├── gcc-runtime_4.9.bb
├── gcc-runtime.inc
├── gcc-target.inc
├── libgcc_4.8.bb
├── libgcc_4.9.bb
├── libgcc-common.inc
├── libgcc.inc
├── libgcc-initial_4.8.bb
├── libgcc-initial_4.9.bb
├── libgcc-initial.inc
├── libgfortran_4.8.bb
├── libgfortran_4.9.bb
└── libgfortran.inc
```

The GNU Binutils package represents the binary tools collection, such as GNU Linker, GNU Assembler, `addr2line`, `ar`, `nm`, `objcopy`, `objdump`, and other tools and related libraries. The Yocto Project offers support for the Binutils version 2.24, and is also dependent on the available toolchain build procedures, as it can be viewed from the inspection of the source code:

```
meta/recipes-devtools/binutils/
├── binutils
├── binutils_2.24.bb
├── binutils-2.24.inc
├── binutils-cross_2.24.bb
├── binutils-cross-canadian_2.24.bb
├── binutils-cross-canadian.inc
├── binutils-cross.inc
├── binutils-crosssdk_2.24.bb
└── binutils.inc
```

The last components is represented by C libraries that are present as components inside the Poky dizzy branch. There are two C libraries available that can be used by developers. The first one is represented by the GNU C library, also known as `glibc`, which is the most used C library in Linux systems. The sources for `glibc` package can be viewed here:

```
meta/recipes-core/glibc/
├── cross-localedef-native
├── cross-localedef-native_2.20.bb
├── glibc
├── glibc_2.20.bb
├── glibc-collateral.inc
├── glibc-common.inc
├── glibc.inc
├── glibc-initial_2.20.bb
├── glibc-initial.inc
├── glibc-ld.inc
├── glibc-locale_2.20.bb
├── glibc-locale.inc
├── glibc-mtrace_2.20.bb
├── glibc-mtrace.inc
├── glibc-options.inc
├── glibc-package.inc
├── glibc-scripts_2.20.bb
├── glibc-scripts.inc
```

```
├── glibc-testing.inc
├── ldconfig-native-2.12.1
├── ldconfig-native_2.12.1.bb
└── site_config
```

From these sources, the same location also includes tools, such as `ldconfig`, a standalone native dynamic linker for runtime dependencies and a binding and cross locale generation tool. In the other C library, called `uClibc`, as previously mentioned, a library designed for embedded systems has fewer recipes, as it can be viewed from the Poky source code:

```
meta/recipes-core/uclibc/
├── site_config
├── uclibc-config.inc
├── uclibc-git
├── uclibc_git.bb
├── uclibc-git.inc
├── uclibc.inc
├── uclibc-initial_git.bb
└── uclibc-package.inc
```

The uClibc is used as an alternative to `glibc` C library because it generates smaller executable footprints. At the same time, `uClibc` is the only package from the ones presented in the preceding list that has a `bbappend` applied to it, since it extends the support for two machines, `genericx86-64` and `genericx86`. The change between `glibc` and `uClibc` can be done by changing the `TCLIBC` variable to the corresponding variable in this way: `TCLIBC = "uclibc"`.

As mentioned previously, the toolchain generation process for the Yocto Project is simpler. It is the first task that is executed before any recipe is built using the Yocto Project. To generate the cross-toolchain inside using Bitbake, first, the `bitbake meta-ide-support` task is executed. The task can be executed for the `qemuarm` architecture, for example, but it can, of course, be generated in a similar method for any given hardware architecture. After the task finishes the execution process, the toolchain is generated and it populates the build directory. It can be used after this by sourcing the `environment-setup` script available in the `tmp` directory:

```
cd poky
source oe-init-build-env ../build-test
```

Set the `MACHINE` variable to the value `qemuarm` accordingly inside the `conf/local.conf` file:

```
bitbake meta-ide-support
source tmp/environment-setup
```

The default C library used for the generation of the toolchain is `glibc`, but it can be changed according to the developer's need. As seen from the presentation in the previous section, the toolchain generation process inside the Yocto Project is very simple and straightforward. It also avoids all the trouble and problems involved in the manual toolchain generation process, making it very easy to reconfigure also.

Summary

In this chapter, you were presented with the necessary information needed to understand the constituent components of a Linux toolchain, and the steps undertaken by developers to work or configure a Linux toolchain that is specific for a board or architecture. You were also presented information on the packages available inside the Yocto Project sources, and how the processes defined inside the Yocto Project are very similar to the ones already used outside of the Yocto Project context.

In the next chapter, we will breeze through information on bootloaders, with special emphasis given to U-Boot bootloader. You will also be given information on a boot sequence and a board's configurations inside the U-Boot sources.

3
Bootloaders

In this chapter, you will be presented with one of the most important components necessary for using a Linux system in an embedded environment. Here, I am referring to the bootloader, a piece of software that offers the possibility of initializing a platform and making it ready to boot a Linux operating system. In this chapter, the benefits and roles of bootloaders will be presented. This chapter mainly focuses on the U-Boot bootloaders, but readers are encouraged to have a look at others, such as Barebox, RedBoot, and so on. All these bootloaders have their respective features and there isn't one in particular that suits every need; therefore, experimentation and curiosity are welcome when this chapter. You have already been introduced to the the Yocto Project reference in the last chapter; hence, you will now be able to understand how this development environment works with various bootloaders, and especially the ones available inside a **Board Support Package** (**BSP**).

The main purpose of this chapter is to present the main properties of embedded bootloaders and firmware, their booting mechanisms, and the problems that appear when firmware is updated or modified. We will also discuss the problems related to safety, installation, or fault tolerance. With regard to bootloader and firmware notions, we have multiple definitions available and a number of them refer to traditional desktop systems, which we are not interested in.

A firmware usually represents a fixed and small program that is used on a system to control hardware. It performs low-level operations and is usually stored on flash, ROM, EPROM, and so on. It is not changed very often. Since there have been situations where this term has confused people and was sometimes used only to define hardware devices or represent data and its instructions, it was avoided altogether. It represents a combination of the two: computer data and information, along with the hardware device combined in a read-only piece of software available on the device.

The bootloader represents the piece of software that is first executed during system initialization. It is used to load, decompress, and execute one or more binary applications, such as a Linux kernel or a root filesystem. Its role involves adding the system in a state where it can execute its primary functions. This is done after loading and starting the correct binary applications that it receives or has already saved on the internal memory. Upon initializing, the hardware bootloader may need to initialize the **phase-locked loop** (**PLL**), set the clocks, or enable access to the RAM memory and other peripherals. However, these initializations are done on a basic level; the rest are done by kernels drivers and other applications.

Today, a number of bootloaders are available. Due to limited space available for this topic, and also the fact that their number is high, we will only discuss the most popular ones. U-Boot is one of the most popular bootloaders available for architectures, such as PowerPC, ARM, MIPS, and others. It will constitute the primary focus of this chapter.

The role of the bootloader

The first time that electricity runs into a development board processor, a great number of hardware components need to be prepared before running a program. For each architecture, hardware manufacturer, and even processor, this initialization process is different. In most cases, it involves a set of configurations and actions are different for a variety of processors and ends up fetching the bootstrap code from a storage device available in the proximity of the processor. This storage device is usually a flash memory and the bootstrap code is the first stage of the bootloader, and the one that initializes the processor and relevant hardware peripherals.

The majority of the available processors when power is applied to them go to a default address location, and after finding the first bytes of binary data, start executing them. Based on this information, the hardware designers define the layout for the flash memory and the address ranges that could later be used to load and boot the Linux operating system from predictable addresses.

In the first stage of initialization, the board init is done, usually in the assembler language specific to the processor and after this is finished, the entire ecosystem is prepared for the operating system booting process. The bootloader is responsible for this; it is the component that offers the possibility to load, locate, and execute primary components of the operating system. Additionally, it can contain other advanced features, such as the capability to upgrade the OS image, validate an OS image, choose between several OS images, and even the possibility to upgrade itself. The difference between the traditional PC BIOS and an embedded bootloader is the fact that in an embedded environment, the bootloader is overwritten after the Linux kernel starts execution. It, in fact, ceases to exist after it offers control to the OS image.

Bootloaders need to carefully initialize peripherals, such as flash or DRAM, before they are used. This is not an easy task to do. For example, the DRAM chips cannot be read or written in a direct method - each chip has a controller that needs to be enabled for read and write operations. At the same time, the DRAM needs to be continually refreshed because the data will be lost otherwise. The refresh operation, in fact, represents the reading of each DRAM location within the time frame mentioned by the hardware manufacturer. All these operations are the DRAM controller's responsibility, and it can generate a lot of frustration for the embedded developer because it requires specific knowledge about the architecture design and DRAM chip.

A bootloader does not have the infrastructure that a normal application has. It does not have the possibility to only be called by its name and start executing. After being switched on when it gains control, it creates its own context by initializing the processor and necessary hardware, such as DRAM, moves itself in the DRAM for faster execution, if necessary and finally, starts the actual execution of code.

The first element that poses as a complexity is the compatibility of the start up code with the processor's boot sequence. The first executable instructions need to be at a predefined location in the flash memory, which is dependent of the processor and even hardware architecture. There is also the possibility for a number of processors to seek for those first executable instructions in several locations based on the hardware signals that are received.

Another possibility is to have the same structure on many of the newly available development boards, such as the Atmel SAMA5D3-Xplained:

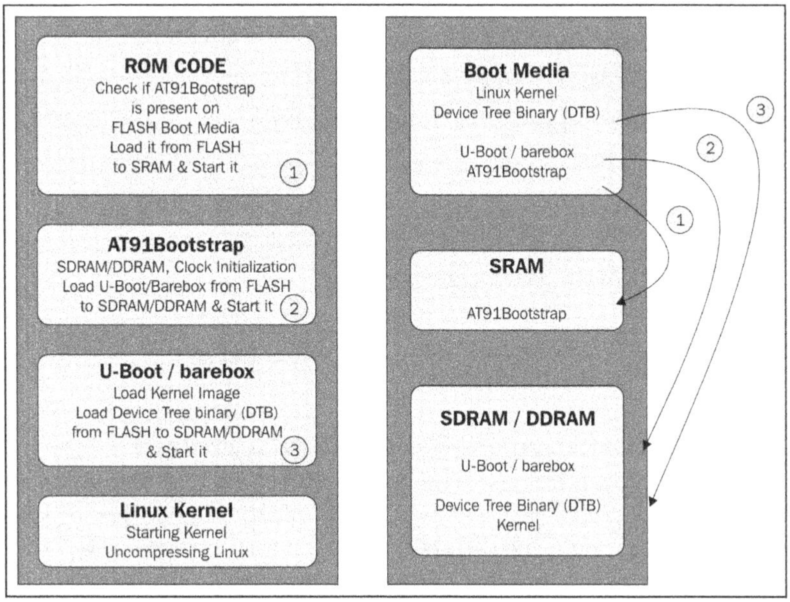

For the Atmel SAMA5D3-Xplained board and others similar to it, the booting starts from an integrated boot code available in the ROM memory called BootROM on AT91 CPUs, which loads the first stage bootloader called AT91Bootstrap on SRAM and starts it. The first stage bootloader initializes the DRAM memory and starts the second stage bootloader, which is U-Boot in this case. More information on boot sequence possibilities can be found in the boot sequence header available, which you'll read about shortly.

The lack of an execution context represents another complexity. Having to write even a simple `"Hello World"` in a system without a memory and, therefore, without a stack on which to allocate information, would look very different from the well-known "Hello World" example. This is the reason why the bootloader initializes the RAM memory to have a stack available and is able to run higher-level programs or languages, such as C.

Comparing various bootloaders

As we read earlier, a number of bootloaders are available for embedded systems. The ones that will be presented here are as follows:

- **U-Boot**: This is also called the Universal Bootloader and is available mostly for PowerPC and ARM architectures for embedded Linux systems
- **Barebox**: This was initially known as U-Boot v2 and was started in 2007 with the scope to solve the limitations of U-Boot; it changed its name over time because the design goals and community changed
- **RedBoot**: This is a RedHat bootloader derived from eCos, an open-source real-time operating system that is portable and devised for embedded systems
- **rrload**: This is a bootloader for ARM and is based on embedded Linux systems
- **PPCBOOT**: This is a bootloader for PowerPC and is based on embedded Linux systems
- **CLR/OHH**: This represents a flash bootloader for embedded Linux systems based on an ARM architecture
- **Alios**: This is a bootloader that is written mostly in assembler, does ROM and RAM initializations, and tries to completely remove the need for firmware on embedded systems

There are a number of bootloaders available and this is a natural outcome of the fact that there are a huge number of different architectures and devices, so many, in fact, that it is almost near impossible to have one that would be good for all systems. The variety of bootloaders is high; the differentiator factors are represented by the board types and structure, SOC differences and even CPUs.

Delving into the bootloader cycle

As mentioned previously, the bootloader is the component that is first run after initializing the system, and prepares the entire ecosystem for the operating system boot process. This process differs from one architecture to the other. For example, for the x86 architecture, the processor has access to BIOS, a piece of software available in a nonvolatile memory, which is usually a ROM. Its role starts out after resetting the system when it is executed and initializes the hardware components that will later be used by the first stage bootloader. It also executes the first stage of the bootloader.

The first stage bootloader is very small in terms of dimensions - in general, it is only 512 bytes and resides on a volatile memory. It performs the initialization for the full bootloader during the second stage. The second stage bootloaders usually reside next to the first stage ones, they contain the most number of features and do most of the work. They also know how to interpret various filesystem formats, mostly because the kernel is loaded from a filesystem.

For x86 processors, there are more bootloader solutions that are available:

- **GRUB**: The Grand Unified Bootloader is the most used and powerful bootloader available for Linux systems from desktop PC platforms. It is a component of the GNU Project and is one of the most potent bootloaders available for x86 architecture systems. This is because it is able to understand a large variety of filesystems and kernel images formats. It is able to change the the boot configuration during boot time. GRUB also has support for a network boot and command-line interface. It has a configuration file that is processed at boot time and can be modified. More information about it can be found at `http://www.gnu.org/software/grub/`.
- **Lilo**: The Linux Loader a bootloader mostly used in commercial Linux distributions. Similar to the previous point, it is available for desktop PC platforms. It has more than one component, the first component for historical reasons is available on the first sector of a disk drive; it is the bootstrap component. Due to the same historical reasons, it is limited to the 512 bytes dimension and it loads and offers control to the second stage bootloader that does most of the bootloader's work. Lilo has a configuration utility that is mainly used as a source of information for the Linux kernel booting process. More information about it can be found at `http://www.tldp.org/HOWTO/LILO.html`.
- **Syslinux**: It is used for removable media or network booting. Syslinux is a Linux operating system bootloader that runs on MS-DOS or Windows FAT filesystems and is mainly used for rescue and first time installations of Linux. More information on it can be found at `http://www.kernel.org/pub/linux/utils/boot/syslinux/`.

For most embedded systems, this booting process does not apply, although there are some that replicate this behavior. There are two types of situations that will be presented next. The first one is a situation where the code execution starts from a fixed address location, and the second one refers to a situation where the CPU has a code available in the ROM memory that is called.

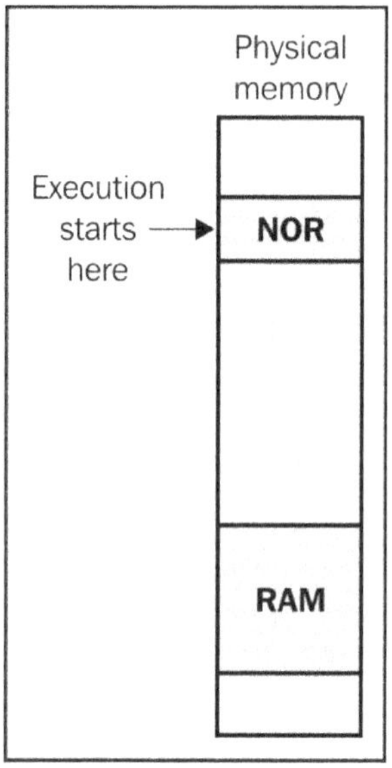

The right-hand side of the image is presented as the previously mentioned booting mechanism. In this case, the hardware requires a NOR flash memory chip, available at the start address to assure the start of the code execution.

A NOR memory is preferred over the NAND one because it allows random address access. It is the place where the first stage bootloader is programmed to start the execution, and this doesn't make it the most practical mechanism of booting.

Although it is not the most practical method used for the bootloader boot process, it is still available. However, it somehow becomes usable only on boards that are not suitable for more potent booting options.

The U-Boot bootloader

There are many open source bootloaders available today. Almost all of them have features to load and execute a program, which usually involves the operating system, and its features are used for serial interface communication. However, not all of them have the possibility to communicate over Ethernet or update themselves. Another important factor is represented by the widespread use of the bootloader. It is very common for organizations and companies to choose only one bootloader for the diversity of boards, processors, and architectures that they support. A similar thing happened with the Yocto Project when a bootloader was chosen to represent the official supported bootloader. They, and other similar companies, chose U-Boot bootloader, which is quite well known in the Linux community.

The U-Boot bootloader, or Das U-Boot as its official name, is developed and maintained by Wolfgang Denx with the support of the community behind it. It is licensed under GPLv2, its source code is freely available inside a `git` repository, as shown in the first chapter, and it has a two month intervals between releases. The release version name is shown as `U-boot vYYYY.MM`. The information about U-Boot loader is available at `http://www.denx.de/wiki/U-Boot/ReleaseCycle`.

The U-Boot source code has a very well defined directory structure. This can be easily seen with this console command:

```
tree -d -L 1

.

├── api

├── arch

├── board

├── common

├── configs

├── disk

├── doc

├── drivers

├── dts
```

```
├── examples
├── fs
├── include
├── lib
├── Licenses
├── net
├── post
├── scripts
├── test
└── tools
19 directories
```

The `arch` directory contains architecture-specific files and directories-specific to each architecture, CPU or development board. An `api` contains external applications that are independent of a machine or architecture type. A `board` contains inside boards with specific names of directories for all board-specific files. A common is a place where `misc` functions are located. A `disk` contains disk drive handling functions, and documentation is available inside the `doc` directory. Drivers are available in the `drivers` directory. The filesystem-specific functionality is available inside the `fs` directory. There are still some directories that would need mentioning here, such as the `include` directory, which contains the header files; the `lib` directory contains generic libraries with support for various utilities, such as the flatten device tree, various decompressions, a `post` (Power On Self-Test) and others, but I will let them be discovered by the reader's curiosity, one small hint would be to inspect the `README` file in the `Directory Hierachy` section.

Moving through the U-Boot sources, which were downloaded in the previous chapter inside the `./include/configs` file, configuration files can be found for each supported board. These configuration file is an `.h` file that contains a number of `CONFIG_` files and defines information on memory mapping, peripherals and their setup, command line output, such as the boot default addresses used for booting a Linux system, and so on. More information on the configuration files could be found inside the `README` file in the *Configuration Options,* section or in a board specific configuration file. For Atmel SAMA5D3-Xplained, the configuration file is `include/configs/sama5d3_xplained.h`. Also, there are two configurations available for this board in the `configs` directory, which are as follows:

- `configs/sama5d3_xplained_mmc_defconfig`
- `configs/sama5d3_xplained_nandflash_defconfig`

These configurations are used to define the board **Secondary Program Loader** (**SPL**) initialization method. SPL represents a small binary built from the U-Boot source code that is placed on the SRAM memory and is used to load the U-Boot into the RAM memory. Usually, it has less than 4 KB of memory, and this is how the booting sequence looks:

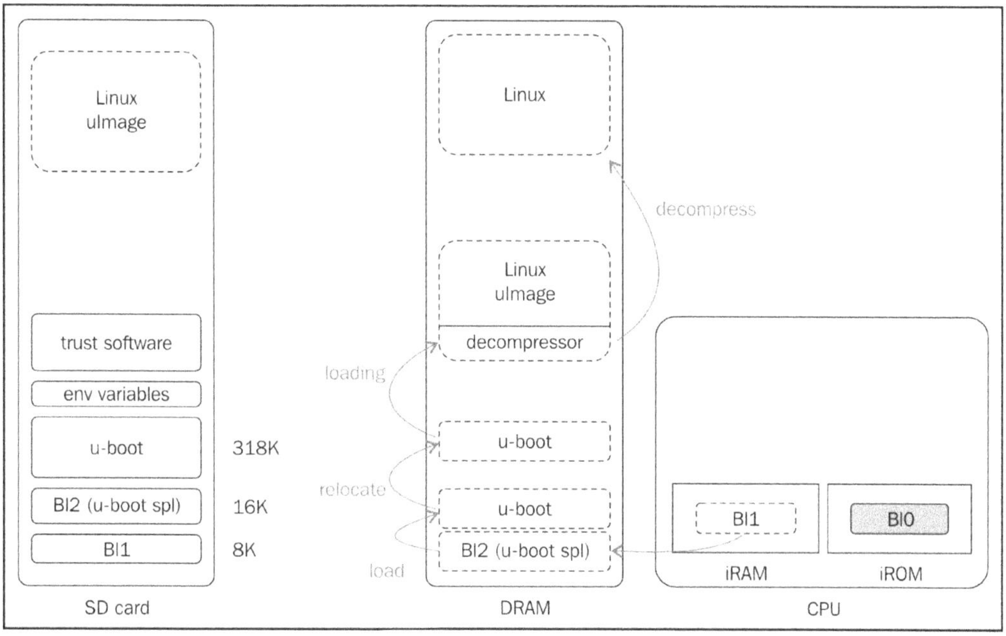

Before actually starting the build for the U-Boot source code for a specific board, the board configuration must be specified. For the Atmel SAMA5_Xplained development board, as presented in the preceding image, there are two available configurations that could be done. The configuration is done with the make `ARCH=arm CROSS_COMPILE=${CC} sama5d3_xplained_nandflash_defconfig` command. Behind this command, the `include/config.h` file is created. This header include definitions that are specific for the chosen board, architecture, CPU, and also board-specific header includes. The defined `CONFIG_*` variable read from the `include/config.h` file includes determining the compilation process. After the configuration is completed, the build can be started for the U-Boot.

Another example that can be very useful when inspected relates to the other scenario of booting an embedded system, one that requires the use of a NOR memory. In this situation, we can take a look at a particular example. This is also well described inside the *Embedded Linux Primer* by Christopher Hallinan, where a processor of the AMCC PowerPC 405GP is discussed. The hardcoded address for this processor is 0xFFFFFFFC and is visible using `.resetvec`, the reset vector placement. There also specifies the fact that the rest of this section is completed with only the value `1` until the end of the 0xFFFFFFFF stack; this implies that an empty flash memory array is completed only with values of `1`. The information about this section is available in `resetvec.S` file, which is located at `arch/powerpc/cpu/ppc4xx/resetvec.S`. The contents of `resetvec.S` file is as follows:

```
 /* Copyright MontaVista Software Incorporated, 2000 */
#include <config.h>
  .section .resetvec,"ax"
#if defined(CONFIG_440)
  b _start_440
#else
#if defined(CONFIG_BOOT_PCI) && defined(CONFIG_MIP405)
  b _start_pci
#else
  b _start
#endif
#endif
```

On inspection of this file's source code, it can be seen that only an instruction is defined in this section independently of the available configuration options.

The configuration for the U-Boot is done through two types of configuration variables. The first one is `CONFIG_*`, and it makes references to configuration options that can be configured by a user to enable various operational features. The other option is called `CFG_*` and this is used for configuration settings and to make references to hardware-specific details. The `CFG_*` variable usually requires good knowledge of a hardware platform, peripherals and processors in general. The configure file for the SAMA5D3 Xplained hardware platform is available inside the `include/config.h` header file, as follows:

```
/* Automatically generated - do not edit */
#define CONFIG_SAMA5D3  1
#define CONFIG_SYS_USE_NANDFLASH        1
#define CONFIG_SYS_ARCH  "arm"
#define CONFIG_SYS_CPU   "armv7"
#define CONFIG_SYS_BOARD "sama5d3_xplained"
#define CONFIG_SYS_VENDOR "atmel"
#define CONFIG_SYS_SOC    "at91"
#define CONFIG_BOARDDIR board/atmel/sama5d3_xplained
#include <config_cmd_defaults.h>
```

```
#include <config_defaults.h>
#include <configs/sama5d3_xplained.h>
#include <asm/config.h>
#include <config_fallbacks.h>
#include <config_uncmd_spl.h>
```

The configuration variables available here represent the corresponding configurations for the SAMA5D3 Xplained board. A part of these configurations refer to a number of standard commands available for user interactions with the bootloader. These commands can be added or removed for the purpose of extending or subtracting commands from the available command line interface.

More information on the U-Boot configurable command interface can be found at `http://www.denx.de/wiki/view/DULG/UBootCommandLineInterface`.

Booting the U-Boot options

In an industrial environment, interaction with the U-Boot is mainly done through the Ethernet interface. Not only does an Ethernet interface enable the faster transfer of operating system images, but it is also less prone to errors than a serial connection.

One of the most important features available inside a bootloader is related to the support for **Dynamic Host Control Protocol** (**DHCP**), **Trivial File Transfer Protocol** (**TFTP**), and even **Bootstrap Protocol** (**BOOTP**). BOOTP and DHPC enable an Ethernet connection to configure itself and acquire an IP address from a specialized server. TFTP enables the download of files through a TFTP server. The messages passed between a target device and the DHCP/BOOTP servers are represented in the following image in a more generic manner. Initially, the hardware platform sends a broadcast message that arrives at all the DHCP/BOOTP servers available. Each server sends back its offer, which also contains an IP address, and the client accepts the one that suits its purposes the best and declines the other ones.

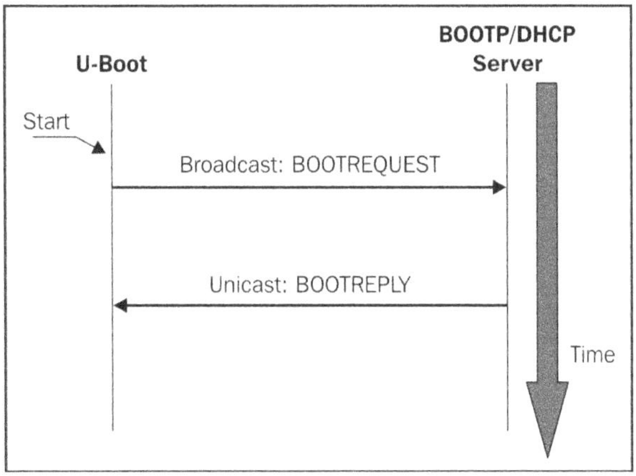

After the target device has finished communication with DHCP/BOOTP, it remains with a configuration that is specific to the target and contains information, such as the hostname, target IP and hardware Ethernet address (MAC address), netmask, tftp server IP address and even a TFTP filename. This information is bound to the Ethernet port and is used later in the booting process.

To boot images, U-Boot offers a number of capabilities that refer to the support of storage subsystems. These options include the RAM boot, MMC boot, NAND boot, NFS boot and so on. The support for these options is not always easy and could imply both hardware and software complexity.

Porting U-Boot

I've mentioned previously that U-Boot is one of the most used and known bootloaders available. This is also due to the fact that its architecture enables the porting of new development platforms and processors in a very easy manner. At the same time, there are a huge number of development platforms available that could be used as references. The first thing that any developer who is interested in porting a new platform should do is to inspect the `board` and `arch` directories to establish their baselines, and, at the same time, also identify their similarities with other CPUs and available boards.

The `board.cfg` file is the starting point to register a new platform. Here, the following information should be added as a table line:

- Status
- Architecture
- CPU
- SOC
- Vendor
- Board name
- Target
- Options
- Maintainers

To port a machine similar to SAMA5D3 Xplained, one of the directories that could be consulted is the arch directory. It contains files, such as board.c, with information related to the initialization process for boards and SOCs. The most notable processes are board_init_r(), which does the setup and probing for board and peripherals after its relocation in the RAM, board_init_f(), which identifies the stack size and reserved address before its relocation in the RAM, and init_sequence[], which is called inside the board_init_f for the setup of peripherals. Other important files inside the same locations are the bootm.c and interrupts.c files. The former has the main responsibility of the boot from memory of the operating system, and the latter is responsible for implementation of generic interrupts.

The board directory also has some interesting files and functions that need to be mentioned here, such as the board/atmel/sama5d3_xplained/sama5d3_xplained.c file. It contains functions, such as board_init(), dram_init(),board_eth_init(), board_mmc_init, spl_board_ init(), and mem_init() that are used for initialization, and some of them called by the arch/arm/lib/board.c file.

Here are some other relevant directories:

- common: This holds information about user commands, middleware, APIs that perform the interfacing between the middleware and user commands, and other functions and functionalities used by all available boards.
- drivers: This contains drivers for various device drivers and middleware APIs, such as drivers/mmc/mmc.c, drivers/pci/pci.c, drivers/watchdog/at91sam9_wdt.c and so on.
- fs: Various supported filesystems, such as USB, SD Card, Ext2 FAT, and so on are available here.
- include: This represents the location where all the headers necessary for most of the boards are present. SOCs and other software is also available. Inside include/configs, board-specific configurations are available, and include the headers imported from Linux; these could be used for various device drivers, porting, or other byte operations.
- tools: This is the place where tools, such as checkpatch.pl, a patch examination tool used as a coding style check, are used before sending it to the mailing list or the mkimage.c tool. This is also used for the U-Boot generic header generation that makes Linux binaries, and assures that they are able to be booted using U-Boot.

More information about the SAMA5D3 Xplained board can be found by inspecting the corresponding doc directory and `README` files, such as `README.at91`, `README.at91-soc`, `README.atmel_mci`, `README.atmel_pmecc`, `README.ARM-memory-map`, and so on.

For people interested in committing to the changes they made while porting a new development board, CPU, or SOC to U-Boot, a few rules should be followed. All of these are related to the `git` interaction and help you to ensure the proper maintenance of your branches.

The first thing that a developer should do is to track the upstream branch that corresponds to a local branch. Another piece of advice would be to forget about `git merge` and instead use `git rebase`. Keeping in contact with the upstream repository can be done using the `git fetch` command. To work with patches, some general rules need to be followed, and patches need to have only one logical change, which can be any one of these:

- Changes should not contain unrelated or different modifications; only one patch is available and acceptable per changeset
- Commits should make the use of `git-bisect` where possible while detecting bugs in sources, when necessary
- If multiple files are impacted by a set of modifications, all of them should be submitted in the same patch
- Patches need to have review, and a very thorough one at that

Let's take a look at following diagram, which illustrates the git rebase operation:

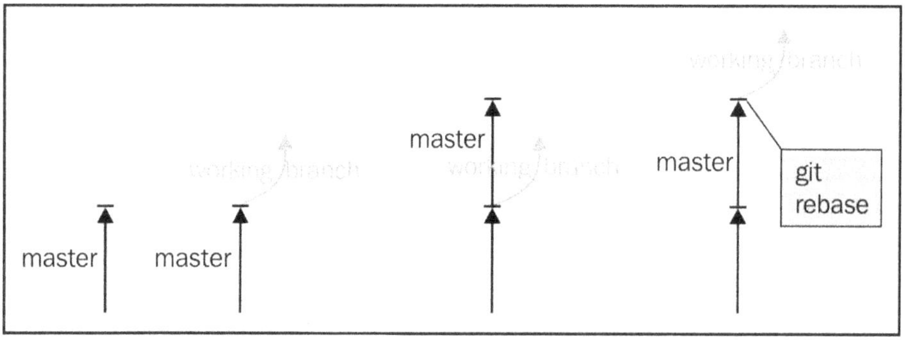

As shown in both the preceding and following diagram, the **git rebase** operation has recreated the work from one branch onto another. Every commit from one branch is made available on the succeeding one, just after the last commit from it.

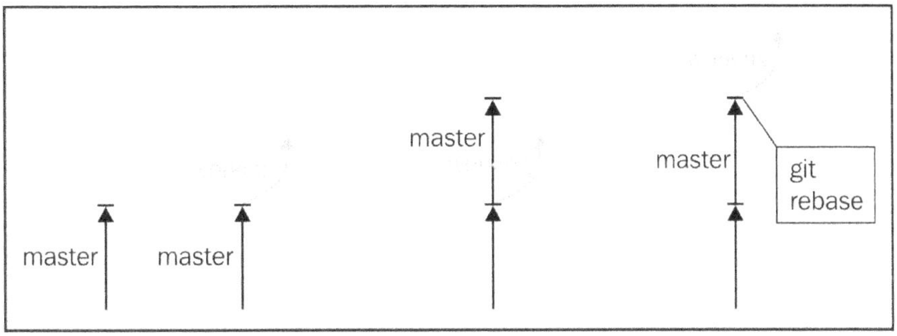

The `git merge` operation, on the other hand, is a new commit that has two parents: the branch from which it was ported, and the new branch on which it was merged. In fact, it gathers a series of commits into one branch with a different commit ID, which is why they are difficult to manage.

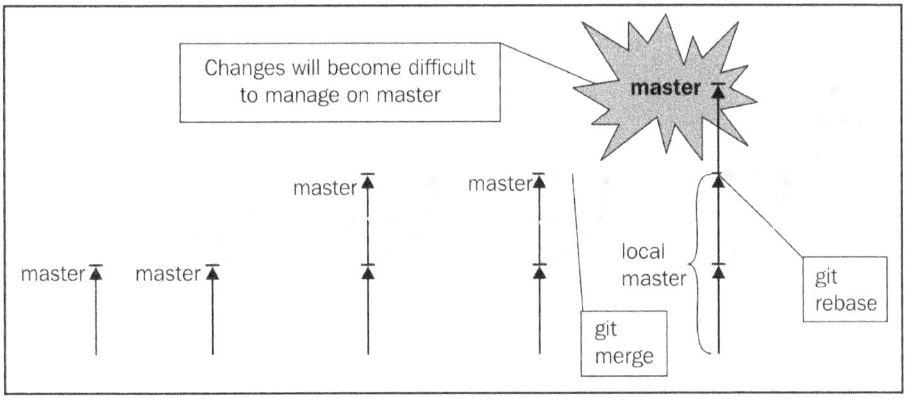

More information related to `git` interactions can be found at `http://git-scm.com/documentation` or `http://www.denx.de/wiki/U-Boot/Patches`.

Almost always when porting a new feature in U-Boot, debugging is involved. For a U-Boot debugger, there are two different situations that can occur:

- The first situation is when `lowlevel_init` was not executed
- The second situation is when the `lowlevel_init` was executed; this is the most well known scenario

In the next few lines, the second situation will be considered: the baseline enabling a debugging session for U-Boot. To make sure that debugging is possible, the `elf` file needs to be executed. Also, it cannot be manipulated directly because the linking address will be relocated. For this, a few tricks should be used:

- The first step is to make sure that the environment is clean and that old objects are not available any more: `make clean`
- The next step would be to make sure the dependencies are cleaned: `find ./ | grep depend | xargs rm`
- After the cleaning is finished, the target build can start and the output can be redirected inside a log file: `make sama5d3_xplained 2>&1 > make.log`
- The generated output should be renamed to avoid debugging problems for multiple boards: `mv u-boot.bin u-boot_sama5d3_xplained.bin`
- It is important to enable DEBUG in the board configuration file; inside `include/configs/ sama5d3_xplained.h`, add the `#define` DEBUG line

An early development platform can be set up after relocation takes place and the proper breakpoint should be set after the relocation has ended. A symbol needs to be reloaded for U-Boot because the relocation will move the linking address. For all of these tasks, a `gdb` script is indicated as `gdb gdb-script.sh`:

```
#!/bin/sh
${CROSS_COMPILE}-gdb u-boot -command=gdb-command-script.txt

vim gdb-command-script.txt
target remote ${ip}:${port}
load
set symbol-reloading
# break the process before calling board_init_r() function
b start.S:79
c
…
# the symbol-file need to be align to the address available after
relocation
add-symbol-file u-boot ${addr}
# break the process at board_init_r() function for single stepping
b board.c:494
```

> More information on relocation can be found at `doc/README.arm-relocation`.

The Yocto Project

The Yocto Project uses various recipes to define interactions to each of the supported bootloaders. Since there are multiple stages of booting, there are also multiple recipes and packages required inside the BSP. The recipes available for various bootloaders are not different from any other recipes available in the Yocto world. However, they have some details that make them unique.

The board that we will focus on here is the `sama5d3_xplained` development board, and it is available inside the `meta-atmel` layer. Inside this layer, the corresponding recipes for the first and second stage bootloaders can be found inside the `recipes-bsp` directory. Here, I am referring to the `at91bootstrap` and `u-boot` recipes. There are some misconceptions about first stage and second stage bootloaders. They might be referred to as second level and third level bootloaders, because the boot ROM code may or may not be taken into account during a discussion. In this book, we prefer to call them as first stage and second stage bootloaders.

The `AT91bootstrap` package represents the first-stage bootloader from Atmel available for their SOCs. It manages hardware initialization and also executes the second stage bootloader download from a boot media inside the memory; it starts it at the end. In the `meta-atmel` layer, the second stage bootloader is `u-boot`, and it is later used for the Linux operating system boot.

Usually, inside a BSP layer, the support for multiple development boards is offered, and this means that multiple versions and bootloader packages are offered as well. The distinction between them, however, is on the basis of machine configurations. For the SAMA5D3 Xplained development board, the machine configuration is available inside the `conf/machine/sama5d3_xplained` file. In this file, the preferred bootloader versions, providers, and configurations are defined. If these configurations are not `MACHINE` specific, they could very well be performed inside the `package` recipe.

This is one example of the configurations available for the `sama5d3_xplained` development board:

```
PREFERRED_PROVIDER_virtual/bootloader = "u-boot-at91"
UBOOT_MACHINE ?= "sama5d3_xplained_nandflash_config"
UBOOT_ENTRYPOINT = "0x20008000"
UBOOT_LOADADDRESS = "0x20008000"

AT91BOOTSTRAP_MACHINE ?= "sama5d3_xplained"
```

Summary

In this chapter, you were presented with information on bootloaders, with particular focus on the U-Boot bootloader. We also discussed topics related to U-Boot interaction, porting, debugging, general information on bootloaders, U-Boot alternatives and a boot sequence inside an embedded environment. There was also a section related to the Yocto Project, where you were introduced to the mechanism used to support various bootloaders available inside BSP. A number of exercises were presented across the chapter, and they offered more clarity on this subject.

In the next chapter, we will discuss the Linux kernel, its features and source code, modules and drivers, and, in general, most of the information needed to interact with the Linux kernel. As you have already been introduced to it, we will also concentrate on the Yocto Project and how it is able to work with various kernel versions for a number of boards and exercises. This should ease the understanding of the information presented to you.

4
Linux Kernel

In this chapter, you will not only learn about the Linux kernel in general, but also specific things about it. The chapter will start with a quick presentation of the history of Linux and its role and will then continue with an explanation of its various features. The steps used to interact with the sources of the Linux kernel will not be omitted. You will only be presented with the steps necessary to obtain a Linux kernel image from a source code, but also information about what porting for an new **ARM machine** implies, and some of the methods used to debug various problems that could appear when working with the Linux kernel sources in general. In the end, the context will be switched to the Yocto Project to show how the Linux kernel can be built for a given machine, and also how an external module can be integrated and used later from a root filesystem image.

This chapter will give you an idea of the Linux kernel and Linux operating system. This presentation would not have been possible without the historical component. Linux and UNIX are usually placed in the same historical context, but although the Linux kernel appeared in 1991 and the Linux operating system quickly became an alternative to the UNIX operating system, these two operating systems are members of the same family. Taking this into consideration, the history of UNIX operating system could not have started from another place. This means that we need to go back in time to more than 40 years ago, to be more precise, about 45 years ago to 1969 when Dennis Ritchie and Ken Thompson started the development of UNIX.

The predecessor of UNIX was **Multiplexed Information and Computing Service** (**Multics**), a multiuser operating system project that was not on its best shape at the time. Since the Multics had become a nonviable solution for Bell Laboratories Computer Sciences Research Center in the summer of 1969, a filesystem design was born and it later became what is known today as UNIX. Over time, it was ported on multiple machines due to its design and the fact that the source code was distributed alongside it. The most prolific contributor to the UNIX was the University of California, Berkeley. They also developed their own UNIX version called **Berkeley Software Distribution** (**BSD**), that was first released in 1977. Until the 1990s, multiple companies developed and offered their own distributions of UNIX, their main inspirations being Berkeley or AT&T. All of them helped UNIX become a stable, robust, and powerful operating system. Among the features that made UNIX strong as an operating system, the following can be mentioned:

- UNIX is simple. The number of system calls that it uses are reduced to only a couple of hundred and their design is basic
- Everything is regarded as a file in UNIX, making the manipulation of data and devices simpler, and it minimizes system calls used for interaction.
- Faster process creation time and the `fork()` system call.
- The UNIX kernel and utilities written in C language as well as a property that makes it easily portable and accessible.
- Simple and robust **interprocess communication** (**IPC**) primitives helps in the creation of fast and simple programs that accomplish only one thing in the best available manner.

Nowadays, UNIX is a mature operating system with support for features, such as virtual memory, TCP/IP networking, demand paging preemptive multiprocessing, and multithreading. The features spread is wide and varies from small embedded devices to systems with hundreds of processors. Its development has moved past the idea that UNIX is a research project, and it has become an operating system that is general-purpose and practically fits any needs. All this has happened due to its elegant design and proven simplicity. It was able to evolve without losing its capability to remain simple.

Linux is as an alternative solution to a UNIX variant called **Minix**, an operating system that was created for teaching purposes, but it lacked easy interaction with the system source code. Any changes made to the source code were not easily integrated and distributed because of Minix's license. Linus Torvalds first started working at a terminal emulator to connect to other UNIX systems from his university. Within the same academic year, emulator evolved in a full-fledged UNIX. He released it to be used by everyone in 1991.

One of the most attractive features of Linux is that it is an open source operating system whose source code is available under the GNU GPL license. When writing the Linux kernel, Linus Torvalds used the best design choices and features from the UNIX available in variations of the operating system kernel as a source of inspiration. Its license is what has propelled it into becoming the powerhouse it is today. It has engaged a large number of developers that helped with code enhancements, bug fixing, and much more.

Today, Linux is an experienced operating system that is able to run on a multitude of architectures. It is able to run on devices that are even smaller than a wristwatch or on clusters of supercomputer. It's the new sensation of our days and is being adopted by companies and developers around the world in an increasingly diversified manner. The interest in the Linux operating system is very strong and this implies not only diversity, but also offers a great number of benefits, ranging from security, new features, embedded solutions to server solution options, and many more.

Linux has become a truly collaborative project developed by a huge community over the internet. Although a great number of changes were made inside this project, Linus has remained its creator and maintainer. Change is a constant factor in everything around us and this applies to Linux and its maintainer, who is now called Greg Kroah-Hartman, and has already been its kernel maintainer for two years now. It may seem that in the period that Linus was around, the Linux kernel was a loose-knit community of developers. This may be because of Linus' harsh comments that are known worldwide. Since Greg has been appointed the kernel maintainer, this image started fading gradually. I am looking forward to the years to come.

The role of the Linux kernel

With an impressive numbers of code lines, the Linux kernel is one of the most prominent open source projects and at the same time, the largest available one. The Linux kernel constitutes a piece of software that helps with the interfacing of hardware, being the lowest-level code available that runs in everyone's Linux operating system. It is used as an interface for other user space applications, as described in the following diagram:

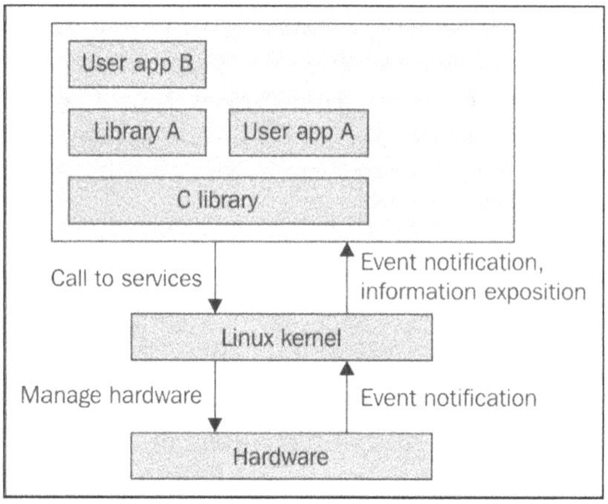

The main roles of the Linux kernel are as follows:

- It provides a set of portable hardware and architecture APIs that offer user space applications the possibility to use necessary hardware resources
- It helps with the management of hardware resources, such as a CPU, input/output peripherals, and memory
- It is used for the management of concurrent accesses and the usage of necessary hardware resources by different applications.

To make sure that the preceding roles are well understood, an example will be very useful. Let's consider that in a given Linux operating system, a number of applications need access to the same resource, a network interface, or a device. For these elements, the kernel needs to multiplex a resource in order to make sure that all applications have access to it.

Delving into the features of the Linux kernel

This section will introduce a number of features available inside the Linux kernel. It will also cover information about each of them, how they are used, what they represent, and any other relevant information regarding each specific functionality. The presentation of each feature familiarizes you with the main role of some of the features available inside the Linux kernel, as well as the Linux kernel and its source code in general.

On a more general note, some of the most valuable features that the Linux kernel has are as follows:

- Stability and reliability
- Scalability
- Portability and hardware support
- Compliance with standards
- Interoperability between various standards
- Modularity
- Ease of programming
- Comprehensive support from the community
- Security

The preceding features does not constitute actual functionalities, but have helped the project along its development process and are still helping it today. Having said this, there are a lot of features that are implemented, such as fast user space mutex (futex), netfileters, Simplified Mandatory Access Control Kernel (smack), and so on. A complete list of these can be accessed and studied at `http://en.wikipedia.org/wiki/Category:Linux_kernel_features`.

Memory mapping and management

When discussing the memory in Linux, we can refer to it as the physical and virtual memory. Compartments of the RAM memory are used for the containment of the Linux kernel variables and data structures, the rest of the memory being used for dynamic allocations, as described here:

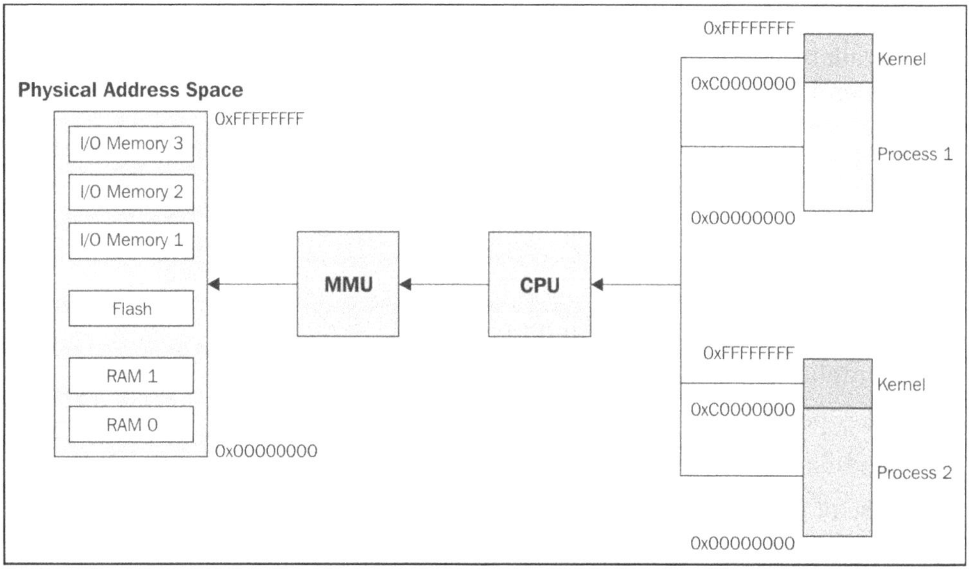

The physical memory defines algorithms and data structures that are able to maintain the memory, and it is done at the page level relatively independently by the virtual memory. Here, each physical page has a `struct page` descriptor associated with it that is used to incorporate information about the physical page. Each page has a `struct page` descriptor defined. Some of the fields of this structure are as follows:

- `_count`: This represents the page counter. When it reaches the `0` value, the page is added to the free pages list.
- `virtual`: This represents the virtual address associated to a physical page. The **ZONE_DMA** and **ZONE_NORMAL** pages are always mapped, while the **ZONE_HIGHMEN** are not always mapped.
- `flags`: This represents a set of flags that describe the attributes of the page.

The zones of the physical memory have been previously. The physical memory is split up into multiple nodes that have a common physical address space and a fast local memory access. The smallest of them is **ZONE_DMA** between 0 to 16Mb. The next is **ZONE_NORMAL**, which is the LowMem area between 16Mb to 896Mb, and the largest one is **ZONE_HIGHMEM**, which is between 900Mb to 4GB/64Gb. This information can be visible both in the preceding and following images:

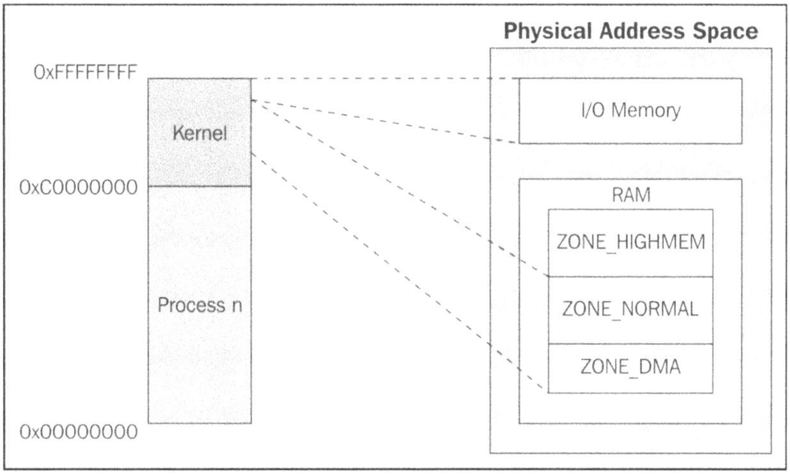

The virtual memory is used both in the user space and the kernel space. The allocation for a memory zone implies the allocation of a physical page as well as the allocation of an address space area; this is done both in the page table and in the internal structures available inside the operating system. The usage of the page table differs from one architecture type to another. For the **Complex instruction set computing** (**CISC**) architecture, the page table is used by the processor, but on a **Reduced instruction set computing** (**RISC**) architecture, the page table is used by the core for a page lookup and **translation lookaside buffer** (**TLB**) add operations. Each zone descriptor is used for zone mapping. It specifies whether the zone is mapped for usage by a file if the zone is read-only, copy-on-write, and so on. The address space descriptor is used by the operating system to maintain high-level information.

The memory allocation is different between the user space and kernel space context because the kernel space memory allocation is not able to allocate memory in an easy manner. This difference is mostly due to the fact that error management in the kernel context is not easily done, or at least not in the same key as the user space context. This is one of the problems that will be presented in this section along with the solutions because it helps readers understand how memory management is done in the context of the Linux kernel.

The methods used by the kernel for memory handling is the first subject that will be discussed here. This is done to make sure that you understand the methods used by the kernel to obtain memory. Although the smallest addressable unit of a processor is a byte, the **Memory Management Unit** (**MMU**), the unit responsible for virtual to physical translation the smallest addressable unit is the page. A page's size varies from one architecture to another. It is responsible for maintaining the system's page tables. Most of 32-bit architectures use 4KB pages, whereas the 64-bit ones usually have 8KB pages. For the Atmel SAMA5D3-Xplained board, the definition of the `struct page` structure is as follows:

```
struct page {
        unsigned long   flags;
        atomic_t          _count;
        atomic_t          _mapcount;
        struct address_space *mapping;
        void        *virtual;
        unsigned long  debug_flags;
        void        *shadow;
        int         _last_nid;

};
```

This is one of the most important fields of the page structure. The `flags` field, for example, represents the status of the page; this holds information, such as whether the page is dirty or not, locked, or in another valid state. The values that are associated with this flag are defined inside the `include/linux/page-flags-layout.h` header file. The `virtual` field represents the virtual address associated with the page, `count` represents the count value for the page that is usually accessible indirectly through the `page_count()` function. All the other fields can be accessed inside the `include/linux/mm_types.h` header file.

The kernel divides the hardware into various zone of memory, mostly because there are pages in the physical memory that are not accessible for a number of the tasks. For example, there are hardware devices that can perform DMA. These actions are done by interacting with only a zone of the physical memory, simply called `ZONE_DMA`. It is accessible between 0-16 Mb for x86 architectures.

There are four main memory zones available and other two less notable ones that are defined inside the kernel sources in the `include/linux/mmzone.h` header file. The zone mapping is also architecture-dependent for the Atmel SAMA5D3-Xplained board. We have the following zones defined:

```
enum zone_type {
#ifdef CONFIG_ZONE_DMA
```

```
        /*
         * ZONE_DMA is used when there are devices that are not able
         * to do DMA to all of addressable memory (ZONE_NORMAL). Then
we
         * carve out the portion of memory that is needed for these
devices.
         * The range is arch specific.
         *
         * Some examples
         *
         * Architecture         Limit
         * ---------------------------
         * parisc, ia64, sparc  <4G
         * s390                 <2G
         * arm                  Various
         * alpha                Unlimited or 0-16MB.
         *
         * i386, x86_64 and multiple other arches
         *                      <16M.
         */
        ZONE_DMA,
#endif
#ifdef CONFIG_ZONE_DMA32
        /*
         * x86_64 needs two ZONE_DMAs because it supports devices that
are
         * only able to do DMA to the lower 16M but also 32 bit
devices that
         * can only do DMA areas below 4G.
         */
        ZONE_DMA32,
#endif
        /*
         * Normal addressable memory is in ZONE_NORMAL. DMA operations
can be
         * performed on pages in ZONE_NORMAL if the DMA devices
support
         * transfers to all addressable memory.
         */
        ZONE_NORMAL,
#ifdef CONFIG_HIGHMEM
        /*
         * A memory area that is only addressable by the kernel
through
```

```
         * mapping portions into its own address space. This is for
example
         * used by i386 to allow the kernel to address the memory
beyond
         * 900MB. The kernel will set up special mappings (page
         * table entries on i386) for each page that the kernel needs
to
         * access.
         */
        ZONE_HIGHMEM,
#endif
        ZONE_MOVABLE,
        __MAX_NR_ZONES
};
```

There are allocations that require interaction with more than one zone. One such example is a normal allocation that is able to use either `ZONE_DMA` or `ZONE_NORMAL`. `ZONE_NORMAL` is preferred because it does not interfere with direct memory accesses, though when the memory is at full usage, the kernel might use other available zones besides the ones that it uses in normal scenarios. The kernel that is available is a **struct zone** structure that defines each zone's relevant information. For the Atmel SAMA5D3-Xplained board, this structure is as shown here:

```
struct zone {
        unsigned long  watermark[NR_WMARK];
        unsigned long  percpu_drift_mark;
        unsigned long  lowmem_reserve[MAX_NR_ZONES];
        unsigned long  dirty_balance_reserve;
        struct per_cpu_pageset __percpu *pageset;
        spinlock_t        lock;
        int        all_unreclaimable;
        struct free_area        free_area[MAX_ORDER];
        unsigned int            compact_considered;
        unsigned int            compact_defer_shift;
        int                     compact_order_failed;
        spinlock_t              lru_lock;
        struct lruvec           lruvec;
        unsigned long         pages_scanned;
        unsigned long         flags;
        unsigned int        inactive_ratio;
        wait_queue_head_t       * wait_table;
        unsigned long         wait_table_hash_nr_entries;
        unsigned long         wait_table_bits;
        struct pglist_data    *zone_pgdat;
```

```
        unsigned long         zone_start_pfn;
        unsigned long         spanned_pages;
        unsigned long         present_pages;
        unsigned long         managed_pages;
        const char              *name;
};
```

As you can see, the zone that defines the structure is an impressive one. Some of the most interesting fields are represented by the `watermark` variable, which contain the high, medium, and low watermarks for the defined zone. The `present_pages` attribute represents the available pages within the zone. The `name` field represents the name of the zone, and others, such as the `lock` field, a spin lock that shields the zone structure for simultaneous access. All the other fields that can be identified inside the corresponding `include/linux/mmzone.h` header file for the Atmel SAMA5D3 Xplained board.

With this information available, we can move ahead and find out how the kernel implements memory allocation. All the available functions that are necessary for memory allocation and memory interaction in general, are inside the `linux/gfp.h` header file. Some of these functions are:

```
struct page * alloc_pages(gfp_t gfp_mask, unsigned int order)
```

This function is used to allocate physical pages in a continuous location. At the end, the return value is represented by the pointer of the first page structure if the allocation is successful, or `NULL` if errors occur:

```
void * page_address(struct page *page)
```

This function is used to get the logical address for a corresponding memory page:

```
unsigned long __get_free_pages(gfp_t gfp_mask, unsigned int order)
```

This one is similar to the `alloc_pages()` function, but the difference is that the return variable is offered in the `struct page * alloc_page(gfp_t gfp_mask)` return argument:

```
unsigned long __get_free_page(gfp_t gfp_mask)
struct page * alloc_page(gfp_t gfp_mask)
```

The preceding two functions are wrappers over similar ones, the difference is that this function returns only one page information. The order for this function has the `zero` value:

```
unsigned long get_zeroed_page(unsigned int gfp_mask)
```

The preceding function does what the name suggests. It returns the page full of `zero` values. The difference between this function and the `__get_free_page()` function is that after being released, the page is filled with `zero` values:

```
void __free_pages(struct page *page, unsigned int order)
void free_pages(unsigned long addr, unsigned int order)
void free_page(unsigned long addr)
```

The preceding functions are used for freeing the given allocated pages. The passing of the pages should be done with care because the kernel is not able to check the information it is provided.

Page cache and page writeback

Usually the disk is slower than the physical memory, so this is one of the reasons that memory is preferred over disk storage. The same applies for processor's cache levels: the closer it resides to the processor the faster it is for the I/O access. The process that moves data from the disk into the physical memory is called **page caching**. The inverse process is defined as **page writeback**. These two notions will be presented in this subsection, but is it mainly about the kernel context.

The first time the kernel calls the `read()` system call, the data is verified if it is present in the page cache. The process by which the page is found inside the RAM is called **cache hit**. If it is not available there, then data needs to be read from the disk and this process is called **cache miss**.

When the kernel issues the **write()** system call, there are multiple possibilities for cache interaction with regard to this system call. The easiest one is to not cache the write system calls operations and only keep the data in the disk. This scenario is called **no-write cache**. When the write operation updates the physical memory and the disk data at the same time, the operation is called **write-through cache**. The third option is represented by **write-back cache** where the page is marked as dirty. It is added to the dirty list and over time, it is put on the disk and marked as not dirty. The best synonym for the dirty keyword is represented by the synchronized key word.

The process address space

Besides its own physical memory, the kernel is also responsible for user space process and memory management. The memory allocated for each user space process is called **process address space** and it contains the virtual memory addressable by a given process. It also contains the related addresses used by the process in its interaction with the virtual memory.

Usually a process receives a flat 32 or 64-bit address space, its size being dependent on the architecture type. However, there are operating systems that allocate a **segmented address space**. The possibility of sharing the address space between the operating systems is offered to threads. Although a process can access a large memory space, it usually has permission to access only an interval of memory. This is called a **memory area** and it means that a process can only access a memory address situated inside a viable memory area. If it somehow tries to administrate a memory address outside of its valid memory area, the kernel will kill the process with the *Segmentation fault* notification.

A memory area contains the following:

- The `text` section maps source code
- The `data` section maps initialized global variables
- The `bss` section maps uninitialized global variables
- The `zero page` section is used to process user space stack
- The `shared libraries text`, `bss` and data-specific sections
- Mapped files
- Anonymous memory mapping is usually linked with functions, such as `malloc()`
- Shared memory segments

A process address space is defined inside the Linux kernel source through a **memory descriptor**. This structure is called `struct mm_struct`, which is defined inside the `include/linux/mm_types.h` header file and contains information relevant for a process address space, such as the number of processes that use the address space, a list of memory areas, the last memory area that was used, the number of memory areas available, start and finish addresses for the code, data, heap and stack sections.

For a kernel thread, no process address space associated with it; for kernel, the process descriptor structure is defined as `NULL`. In this way, the kernel mentions that a kernel thread does not have a user context. A kernel thread only has access to the same memory as all the other processes. A kernel thread does not have any pages in a user space or access to the user space memory.

Since the processors work only with physical addresses, the translation between physical and virtual memory needs to be made. These operations are done by the page tables that split the virtual addresses into smaller components with associated indexes that are used for pointing purposes. In the majority of available boards and architectures in general, the page table lookup is handled by the hardware; the kernel is responsible for setting it up.

Process management

A process, as presented previously, is a fundamental unit in a Linux operating system and at the same time, is a form of abstraction. It is, in fact, a program in execution, but a program by itself is not a process. It needs to be in an active state and have associated resources. A process is able to become a parent by using the `fork()` function, which spawns a child process. Both parent and child processes reside in separate address spaces, but both of them have the same content. The `exec()` family of function is the one that is able to execute a different program, create an address space, and load it inside that address space.

When `fork()` is used, the resources that the parent process has are reproduced for the child. This function is implemented in a very interesting manner; it uses the `clone()` system call that, at it's base, contains the `copy_process()` function. This functions does the following:

- Calls the `dup_task_struct()` function to create a new kernel stack. The `task_struct` and `thread_info` structures are created for a new process.
- Checks that the child does not go beyond the limits of the memory area.
- The child process distinguishes itself from its parent.
- It is set as `TASK_UNINTERRUPTIBLE` to make sure it does not run.
- Flags are updated.
- `PID` is associated with the child process.
- The flags that are already set are inspected and proper action is performed with respect to their values.
- The clean process is performed at the end when the child process pointer is obtained.

Threads in Linux are very similar to processes. They are viewed as processes that share various resources, such as memory address space, open files, and so on. The creation of threads is similar to a normal task, the exception being the `clone()` function, which passes flags that mention shared resources. For example, the clone function calls for a thread, which is `clone(CLONE_VM | CLONE_FS | CLONE_FILES | CLONE_SIGHAND, 0)`, while for the normal fork looks similar to `clone(SIGCHLD, 0)`.

The notion of kernel threads appeared as a solution to problems involving tasks running in the background of the kernel context. The kernel thread does not have an address space and is only available inside the kernel context. It has the same properties as a normal process, but is only used for special tasks, such as `ksoftirqd`, `flush`, and so on.

At the end of the execution, the process need to be terminated so that the resources can be freed, and the parent of the executing process needs to be notified about this. The method that is most used to terminate a process is done by calling the `exit()` system call. A number of steps are needed for this process:

1. The `PF_EXITING` flag is set.
2. The `del_timer_sync()` function is called to remove the kernel timers.
3. The `acct_update_integrals()` function is called when writing accounting and logging information.
4. The `exit_mm()` is called to release the `mm_struct` structure for the process.
5. The `exit_sem()` is called to dequeue the process from the IPC semaphore.
6. The `exit_files()` and `exit_fs()` function are called to remove the links to various files descriptors.
7. The task exit code should be set.
8. Call `exit_notify()` to notify the parent and set the task exit state to `EXIT_ZOMBIE`.
9. Call `schedule()` to switch to a new process.

After the preceding steps are performed, the object associated with this task is freed and it becomes unrunnable. Its memory exists solely as information for its parent. After its parent announces that this information is of no use to it, this memory is freed for the system to use.

Process scheduling

The process scheduler decides which resources are allocated for a runnable process. It is a piece of software that is responsible for multitasking, resource allocation to various processes, and decides how to best set the resources and processor time. it also decides which processes should run next.

The first design of the Linux scheduler was very simplistic. It was not able to scale properly when the number of processes increased, so from the 2.5 kernel version, a new scheduler was developed. It is called **O(1) scheduler** and offers a constant time algorithm for time slice calculation and a run queue that is defined on a per-processor basis. Although it is perfect for large servers, it is not the best solution for a normal desktop system. From the 2.6 kernel version, improvements have been made to the O(1) scheduler, such as the fair scheduling concept that later materialized from the kernel version 2.6.23 into the **Completely Fair Scheduler** (**CFS**), which became the defacto scheduler.

The CFC has a simple idea behind. It behaves as if we have a perfect multitasking processor where each process gets `1/n` slice of the processor's time and this time slice is an incredibly small. The `n` value represents the number of running processes. Con Kolivas is the Australian programmer that contributed to the fair scheduling implementation, also known as **Rotating Staircase Deadline Scheduler** (**RSDL**). Its implementation required a red-black tree for the priorities of self-balancing and also a time slice that is calculated at the nanosecond level. Similarly to the O(1) scheduler, CFS applies the notion of weight, which implies that some processes wait more than others. This is based on the weighed fair queuing algorithm.

A process scheduler constitutes one of the most important components of the Linux kernel because it defines the user interaction with the operating system in general. The Linux kernel CFS is the scheduler that appeals to developers and users because it offers scalability and performance with the most reasonable approach.

System calls

For processes to interact with a system, an interface should be provided to give the user space application the possibility of interacting with hardware and other `processes.System` calls. These are used as an interface between the hardware and the user space. They are also used to ensure stability, security, and abstraction, in general. These are common layers that constitute an entry point into the kernel alongside traps and exceptions, as described here:

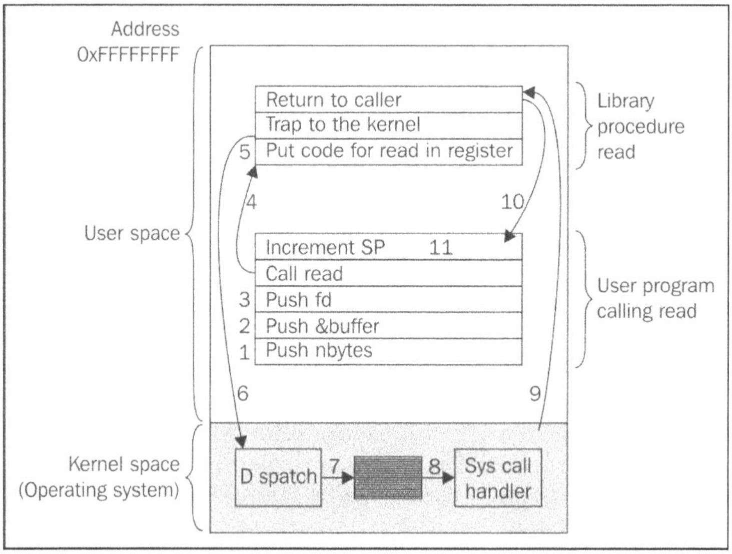

The interaction with most of the system calls that are available inside the Linux system is done using the C library. They are able to define a number of arguments and return a value that reveals whether they were successful or not. A value of `zero` usually means that the execution ended with success, and in case errors appear, an error code will be available inside the `errno` variable. When a system call is done, the following steps are followed:

1. The switch into kernel mode is made.
2. Any restrictions to the kernel space access are eliminated.
3. The stack from the user space is passed into the kernel space.
4. Any arguments from the user space are checked and copied into the kernel space.
5. The associated routine for the system call is identified and run.
6. The switch to the user space is made and the execution of the application continues.

A system call has a `syscall` number associated with it, which is a unique number used as a reference for the system call that cannot be changed (there is no possibility of implementing a system call). A symbolic constant for each system call number is available in the `<sys/syscall.h>` header file. To check the existence of a system call, `sys_ni_syscall()` is used, which returns the `ENOSYS` error for an invalid system call.

The virtual file system

The Linux operating system is able to support a large variety of filesystem options. This is done due to the existence of **Virtual File System** (**VFS**), which is able to provide a common interface for a large number of filesystem types and handle the systems calls relevant to them.

The filesystem types supported by the VFS can be put in these three categories:

- **Disk-based filesystems**: These manage the memory on a local disk or devices that are used for disk emulation. Some of the most well known ones are:
    - Linux filesystems, such as Second Extended Filesystem (Ext2), Third Extended Filesystem (Ext3), and Forth Extended Filesystem (Ext4)
    - UNIX filesystems, such as sysv filesystem, UFS, Minix filesystem, and so on
    - Microsoft filesystems, such as MS-DOS, NTFS (available since Windows NT), and VFAT (available since Windows 95)

    - ISO966 CD-ROM filesystem and disk format DVD filesystem
    - Proprietary filesystems, such as the ones from Apple, IBM, and other companies

- **Network filesystems**: They are allowed to access various filesystem types over a network on other computers. One of the most well known ones is NFS. Of course, there are others but they are not as well known. These include **Andrew filesystem** (**AFS**), **Novel's NetWare Core Protocol** (**NCP**), **Constant Data Availability** (**Coda**), and so on.
- **Special filesystems**: The `/proc` filesystem is the perfect example for this category of filesystems. This category of filesystems enables an easier access for system applications to interrogate data structures of kernels and implement various features.

The virtual filesystem system call implementation is very well summarized in this image:

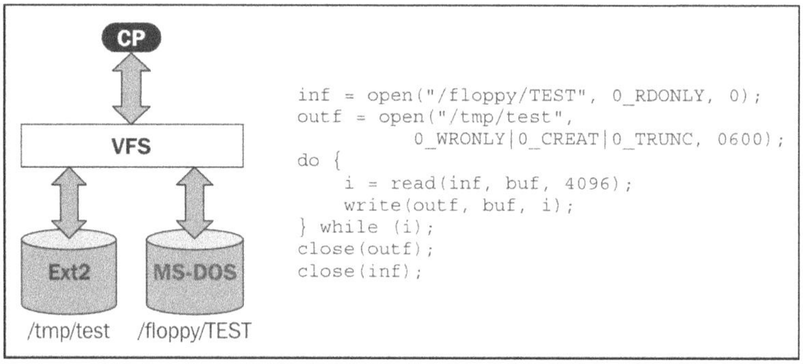

In the preceding image, it can be seen how easily the copy is handled from one filesystem type to another. It only uses the basic `open()`, `close()`, `read()`, `write()` functions available for all the other filesystem interaction. However, all of them implement the specific functionality underneath for the chosen filesystem. For example, the `open()` system calls `sys_open()` and it takes the same arguments as `open()` and returns the same result. The difference between `sys_open()` and `open()` is that `sys_open()` is a more permissive function.

All the other three system calls have corresponding `sys_read()`, `sys_write()`, and `sys_close()` functions that are called internally.

Interrupts

An interrupt is a representation of an event that changes the succession of instructions performed by the processor. Interrupts imply an electric signal generated by the hardware to signal an event that has happened, such as a key press, reset, and so on. Interrupts are divided into more categories depending on their reference system, as follows:.

- Software interrupts: These are usually exceptions triggered from external devices and user space programs
- Hardware interrupts: These are signals from the system that usually indicate a processor specific instruction

The Linux interrupt handling layer offers an abstraction of interrupt handling for various device drivers through comprehensive API functions. It is used to request, enable, disable, and free interrupts, making sure that portability is guaranteed on multiple platforms. It handles all available interrupt controller hardware.

The generic interrupt handling uses the `__do_IRQ()` handler, which is able to deal with all the available types of the interrupt logic. The handling layers are divided in two components:

- The top half component is used to respond to the interrupt
- The bottom half component is scheduled by the top half to run at a later time

The difference between them is that all the available interrupts are permitted to act in the bottom half context. This helps the top half respond to another interrupt while the bottom half is working, which means that it is able to save its data in a specific buffer and it permits the bottom half to operate in a safe environment.

For the bottom half processing, there are four defined mechanisms available:

- **Softirqs**
- **Tasklets**
- **Work queues**
- **Kernel threads**

The available mechanisms are well presented here:

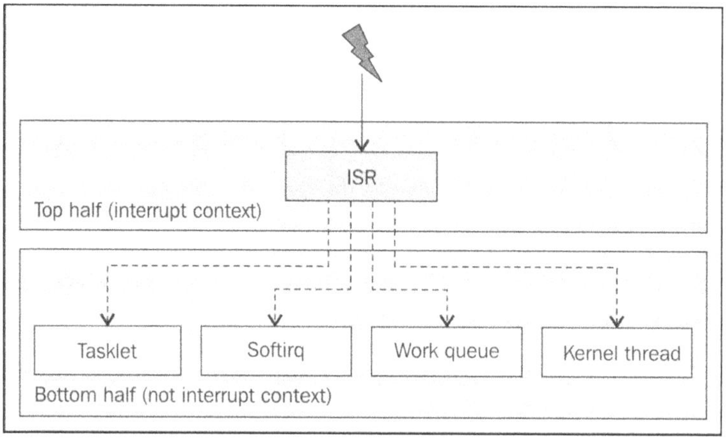

Although the model for the top and bottom half interrupt mechanism looks simple, it has a very complicated function calling mechanism model. This example shows this fact for the ARM architecture:

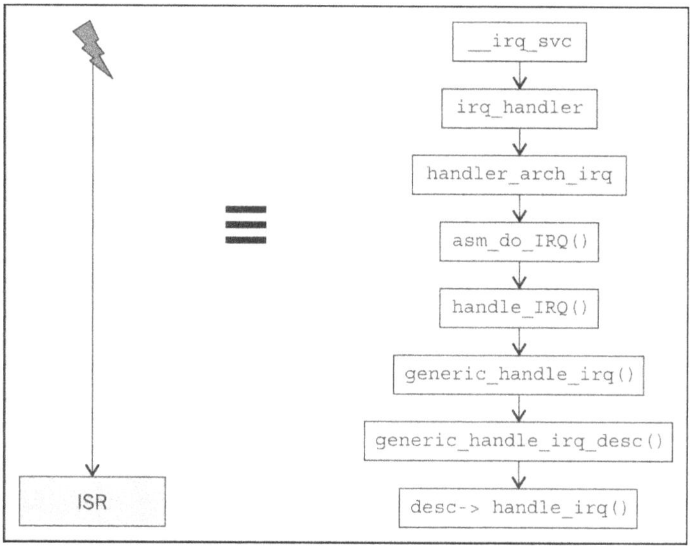

For the top half component of the interrupt, there are three levels of abstraction in the interrupt source code. The first one is the high-level driver API that has functions, such as `request_irq()`, `free_irq`, `disable_irq()`, `enable_irq()`, and so on. The second one is represented by the high-level IRQ flow handlers, which is a generic layer with predefined or architecture-specific interrupt flow handlers assigned to respond to various interrupts during device initialization or boot time. It defines a number of predefined functions, such as `handle_level_irq()`, `handle_simple_irq()`, `handle_percpu_irq()`, and so on. The third is represented by chip-level hardware encapsulation. It defines the `struct irq_chip` structure that holds chip-relevant functions used in the IRQ flow implementation. Some of the functions are `irq_ack()`, `irq_mask()`, and `irq_unmask()`.

A module is required to register an interrupt channel and release it afterwards. The total number of supported requests is counted from the `0` value to the number of IRQs-1. This information is available inside the `<asm/irq.h>` header file. When the registration is done, a handler flag is passed to the `request_irq()` function to specify the interrupt handler's type, as follows:

- `SA_SAMPLE_RANDOM`: This indicates that the interrupt can contribute to the entropy pool, that is, a pool with bits that possess a strong random property, by sampling unpredictable events, such as mouse movement, inter-key press time, disk interrupts, and so on
- `SA_SHIRQ`: This shows that the interrupt is sharable between devices.
- `SA_INTERRUPT`: This indicates a fast interrupt handler, so interrupts are disabled on the current processor-it does not represent a situation that is very desirable

Bottom halves

The first mechanism that will be discussed regarding bottom half interrupt handling is represented by `softirqs`. They are rarely used but can be found on the Linux kernel source code inside the `kernel/softirq.c` file. When it comes to implementation, they are statically allocated at the compile step. They are created when an entry is added in the `include/linux/interrupt.h` header file and the system information they provide is available inside the `/proc/softirqs` file. Although not used too often, they can be executed after exceptions, interrupts, system calls, and when the `ksoftirkd` daemon is run by the scheduler.

Next on the list are tasklets. Although they are built on top of `softirqs`, they are more commonly used for bottom half interrupt handling. Here are some of the reasons why this is done:

- They are very fast
- They can be created and destroyed dynamically
- They have atomic and nonblocking code
- They run in a soft interrupt context
- They run on the same processor that they were scheduled for

Tasklets have a **struct tasklet_struct** structure available. These are also available inside the `include/linux/interrupt.h` header file, and unlike `softirqs`, tasklets are non-reentrant.

Third on the list are work queues that represent a different form of doing the work allotted in comparison to previously presented mechanisms. The main differences are as follows:

- They are able run in the same time on more the one CPU
- They are allowed to go to sleep
- They runs on a process context
- They can be scheduled or preempted

Although they might have a latency that is slightly bigger the tasklets, the preceding qualities are really useful. The tasklets are built around the `struct workqueue_struct` structure, available inside the `kernel/workqueue.c` file.

The last and the newest addition to the bottom half mechanism options is represented by the kernel threads that are operated entirely in the kernel mode since they are created/destroyed by the kernel. They appeared during the 2.6.30 kernel release, and also have the same advantages as the work queues, along with some extra features, such as the possibility of having their own context. It is expected that eventually the kernel threads will replace the work queues and tasklets, since they are similar to the user space threads. A driver might want to request a threaded interrupt handler. All it needs to do in this case is to use `request_threaded_irq()` in a similar way to `request_irq()`. The `request_threaded_irq()` function offers the possibility of passing a handler and `thread_fn` to split the interrupt handling code into two parts. In addition to this, `quick_check_handler` is called to check if the interrupt was called from a device; if that is the case, it will need to call `IRQ_WAKE_THREAD` to wake up the handler thread and execute `thread_fn`.

Methods to perform kernel synchronization

The number of requests with which a kernel is dealing is likened to the number of requests a server has to receive. This situation can deal with race conditions, so a good synchronization method would be required. A number of policies are available for the way the kernel behaves by defining a kernel control path. Here is an example of a kernel control path:

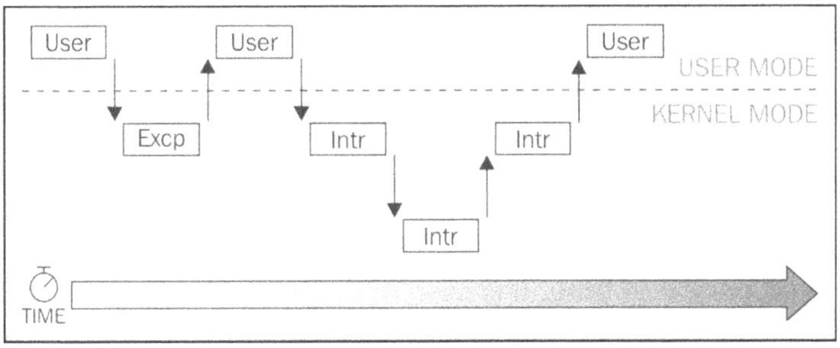

The preceding image offers a clear picture as to why synchronization is necessary. For example, a race condition can appear when more than one kernel control path is interlinked. To protect these critical regions, a number of measures should be taken. Also, it should be taken into consideration that an interrupt handler cannot be interrupted and `softirqs` should not be interleaved.

A number of synchronization primitives have been born:

- **Per-CPU variables**: This is one of the most simple and efficient synchronization methods. It multiplies a data structure so that each one is available for each CPU.
- **Atomic operations**: This refers to atomic read-modify-write instructions.
- **Memory barrier**: This safeguards the fact that the operations done before the barrier are all finished before starting the operations after it.
- **Spin lock**: This represents a type of lock that implements bust waiting.
- **Semaphore**: This is a form of locking that implements sleep or blocking waiting.
- **Seqlocks**: This is similar to spin locks, but is based on an access counter.
- **Local interrupt disabling**: This forbids the use of functions that can be postponed on a single CPU.
- **Read-copy-update(RCU)**: This is a method designed to protect the most used data structures used for reading. It offers a lock-free access to shared data structures using pointers.

With the preceding methods, race condition situations try to be fixed. It is the job of the developer to identify and solve all the eventual synchronization problems that might appear.

Timers

Around the Linux kernel, there are a great number of functions that are influenced by time. From the scheduler to the system uptime, they all require a time reference, which includes both absolute and relative time. For example, an event that needs to be scheduled for the future, represents a relative time, which, in fact, implies that there is a method used to count time.

The timer implementation can vary depending on the type of the event. The periodical implementations are defined by the system timer, which issues an interrupt at a fixed period of time. The system timer is a hardware component that issues a timer interrupt at a given frequency to update the system time and execute the necessary tasks. Another one that can be used is the real-time clock, which is a chip with a battery attached that keeps counting time long after the system was shut down. Besides the system time, there are dynamic timers available that are managed by the kernel dynamically to plan events that run after a particular time has passed.

The timer interrupt has an occurrence window and for ARM, it is 100 times per second. This is called the **system timer frequency** or **tick rate** and its unit of measurement is **hertz** (**Hz**). The tick rate differs from one architecture to another. If for the most of them, we have the value of 100 Hz, there are others that have values of 1024 Hz, such as the Alpha and Itanium (IA-64) architectures, for example. The default value, of course, can be changed and increased, but this action has its advantages and disadvantages.

Some of the advantages of higher frequency are:

- The timer will be executed more accurately and in a larger number
- System calls that use a timeout are executed in a more precise manner
- Uptime measurements and other similar measurements are becoming more precise
- The preemption of process is more accurate

The disadvantages of higher frequency on the other hand, implies a higher overhead. The processors spend more time in a timer interrupt context; also, an increase in power consumption will take place because more computing is done.

The total number of ticks done on a Linux operation system from the time it started booting is stored in a variable called **jiffies** inside the `include/linux/jiffies.h` header file. At boot time, this variable is initialized to zero and one is added to its value each time an interrupt happens. So, the actual value of the system uptime can be calculated in the form of jiffies/Hz.

Linux kernel interaction

Until now, you were introduced to some of features of the Linux kernel. Now, it is time to present more information about the development process, versioning scheme, community contributions, and and interaction with the Linux kernel.

The development process

Linux kernel is a well known open source project. To make sure that developers know how to interact with it, information about how the `git` interaction is done with this project, and at the same time, some information about its development and release procedures will be presented. The project has evolved and its development processes and release procedures have evolved with it.

Before presenting the actual development process, a bit of history will be necessary. Until the 2.6 version of the Linux kernel project, one release was made every two or three years, and each of them was identified by even middle numbers, such as 1.0.x, 2.0.x, and 2.6.x. The development branches were instead defined using even numbers, such as 1.1.x, 2.1.x, and 2.5.x, and they were used to integrate various features and functionalities until a major release was prepared and ready to be shipped. All the minor releases had names, such as 2.6.32 and 2.2.23, and they were released between major release cycles.

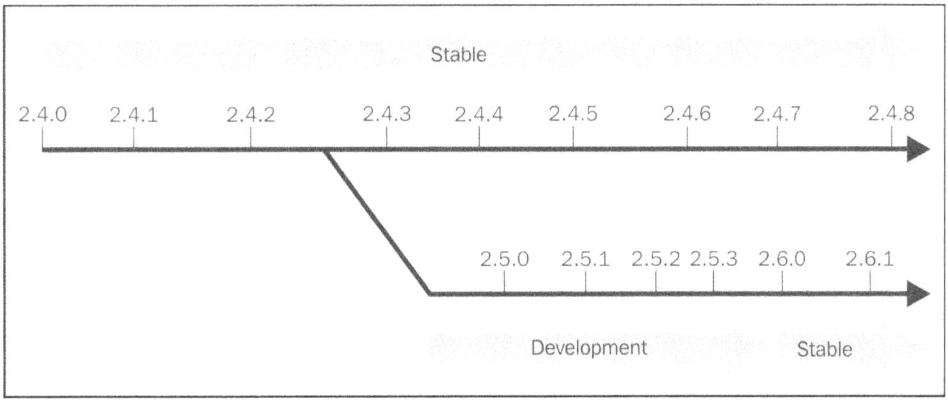

This way of working was kept up until the 2.6.0 version when a large number of features were added inside the kernel during every minor release, and all of them were very well put together as to not cause the need for the branching out of a new development branch. This implied a faster pace of release with more features available. So, the following changes have appeared since the release of the 2.6.14 kernel:

- All the new minor release versions, such as 2.6.x, contain a two week merge window in which a number of features could be introduced in the next release
- This merge window will be closed with a release test version called 2.6.(x+1)-rc1
- Then a 6-8 weeks bug fixing period follows when all the bugs introduced by the added features should be fixed
- In the bug fixing interval, tests were run on the release candidate and the 2.6.(x+1)-rcY test versions were released
- After the final test were done and the last release candidate is considered sufficiently stable, a new release will be made with a name, such as 2.6.(x+1), and this process will be continued once again

This process worked great but the only problem was that the bug fixes were only released for the latest stable versions of the Linux kernel. People needed long term support versions and security updates for their older versions, general information about these versions that were long time supported, and so on.

This process changed in time and in July 2011, the 3.0 Linux kernel version appeared. It appeared with a couple of small changes designed to change the way the interaction was to be done to solve the previously mentioned requests. The changes were made to the numbering scheme, as follows:

- The kernel official versions would be named 3.x (3.0, 3.1, 3.2, and so on)
- The stable versions would be named 3.x.y (3.0.1, 3.1.3, and so on)

Although it only removed one digit from the numbering scheme, this change was necessary because it marked the 20th anniversary of the Linux kernel.

Since a great number of patches and features are included in the Linux kernel everyday, it becomes difficult to keep track of all the changes, and the bigger picture in general. This changed over time because sites, such as `http://kernelnewbies.org/LinuxChanges` and `http://lwn.net/`, appeared to help developers keep in touch with the world of Linux kernel.

Besides these links, the `git` versioning control system can offer much needed information. Of course, this requires the existence of Linux kernel source clones to be available on the workstation. Some of the commands that offer a great deal of information are:

- `git log`: This lists all the commits with the latest situated on top of the list
- `git log -p`: This lists all the commits and with their corresponding `diffs`
- `git tag -l`: This lists the available tags
- `git checkout <tagname>`: This checks out a branch or tag from a working repository
- `git log v2.6.32..master`: This lists all the changes between the given tag and the latest version
- `git log -p V2.6.32..master MAINTAINERS`: This lists all the differences between the two given branches in the `MAINTAINERS` file

Of course, this is just a small list with helpful commands. All the other commands are available at `http://git-scm.com/docs/`.

Kernel porting

The Linux kernel offers support for a large variety of CPU architectures. Each architecture and individual board have their own maintainers, and this information is available inside the `MAINTAINERS` file. Also, the difference between board porting is mostly given by the architecture, PowerPC being very different from ARM or x86. Since the development board that this book focuses on is an Atmel with an ARM Cortex-A5 core, this section will try to focus on ARM architecture.

The main focus in our case is the `arch/arm` directory, which contains sub directories such as, `boot`, `common`, `configs`, `crypto`, `firmware`, `kernel`, `kvm`, `lib`, `mm`, `net`, `nwfpe`, `oprofile`, `tools`, `vfp`, and `xen`. It also contains an important number of directories that are specific for different CPU families, such as the `mach-*` directories or the `plat-*` directories. The first `mach-*` category contains support for the CPU and several boards that use that CPU, and the second `plat-*` category contains platform-specific code. One example is `plat-omap`, which contains common code for both `mach-omap1` and `mach-omap2`.

The development for the ARM architecture has suffered a great change since 2011. If until then ARM did not use a device tree, it was because it needed to keep a large portion of the code inside the `mach-*` specific directory, and for each board that had support inside the Linux kernel, a unique machine ID was associated and a machine structure was associates with each board that contained specific information and a set of callbacks. The boot loader passed this machine ID to a specific ARM registry and in this way, the kernel knew the board.

The increase in popularity of the ARM architecture came with the refactoring of the work and the introduction of the **device tree** that dramatically reduced the amount of code available inside the `mach-*` directories. If the SoC is supported by the Linux kernel, then adding support for a board is as simple as defining a device tree in the `/arch/arm/boot/dts` directory with an appropriate name. For example, for `<soc-name>-<board-name>.d`, include the relevant `dtsi` files if necessary. Make sure that you build the **device tree blob** (**DTB**) by including the device tree into **arch/arm/boot/dts/Makefile** and add the missing device drivers for board.

In the eventuality that the board does not have support inside the Linux kernel, the appropriate additions would be required inside the `mach-*` directory. Inside each `mach-*` directory, there are three types of files available:

- **Generic code files**: These usually have a single word name, such as `clock.c`, `led.c`, and so on
- **CPU specific code**: This is for the machine ID and usually has the `<machine-ID>*.c` form - for example, `at91sam9263.c`, `at91sam9263_devices.c`, `sama5d3.c`, and so on
- **Board specific code**: This usually is defined as board-*.c, such as `board-carmeva.c`, `board-pcontrol-g20.c`, `board-pcontrol-g20.c`, and so on

For a given board, the proper configuration should be made first inside the `arch/arm/mach-*/Kconfig` file; for this, the machine ID should be identified for the board CPU. After the configuration is done, the compilation can begin, so for this, `arch/arm/mach-*/Makefile` should also be updated with the required files to ensure board support. Another step is represented by the machine structure that defines the board and the machine type number that needs to be defined in the `board-<machine>.c` file.

The machine structure uses two macros: `MACHINE_START` and `MACHINE_END`. Both are defined inside `arch/arm/include/asm/march/arch.h` and are used to define the `machine_desc` structure. The machine type number is available inside the `arch/arm/tools/mach_types` file. This file is used to generate the `include/asm-arm/mach-types.h` file for the board.

> The updated number list of the machine type is available at http://www.arm.linux.org.uk/developer/machines/download.php.

When the boot process starts in the first case, only the dtb is necessary to pass to the boot loader and loaded to initialize the Linux kernel, while in the second case, the machine type number needs to be loaded in the R1 register. In the early boot process, __lookup_machine_type looks for the machine_desc structure and loads it for the initialization of the board.

Community interaction

After this information has been presented to you, and if you are eager to contribute to the Linux kernel, then this section should be read next. If you want to really contribute to the Linux kernel project, then a few steps should be performed before starting this work. This is mostly related to documentation and investigation of the subject. No one wants to send a duplicate patch or replicate the work of someone else in vain, so a search on the Internet on the topic of your interest could save a lot of time. Other useful advice is that after you've familiarized yourself with the subject, avoid sending a workaround. Try to reach the problem and offer a solution. If not, report the problem and describe it thoroughly. If the solution is found, then make both the problem and solution available in the patch.

One of the most valuable things in the open source community is the help you can get from others. Share your question and issues, but do not forget to mention the solution also. Ask the questions in appropriate mailing lists and try to avoid the maintainers, if possible. They are usually very busy and have hundreds and thousands of e-mails to read and reply. Before asking for help, try to research the question you want to raise, it will help both when formulating it but also it could offer an answer. Use IRC, if available, for smaller questions and lastly, but most importantly, try to not overdo it.

When you are preparing for a patch, make sure that it is done on the corresponding branch, and also that you read the Documentation/BUG-HUNTING file first. Identify bug reports, if any, and make sure you link your patch to them. Do not hesitate to read the Documentation/SubmittingPatches guidelines before sending. Also, do not send your changes before testing them properly. Always sign your patches and make the first description line as suggestive as possible. When sending the patches, find appropriate mailing lists and maintainers and wait for the replies. Solve comments and resubmit them if this is needed, until the patch is considered acceptable.

Kernel sources

The official location for the Linux kernel is available at `http://www.kernel.org`, but there a lot of smaller communities that contribute to the Linux kernel with their features or even maintain their own versions.

Although the Linux core contains the scheduler, memory management, and other features, it is quite small in size. The extremely large number of device drivers, architectures and boards support together with filesystems, network protocols and all the other components were the ones that made the size of the Linux kernel really big. This can be seen by taking a look at the size of the directories of the Linux.

The Linux source code structure contains the following directories:

- `arch`: This contains architecture-dependent code
- `block`: This contains the block layer core
- `crypto`: This contains cryptographic libraries
- `drivers`: This gathers all the implementation of the device drivers with the exception of the sound ones
- `fs`: This gathers all the available implementations of filesystem
- `include`: This contains the kernel headers
- `init`: This has the Linux initialization code
- `ipc`: This holds the interprocess communication implementation code
- `kernel`: This is the core of the Linux kernel
- `lib`: This contains various libraries, such as `zlibc`, `crc`, and so on
- `mm`: This contains the source code for memory management
- `net`: This offers access to all the network protocol implementations supported inside Linux
- `samples`: This presents a number of sample implementations, such as `kfifo`, `kobject`, and so on
- `scripts`: This is used both internally and externally
- `security`: This has a bunch of security implementation, such as `apparmor`, `selinux`, `smack`, and so on
- `sound`: This contains sound drivers and support code
- `usr`: This is the `initramfs cpio` archive that generates sources
- `virt`: This holds the source code for the virtualization support
- `COPYING`: This represents the Linux license and the definition copying conditions

- `CREDITS`: This represents the collection of Linux's main contributors
- `Documentation`: This contains corresponding documentation of kernel sources
- `Kbuild`: This represents the top-level kernel build system
- `Kconfig`: This is the top-level descriptor for configuration parameters
- `MAINTAINERS`: This a list with the maintainers of each kernel component
- `Makefile`: This represents the top-level makefile
- `README`: This file describes what Linux is, it is the starting point for understanding the project
- `REPORTING-BUGS`: This offers information regarding the bug report procedure

As it can be seen, the source code of the Linux kernel is quite large, so a browsing tool would be required. There are a number of tools that can be used, such as **Cscope**, **Kscope**, or the web browser, **Linux Cross Reference** (**LXR**). Cscope is a huge project that can be also available with extensions for `vim` and `emacs`.

Configuring kernel

Before building a Linux kernel image, the proper configuration needs to be done. This is hard, taking into consideration that we have access to hundreds and thousands of components, such as drivers, filesystems, and other items. A selection process is done inside the configuration stage, and this is possible with the help of dependency definitions. The user has the chance to use and define a number of options that are enabled in order to define the components that will be used to build a Linux kernel image for a specific board.

All the configurations specific for a supported board are located inside a configuration file, simply named `.config`, and it is situated on the same level as the previously presented files and directory locations. Their form is usually represented as `configuration_key=value`. There are, of course, dependencies between these configurations, so they are defined inside the `Kconfig` files.

Here are a number of variable options available for a configuration key:

- `bool`: These are the options can have true or false values
- `tristate`: This, besides the true and false options, also appears as a module option
- `int` : These values, are not that spread but they usually have a well-established value range
- `string` : These values, are also not the most spread ones but usually contain some pretty basic information

With regard to the `Kconfig` files, there are two options available. The first one makes option A visible only when option B is enabled and is defined as *depends on*, and the second option offers the possibility of enabling option A. This is done when the option is enabled automatically and is defined as *select*.

Besides the manual configuration of the `.config` file, configuration is the worst option for a developer, mostly because it can miss dependencies between some of the configurations. I would like to suggest to developers to use the make `menuconfig` command that will launch a text console tool for the configuration of a kernel image.

Compiling and installing the kernel

After the configuration is done, the compilation process can be started. A piece of advice I would like to give is to use as many threads as possible if the host machine offers this possibility because it would help with the build process. An example of the build process start command is `make -j 8`.

At the end of the build process, a `vmlinux` image is offered and also some architecture-dependent images are made available inside the architecture-specific files for the ARM architecture. The result of this is available inside `arch/arm/boot/*Image`. Also, the Atmel SAMA5D3-Xplained board will offer a specific device tree file that is available in `arch/arm/boot/dts/*.dtb`. If the `vmlinux` image file is an ELF file with debug information that cannot be used for booting except for debug purposes, the `arch/arm/boot/*Image` file is the solution for this purpose.

The installation is the next step when development is done for any other application. The same also takes place for the Linux kernel, but in an embedded environment, this step seems kind of unnecessary. For Yocto enthusiasts, this step is also available. However, in this step, proper configurations are done for the kernel source and headers are to be used by the dependencies that do the storing for the deploy step.

The kernel modules, as mentioned in the cross-compilation chapter, need to be later used for the compiler build. The install for the kernel modules could be done using the make `modules_install` command, and this offers the possibility to install the sources available inside the `/lib/modules/<linux-kernel-version>` directory with all the module dependencies, symbols, and aliases.

Cross-compiling the Linux kernel

In an embedded development, the compilation process implies cross-compilation, the most visible difference with the native compilation process being the fact that it has a prefix with the target architecture available in the naming. The prefix setup can be done using the `ARCH` variable that defines the name of the architecture of the target board and the `CROSS_COMPILE` variable that defines the prefix for the cross-compilation toolchain. Both of them are defined in the top-level `Makefile`.

The best option would be to set these variables as environment variables to make sure that a make process is not run for the host machine. Although it only works in the current terminal, it will be the best solution in the situation that no automation tool is available for these tasks, such as the Yocto Project. It is not recommended though to update the `.bashrc` shell variables if you are planning to use more than one toolchain on the host machine.

Devices and modules

As I mentioned previously, the Linux kernel has a lot of kernel modules and drivers that are already implemented and available inside the source code of the Linux kernel. A number of them, being so many, are also available outside the Linux kernel source code. Having them outside not only reduces the boot time by not initializing them at boot time, but is done instead at the request and needs of users. The only difference is that the loading and unloading of the modules requires root access.

Loading and interacting with the Linux kernel modules requires logging information to be made available. The same happens for any kernel module dependencies. The logging information is available through the `dmesg` command and the level of logging enables manual configuration using the `loglevel` parameter or it can be disabled with the quite parameter. Also for the kernel dependencies, information about them is available inside the `/lib/modules/<kernel-version>/modules.dep` file.

For module interaction, multiple utilities used for multiple operations are available, such as `modinfo`, which is used for information gathering about modules; `insmod` is able for loading a module when the fill path to the kernel module is given. Similar utilities for a module are available. One of them is called `modprobe` and the difference in `modprobe` is that the full path is not necessary, as it is responsible for loading dependent modules of the chosen kernel object before loading itself. Another functionality that `modprobe` offers is the `-r` option. It is the remove functionality which offers support for removing the module and all its dependencies. An alternative to this is the `rmmod` utility, which removes modules not used anymore. The last utility available is `lsmod`, which lists the loaded modules.

The simplest kernel module example that can be written looks something similar to this:

```
#define MODULE
#define LINUX
#define __KERNEL__

#include <linux/init.h>
#include <linux/module.h>
#include <linux/kernel.h>

static int hello_world_init(void)
{
   printk(KERN_ALERT "Hello world!\n");
   return 0;
}

static void hello_world_exit(void)
{
   printk(KERN_ALERT "Goodbye!\n");
}

module_init(hello_world_init);
module_exit(hello_world_exit);

MODULE_LICENSE("GPL");
```

This is a simple `hello world kernel` module. Useful information that can be gathered from the preceding example is that every kernel module needs a start function defined in the preceding example as `hello_world_init()`. It is called when the module is inserted, and a cleanup function called `hello_world_exit()` is called when the module is removed.

Since the Linux kernel version 2.2, there is a possibility of using the `_init and __ exit` macros in this way:

```
static int __init hello_world_init (void)
static void __exit hello_world_exit (void)
```

The preceding macros are removed, the first one after the initialization, and the second one when the module is built-in within the Linux kernel sources.

> More information about the Linux kernel modules can be found in the Linux **Kernel Module Programming Guide** available at `http://www.tldp.org/LDP/lkmpg/2.6/html/index.html`.

As mentioned previously, a kernel module is not only available inside a Linux kernel, but also outside of the Linux kernel tree. For a built-in kernel module, the compile process is similar to the one of other available kernel modules and a developer can inspire its work from one of them. The kernel module available outside of the Linux kernel drivers and the build process requires access to the sources of the Linux kernel or the kernel headers.

For a kernel module available outside of the Linux kernel sources, a `Makefile` example is available, as follows:

```
KDIR := <path/to/linux/kernel/sources>
PWD := $(shell pwd)
obj-m := hello_world.o
all:
$(MAKE) ARCH=arm CROSS_COMPILE=<arm-cross-compiler-prefix> -C
$(KDIR) M=$(PWD)
```

For a module that is implemented inside a Linux kernel, a configuration for the module needs to be made available inside the corresponding `Kconfig` file with the correct configuration. Also, the `Makefile` near the `Kconfig` file needs to be updated to let the `Makefile` system know when the configuration for the module is updated and the sources need to be built. We will see an example of this kind for a kernel device driver here.

An example of the `Kconfig` file is as follows:

```
config HELLO_WORLD_TEST
  tristate "Hello world module test"
  help
    To compile this driver as a module chose the M option.
     otherwise chose Y option.
```

An example of the `Makefile` is as follows:

```
obj-$(CONFIG_ HELLO_WORLD_TEST)  += hello_world.c
```

In both these examples, the source code file is `hello_world.c` and the resulting kernel module if it is not built-in is called `hello_world.ko`.

A driver is usually used as an interface with a framework that exposes a number of hardware features, or with a bus interface used to detect and communicate with the hardware. The best example is shown here:

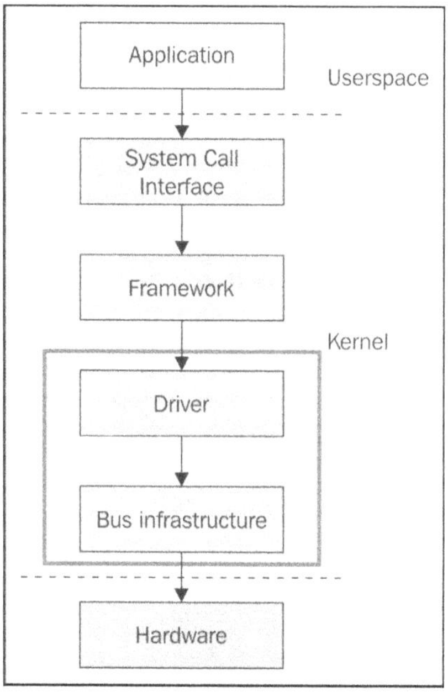

Since there are multiple scenarios of using a device driver and three device mode structures are available:

- `struct bus_type`: This represents the types of busses, such as I2C, SPI, USB, PCI, MMC, and so on
- `struct device_driver`: This represents the driver used to handle a specific device on a bus
- `struct device`: This is used to represent a device connected to a bus

An inheritance mechanism is used to create specialized structures from more generic ones, such as `struct device_driver` and `struct device` for every bus subsystem. The bus driver is the one responsible for representing each type of bus and matching the corresponding device driver with the detected devices, detection being done through an adapter driver. For nondiscoverable devices, a description is made inside the device tree or the source code of the Linux kernel. They are handled by the platform bus that supports platform drivers and in return, handles platform devices.

Debugging a kernel

Having to debug the Linux kernel is not the most easy task, but it needs to be accomplished to make sure that the development process moves forward. Understanding the Linux kernel is, of course, one of the prerequisites. Some of the available bugs are very hard to solve and may be available inside the Linux kernel for a long period of time.

For most of the trivial ones, some of the following steps should be taken. First, identify the bug properly; it is not only useful when define the problem, but also helps with reproducing it. The second step involves finding the source of the problem. Here, I am referring to the first kernel version in which the bug was first reported. Good knowledge about the bug or the source code of the Linux kernel is always useful, so make sure that you understand the code before you start working on it.

The bugs inside the Linux kernel have a wide spread. They vary from a variable not being stored properly to race conditions or hardware management problems, they have widely variable manifestations and a chain of events. However, debugging them is not as difficult as it sounds. Besides some specific problems, such as race conditions and time constraints, debugging is very similar to the debugging of any large user space application.

The first, easiest, and most handy method to debug the kernel is the one that involves the use of the `printk()` function. It is very similar to the `printf()` C library function, and although old and not recommended by some, it does the trick. The new preferred method involves the usage of the `pr_*()` functions, such as `pr_emerg()`, `pr_alert()`, `pr_crit()`, `pr_debug()`, and so on. Another method involves the usage of the `dev_*()` functions, such as `dev_emerg()`, `dev_alert()`, `dev_crit()`, `dev_dbg()`, and so on. They correspond to each logging level and also have extra functions that are defined for debugging purposes and are compiled when `CONFIG_DEBUG` is enabled.

> More information about the `pr_*()` and `dev_*()` family of functions can be found inside the Linux kernel source code at `Documentation/dynamic-debug-howto.txt`. You can also find more information about `loglevel` at `Documentation/kernel-parameters.txt`.

When a kernel **oops** crash appears, it signals that the kernel has made a mistake. Not being able to fix or kill itself, it offers access to a bunch of information, such as useful error messages, registers content, and back trace information.

The `Magic SysRq` key is another method used in debugging. It is enabled by `CONFIG_MAGIC_SYSRQ config` and can be used to debug and rescue kernel information, regardless of its activity. It offers a series of command-line options that can be used for various actions, ranging from changing the nice level to rebooting the system. Plus, it can be toggled on or off by changing the value in the `/proc/sys/kernel/sysrq` file. More information about the system request key can be found at `Documentation/sysrq.txt`.

Although Linus Torvalds and the Linux community do not believe that the existence of a kernel debugger will do much good to a project, a better understanding of the code is the best approach for any project. There are still some debugger solutions that are available to be used. GNU debugger (`gdb`) is the first one and it can be used in the same way as for any other process. Another one is the `kgdb` a patch over `gdb` that permits debugging of serial connections.

If none of the preceding methods fail to help solve the problem and you've tried everything but can't seem to arrive at a solution, then you can contact the open source community for help. There will always will be developers there who will lend you a hand.

> To acquire more information related to the Linux kernel, there are a couple of books that can be consulted. I will present a bunch of their names here: *Embedded Linux Primer* by Christopher Hallinan, *Linux Kernel Development* by Robert Love, *Linux Kernel In A Nutshell* by Greg Kroah-Hartman, and last but not the least, *Understanding the Linux Kernel* by Daniel P. Bovet and Marco Cesati.

The Yocto Project reference

Moving on to the Yocto Project, we have recipes available for every kernel version available inside the BSP support for each supported board, and recipes for kernel modules that are built outside the Linux kernel source tree.

The Atmel SAMA5D3-Xplained board uses the `linux-yocto-custom` kernel. This is defined inside the `conf/machine/sama5d3-xplained.conf` machine configuration file using the `PREFERRED_PROVIDER_virtual/kernel` variable. No `PREFERRED_VERSION` is mentioned, so the latest version is preferred; in this case, we are talking about the `linux-yocto-custom_3.10.bb` recipe.

The `linux-yocto-custom_3.10.bb` recipe fetches the kernel sources available inside Linux Torvalds' `git` repository. After a quick look at the sources once the `do_fetch` task is finished, it can be observed that the Atmel repository was, in fact, fetched. The answer is available inside the `linux-yocto-custom_3.10.bbappend` file, which offers another `SR_URI` location. Other useful information you can gather from here is the one available in bbappend file, inside it is very well stated that the SAMA5D3 Xplained machine is a `COMPATIBLE_MACHINE`:

```
KBRANCH = "linux-3.10-at91"
SRCREV = "35158dd80a94df2b71484b9ffa6e642378209156"
PV = "${LINUX_VERSION}+${SRCPV}"

PR = "r5"

FILESEXTRAPATHS_prepend := "${THISDIR}/files/${MACHINE}:"

SRC_URI = "git://github.com/linux4sam/linux-at91.git;protocol=git;bran
ch=${KBRANCH};nocheckout=1"
SRC_URI += "file://defconfig"

SRCREV_sama5d4-xplained = "46f4253693b0ee8d25214e7ca0dde52e788ffe95"

do_deploy_append() {
  if [ ${UBOOT_FIT_IMAGE} = "xyes" ]; then
    DTB_PATH="${B}/arch/${ARCH}/boot/dts/"
    if [ ! -e "${DTB_PATH}" ]; then
      DTB_PATH="${B}/arch/${ARCH}/boot/"
    fi

    cp ${S}/arch/${ARCH}/boot/dts/${MACHINE}*.its ${DTB_PATH}
    cd ${DTB_PATH}
    mkimage -f ${MACHINE}.its ${MACHINE}.itb
    install -m 0644 ${MACHINE}.itb ${DEPLOYDIR}/${MACHINE}.itb
    cd -
  fi
}

COMPATIBLE_MACHINE = "(sama5d4ek|sama5d4-xplained
|sama5d3xek|sama5d3-xplained|at91sam9x5ek
|at91sam9rlek|at91sam9m10g45ek)"
```

The recipe firstly defines repository-related information. It is defined through variables, such as SRC_URI and SRCREV. It also indicates the branch of the repository through the KBRANCH variable, and also the place from where defconfig needs to be put into the source code to define the .config file. As seen in the recipe, there is an update made to the do_deploy task for the kernel recipe to add the device driver to the tmp/deploy/image/sama5d3-xplained directory alongside the kernel image and other binaries.

The kernel recipe inherits the kernel.bbclass and kernel-yocto.bbclass files, which define most of its tasks actions. Since it also generates a device tree, it needs access to linux-dtb.inc, which is available inside the meta/recipes-kernel/linux directory. The information available in the linux-yocto-custom_3.10.bb recipe is rather generic and overwritten by the bbappend file, as can be seen here:

```
SRC_URI = "git://git.kernel.org/pub/scm/linux/kernel/git/torvalds/
linux.git;
protocol=git;nocheckout=1"

LINUX_VERSION ?= "3.10"
LINUX_VERSION_EXTENSION ?= "-custom"

inherit kernel
require recipes-kernel/linux/linux-yocto.inc

# Override SRCREV to point to a different commit in a bbappend
file to
# build a different release of the Linux kernel.
# tag: v3.10 8bb495e3f02401ee6f76d1b1d77f3ac9f079e376"
SRCREV = "8bb495e3f02401ee6f76d1b1d77f3ac9f079e376"

PR = "r1"
PV = "${LINUX_VERSION}+git${SRCPV}"

# Override COMPATIBLE_MACHINE to include your machine in a bbappend
# file. Leaving it empty here ensures an early explicit build
failure.
COMPATIBLE_MACHINE = "(^$)"

# module_autoload is used by the kernel packaging bbclass
module_autoload_atmel_usba_udc = "atmel_usba_udc"
module_autoload_g_serial = "g_serial"
```

After the kernel is built by running the `bitbake virtual/kernel` command, the kernel image will be available inside the `tmp/deploy/image/sama5d3-xplained` directory under the `zImage-sama5d3-xplained.bin` name, which is a symbolic link to the full name file and has a larger name identifier. The kernel image was deployed here from the place where the Linux kernel tasks were executed. The simplest method to discover that place would be to run `bitbake -c devshell virtual/kernel`. A development shell will be available to the user for direct interaction with the Linux kernel source code and access to task scripts. This method is preferred because the developer has access to the same environment as `bitbake`.

A kernel module, on the other hand, has a different kind of behavior if it is not built-in inside the Linux kernel source tree. For the modules that are build outside of the source tree, a new recipe need to be written, that is, a recipe that inherits another `bitbake` class this time called `module.bbclass`. One example of an external Linux kernel module is available inside the `meta-skeleton` layer in the `recipes-kernel/hello-mod` directory:

```
SUMMARY = "Example of how to build an external Linux kernel module"
LICENSE = "GPLv2"
LIC_FILES_CHKSUM = "file://COPYING;md5=12f884d2ae1ff87c09e5b7ccc2c4ca
7e"

inherit module

PR = "r0"
PV = "0.1"

SRC_URI = "file://Makefile \
           file://hello.c \
           file://COPYING \
          "

S = "${WORKDIR}"

# The inherit of module.bbclass will automatically name module
packages with
# "kernel-module-" prefix as required by the oe-core build
environment.
```

As mentioned in the example of the Linux kernel external module, the last two lines of each kernel module that is external or internal is packaged with the `kernel-module-` prefix to make sure that when the `IMAGE_INSTALL` variable is available, the value kernel-modules are added to all kernel modules available inside the `/lib/modules/<kernel-version>` directory. The kernel module recipe is very similar to any available recipe, the major difference being in the form of the module inherited, as shown in the line inherit module.

Inside the Yocto Project, there are multiple commands available to interact with the kernel and kernel module recipes. The simplest command is, of course, `bitbake <recipe-name>`, but for the Linux kernel, there are a number of commands available to make the interaction easier. The most used one is the `bitbake -c menuconfig virtual/kernel` operation, which offers access to the kernel configuration menu.

Besides already known tasks, such as `configure`, `compile`, and `devshell`, that are used mostly in the development process, there are other ones, such as `diffconfig`, which uses the `diffconfig` script available in the Linux kernel `scripts` directory. The difference between the implementation of the Yocto Project and the available script of the Linux kernel is the fact that the former adds the kernel `config` creation phase. These `config` fragments are used to add kernel configurations into the `.config` file as part of the automation process.

Summary

In this chapter, you learned about the Linux kernel in general, about its features and methods of interacting with it. There was also information about debugging and porting features. All this was done to make sure that you would get enough information about the whole ecosystem before interacting with it. It is my opinion that if you understand the whole picture first, it will become easier to focus on the more specific things. This is also one of the reasons that the Yocto Project reference was kept toward the end. You were introduced to how a Linux kernel recipe and a Linux kernel external module are defined and used later by a given machine. More information on Linux kernels will also be available in the next chapter, which will gather all the previously presented information and will show you how a developer can interact with a Linux operating system image.

Besides this information, in the next chapter, there will be an explanation about the organization of the root file system and the principles behind it, its content, and device drivers. Busybox is another interesting subject that will be discussed and also the various support for file systems that are available. Since it tends to become larger, information about what a minimal file system should look like will also be presented. Having said this, we shall proceed to the next chapter.

5
The Linux Root Filesystem

In this chapter, you will learn about the root filesystem and its structure. You will also be presented with information about the root filesystem's content, the various device drivers available, and its the communication with the Linux kernel. We will slowly make the transition to the Yocto Project and the method used to define the Linux root filesystem's content. The necessary information will be presented to make sure that a user will be also able to customize the `rootfs` filesystem according to its needs.

The special requirements of the root filesystem will be presented. You will be given information on its content, subdirectories, defined purposes, the various filesystem options available, the BusyBox alternative, and also a lot of interesting features.

When interacting with an embedded environment, a lot of developers would start from a minimal root filesystem made available by a distribution provider, such as Debian, and using a cross-toolchain will enhance it with various packages, tools, and utilities. If the number of packages to be added is big, it can be very troublesome work. Starting from scratch would be an even bigger nightmare. Inside the Yocto Project, this job is automatized and there is no need for manual work. The development is started from scratch, and it offers a large number of packages inside the root filesystem to make the work fun and interesting. So, let's move ahead and take a look at this chapter's content to understand more about root filesystems in general.

Interacting with the root filesystem

A root filesystem consists of a directory and file hierarchy. In this file hierarchy, various filesystems can be mounted, revealing the content of a specific storage device. The mounting is done using the mount command, and after the operation is done, the mount point is populated with the content available on the storage device. The reverse operation is called `umount` and is used to empty the mount point of its content.

The preceding commands are very useful for the interaction of applications with various files available, regardless of their location and format. For example, the standard form for the `mount` command is `mount -t type device directory`. This command asks the kernel to connect the filesystem from the device that has the `type` format mentioned in the command line, along with the directory mentioned in the same command. The `umount` command needs to be given before removing the device to make sure the kernel caches are written in the storage point.

A root filesytem is available in the root hierarchy, also known as `/`. It is the first available filesystem and also the one on which the `mount` command is not used, since it is mounted directly by the kernel through the `root= argument`. The following are the multiple options to load the root filesystem:

- From the memory
- From the network using NFS
- From a NAND chip
- From an SD card partition
- From a USB partition
- From a hard disk partition

These options are chosen by hardware and system architects. To make use of these, the kernel and bootloader need to be configured accordingly.

Besides the options that require interaction with a board's internal memory or storage devices, one of the most used methods to load the root filesystem is represented by the NFS option, which implies that the root filesystem is available on your local machine and is exported over the network on your target. This option offers the following advantages:

- The size of the root filesystem will not be an issue due to the fact that the storage space on the development machine is much larger than the one available on the target
- The update process is much easier and can be done without rebooting
- Having access to an over the network storage is the best solution for devices with small even inexistent internal or external storage devices

The downside of the over the network storage is the fact that a sever client architecture is needed. So, for NFS, an NFS server functionality will need to be available on the development machine. For a Ubuntu host, the required configuration involves installing the `nfs-kernel-server` package, `sudo apt-get install nfs-kernel-server`. After the package is installed, the exported directory location needs to be specified and configured. This is done using the `/etc/exports` file; here, configuration lines similar to `/nfs/rootfs <client-IP-address> (rw,no_root_squash,no_subtree_check)` appear, where each line defines a location for the over the network shared locations with the NFS client. After the configuration is finished, the NFS server needs to be restarted in this way: `sudo /etc/init.d/nfs-kernel-server restart`.

For the client side available on the target, the Linux kernel needs to be configured accordingly to make sure that the NFS support is enabled, and also that an IP address will be available at boot time. This configurations are `CONFIG_NFS_FS=y`, `CONFIG_IP_PNP=y`, and `CONFIG_ROOT_NFS=y`. The kernel also needs to be configured with the `root=/dev/nfs` parameter, the IP address for the target, and the NFS server `nfsroot=192.168.1.110:/nfs/rootfs` information. Here is an example of the communication between the two components:

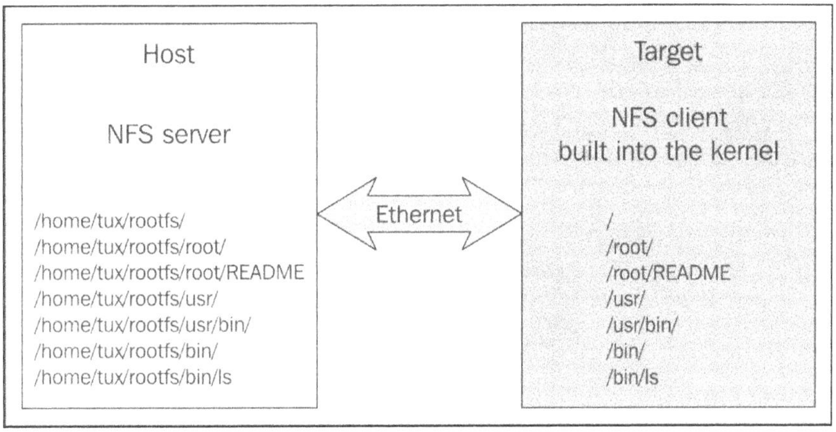

There is also the possibility of having a root filesystem integrated inside the kernel image, that is, a minimal root filesytem whose purpose is to start the full featured root filesystem. This root filesystem is called `initramfs`. This type of filesystem is very helpful for people interested in fast booting options of smaller root filesystems that only contain a number of useful features and need to be started earlier. It is useful for the fast loading of the system at boot time, but also as an intermediate step before starting the real root filesystem available on one of the available storage locations. The root filesystem is first started after the kernel booting process, so it makes sense for it to be available alongside the Linux kernel, as it resides near the kernel on the RAM memory. The following image explains this:

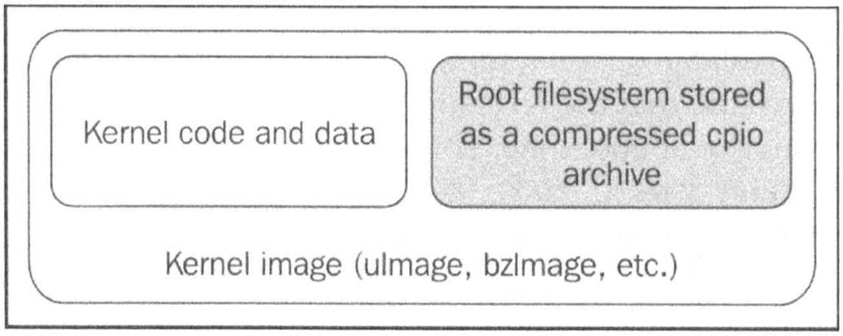

To create `initramfs`, configurations need to be made available. This happens by defining either the path to the root filesystem directory, the path to a `cpio` archive, or even a text file describing the content of the `initramfs` inside the `CONFIG_INITRAMFS_SOURCE`. When the kernel build starts, the content of `CONFIG_INITRAMFS_SOURCE` will be read and the root filesystem will be integrated inside the kernel image.

> More information about the `initramfs` filesystem's options can be found inside the kernel documentations files at `Documentation/filesystems/ramfs-rootfs-initramfs.txt` and `Documentation/early-userspace/README`.

The initial RAM disk or `initrd` is another mechanism of mounting an early root filesystem. It also needs the support enabled inside the Linux kernel and is loaded as a component of the kernel. It contains a small set of executables and directories and represents a transient stage to the full featured root filesystem. It only represents the final stage for embedded devices that do not have a storage device capable of fitting a bigger root filesystem.

On a traditional system, the `initrd` is created using the `mkinitrd` tool, which is, in fact, a shell script that automates the steps necessary for the creation of `initrd`. Here is an example of its functionality:

```
#!/bin/bash

# Housekeeping...
rm -f /tmp/ramdisk.img
rm -f /tmp/ramdisk.img.gz

# Ramdisk Constants
RDSIZE=4000
BLKSIZE=1024

# Create an empty ramdisk image
dd if=/dev/zero of=/tmp/ramdisk.img bs=$BLKSIZE count=$RDSIZE

# Make it an ext2 mountable file system
/sbin/mke2fs -F -m 0 -b $BLKSIZE /tmp/ramdisk.img $RDSIZE

# Mount it so that we can populate
mount /tmp/ramdisk.img /mnt/initrd -t ext2 -o loop=/dev/loop0

# Populate the filesystem (subdirectories)
mkdir /mnt/initrd/bin
mkdir /mnt/initrd/sys
mkdir /mnt/initrd/dev
mkdir /mnt/initrd/proc

# Grab busybox and create the symbolic links
pushd /mnt/initrd/bin
cp /usr/local/src/busybox-1.1.1/busybox .
```

```
ln -s busybox ash
ln -s busybox mount
ln -s busybox echo
ln -s busybox ls
ln -s busybox cat
ln -s busybox ps
ln -s busybox dmesg
ln -s busybox sysctl
popd

# Grab the necessary dev files
cp -a /dev/console /mnt/initrd/dev
cp -a /dev/ramdisk /mnt/initrd/dev
cp -a /dev/ram0 /mnt/initrd/dev
cp -a /dev/null /mnt/initrd/dev
cp -a /dev/tty1 /mnt/initrd/dev
cp -a /dev/tty2 /mnt/initrd/dev

# Equate sbin with bin
pushd /mnt/initrd
ln -s bin sbin
popd

# Create the init file
cat >> /mnt/initrd/linuxrc << EOF
#!/bin/ash
echo
echo "Simple initrd is active"
echo
mount -t proc /proc /proc
mount -t sysfs none /sys
/bin/ash --login
EOF

chmod +x /mnt/initrd/linuxrc
```

```
# Finish up...
umount /mnt/initrd
gzip -9 /tmp/ramdisk.img
cp /tmp/ramdisk.img.gz /boot/ramdisk.img.gz
```

> More information on `initrd` can be found at `Documentation/initrd.txt`.

Using `initrd` is not as simple as `initramfs`. In this case, an archive needs to be copied in a similar manner to the one used for the kernel image, and the bootloader needs to pass its location and size to the kernel to make sure that it has started. Therefore, in this case, the bootloader also requires the support of `initrd`. The central point of the `initrd` is constituted by the `linuxrc` file, which is the first script started and is usually used for the purpose of offering access to the final stage of the system boot, that is, the real root filesytem. After `linuxrc` finishes the execution, the kernel unmounts it and continues with the real root filesystem.

Delving into the filesystem

No matter what their provenience is, most of the available root filesystems have the same organization of directories, as defined by the **Filesystem Hierarchy Standard** (**FHS**), as it is commonly called. This organization is of great help to both developers and users because it not only mentions a directory hierarchy, but also the purpose and content of the directories The most notable ones are:

- `/bin`: This refers to the location of most programs
- `/sbin`: This refers to the location of system programs
- `/boot`: This refers to the location for boot options, such as the `kernel image`, `kernel config`, `initrd`, `system maps`, and other information
- `/home`: This refers to the user home directory
- `/root`: This refers to the location of the root user's home location
- `/usr`: This refers to user-specific programs and libraries, and mimics parts of the content of the root filesystem
- `/lib`: This refers to the location of libraries
- `/etc`: This refers to the system-wide configurations
- `/dev`: This refers to the location of device files
- `/media`: This refers to the location of mount points of removable devices
- `/mnt`: This refers to the mount location point of static media

- `/proc`: This refers to the mounting point of the `proc` virtual filesystem
- `/sys`: This refers to the mounting point of the `sysfs` virtual filesystem
- `/tmp`: This refers to the location temporary files
- `/var`: This refers to data files, such as logging data, administrative information, or the location of transient data

The FHS changes over time, but not very much. Most of the previously mentioned directories remain the same for various reasons - the simplest one being the fact that they need to ensure backward compatibility.

> The latest available information of the FHS is available at `http://refspecs.linuxfoundation.org/FHS_2.3/fhs-2.3.pdf`.

The root filesystems are started by the kernel, and it is the last step done by the kernel before it ends the boot phase. Here is the exact code to do this:

```
/*
  * We try each of these until one succeeds.
  *
  * The Bourne shell can be used instead of init if we are
  * trying to recover a really broken machine.
  */
  if (execute_command) {
    ret = run_init_process(execute_command);
    if (!ret)
      return 0;
    pr_err("Failed to execute %s (error %d).  Attempting
defaults...\n",execute_command, ret);
  }
  if (!try_to_run_init_process("/sbin/init") ||
    !try_to_run_init_process("/etc/init") ||
    !try_to_run_init_process("/bin/init") ||
    !try_to_run_init_process("/bin/sh"))
      return 0;

  panic("No working init found.  Try passing init= option to
kernel." "See Linux Documentation/init.txt for guidance.");
```

In this code, it can easily be identified that there are a number of locations used for searching the `init` process that needs to be started before exiting from the Linux kernel boot execution. The `run_init_process()` function is a wrapper around the `execve()` function that will not have a return value if no errors are encountered in the call procedure. The called program overwrites the memory space of the executing process, replacing the calling thread and inheriting its `PID`.

This initialization phase is so old that a similar structure inside the Linux 1.0 version is also available. This represents the user space processing start. If the kernel is not able to execute one of the four preceding functions in the predefined locations, then the kernel will halt and a panic message will be prompted onto the console to issue an alert that no init processes can be started. So, the user space processing will not start until the kernel space processing is finished.

For the majority of the available Linux systems, `/sbin/init` is the location where the kernel spawns the init process; the same affirmation is also true for the Yocto Project's generated root filesystems. It is the first application run in the user space context, but it isn't the only necessary feature of the root filesystem. There are a couple of dependencies that need to be resolved before running any process inside the root filesystem. There are dependencies used to solve dynamically linked dependencies references that were not solved earlier, and also dependencies that require external configurations. For the first category of dependencies, the `ldd` tool can be used to spot the dynamically linked dependencies, but for the second category, there is no universal solution. For example, for the `init` process, the configuration file is `inittab`, which is available inside the `/etc` directory.

For developers not interested in running another `init` process, this option is available and can be accessed using the kernel command line with the available `init=` parameter, where the path to the executed binary should be made available. This information is also available in the preceding code. The customization of the `init` process is not a method commonly used by developers, but this is because the `init` process is a very flexible one, which makes a number of start up scripts available.

Every process started after `init` uses the parent-child relationship, where `init` acts as the parent for all the processes run in the user space context, and is also the provider of environment parameters. Initially, the init process spawns processes according to the information available inside the `/etc/inittab` configuration file, which defines the runlevel notion. A runlevel represents the state of the system and defines the programs and services that have been started. There are eight runlevels available, numbered from `0` to `6`, and a special one that is noted as `S`. Their purpose is described here:

Runlevel value	Runlevel purpose
0	It refers to the shutdown and power down command for the whole system
1	It is a single-user administrative mode with a standard login access
2	It is multiuser without a TCP/IP connection
3	It refers to a general purpose multiuser
4	It is defined by the system's owner
5	It refers to graphical interface and TCP/IP connection multiuser systems
6	It refers to a system reboot
s	It is a single user mode that offers access to a minimal root shell

Each runlevel starts and kills a number of services. The services that are started begin with `S`, and the ones that a killed begin with `K`. Each service is, in fact, a shell script that defines the behaviour of the provides that it defines.

The `/etc/inittab` configuration script defines the runlevel and the instructions applied to all of them. For the Yocto Project, the `/etc/inittab` looks similar to this:

```
# /etc/inittab: init(8) configuration.
# $Id: inittab,v 1.91 2002/01/25 13:35:21 miquels Exp $

# The default runlevel.
id:5:initdefault:

# Boot-time system configuration/initialization script.
# This is run first except when booting in emergency (-b) mode.
si::sysinit:/etc/init.d/rcS

# What to do in single-user mode.
~~:S:wait:/sbin/sulogin

# /etc/init.d executes the S and K scripts upon change
# of runlevel.
#
# Runlevel 0 is halt.
# Runlevel 1 is single-user.
# Runlevels 2-5 are multi-user.
# Runlevel 6 is reboot.
```

```
l0:0:wait:/etc/init.d/rc 0
l1:1:wait:/etc/init.d/rc 1
l2:2:wait:/etc/init.d/rc 2
l3:3:wait:/etc/init.d/rc 3
l4:4:wait:/etc/init.d/rc 4
l5:5:wait:/etc/init.d/rc 5
l6:6:wait:/etc/init.d/rc 6
# Normally not reached, but fallthrough in case of emergency.
z6:6:respawn:/sbin/sulogin
S0:12345:respawn:/sbin/getty 115200 ttyS0
# /sbin/getty invocations for the runlevels.
#
# The "id" field MUST be the same as the last
# characters of the device (after "tty").
#
# Format:
#  <id>:<runlevels>:<action>:<process>
#

1:2345:respawn:/sbin/getty 38400 tty1
```

When the preceding `inittab` file is parsed by the `init`, the first script that is executed is the `si::sysinit:/etc/init.d/rcS` line, identified through the `sysinit` tag. Then, `runlevel 5` is entered and the processing of instructions continues until the last level, until a shell is finally spawned using `/sbin/getty symlink`. More information on either `init` or `inittab` can be found by running `man init` or `man inittab` in the console.

The last stage of any Linux system is represented by the power off or shutdown command. It is very important, because if it's not done appropriately, it can affect the system by corrupting data. There are, of course, multiple options to implement the shutdown scheme, but the handiest ones remain in the form of utilities, such as `shutdown`, `halt`, or `reboot`. There is also the possibility to use `init 0` to halt the system, but, in fact, what all of them have in common is the use of the `SIGTERM` and `SIGKILL` signals. `SIGTERM` is used initially to notify you about the decision to shut down the system, to offer the chance to the system to perform necessary actions. After this is done, the `SIGKILL` signal is sent to terminate all the processes.

Device drivers

One of the most important challenges for the Linux system is the access allowed to applications to various hardware devices. Notions, such as virtual memory, kernel space, and user space, do not help in simplifying things, but add another layer of complexity to this information.

A device driver has the sole purpose of isolating hardware devices and kernel data structures from user space applications. A user does not need to know that to write data to a hard disk, he or she will be required to use sectors of various sizes. The user only opens a file to write inside it and close when finished. The device driver is the one that does all the underlying work, such as isolating complexities.

Inside the user space, all the device drivers have associated device nodes, which are, in fact, special files that represent a device. All the device files are located in the `/dev` directory and the interaction with them is done through the `mknod` utility. The device nodes are available under two abstractions:

- **Block devices**: These are composed of fixed size blocks that are usually used when interacting with hard disks, SD cards, USB sticks, and so on
- **Character devices**: These are streams of characters that do not have a size, beginning, or end; they are mostly not in the form of block devices, such as terminals, serial ports, sound card and so on

Each device has a structure that offers information about it:

- `Type` identifies whether the device node is a character or block
- `Major` identifies the category for the device
- `Minor` holds the identifier of the device node

The `mknod` utility that creates the device node uses a triplet of information, such as `mknod /dev/testdev c 234 0`. After the command is executed, a `new /dev/testdev` file appears. It should bind itself to a device driver that is already installed and has already defined its properties. If an `open` command is issued, the kernel looks for the device driver that registered with the same major number as the device node. The minor number is used for handling multiple devices, or a family of devices, with the same device driver. It is passed to the device driver so that it can use it. There is no standard way to use the minor, but usually, it defines a specific device from a family of the devices that share the same major number.

Using the `mknod` utility requires manual interaction and root privileges, and lets the developer do all the heavy lifting needed to identify the properties of the device node and its device driver correspondent. The latest Linux system offers the possibility to automate this process and to also complete these actions every time devices are detected or disappear. This is done as follows:

- `devfs`: This refers to a device manager that is devised as a filesystem and is also accessible on a kernel space and user space.
- `devtmpfs`: This refers to a virtual filesystem that has been available since the 2.6.32 kernel version release, and is an improvement to `devfs` that is used for boot time optimizations. It only creates device nodes for hardware available on a local system.
- `udev`: This refers to a daemon used on servers and desktop Linux systems. More information on this can be referred to by accesing `https://www.kernel.org/pub/linux/utils/kernel/hotplug/udev/udev.html`. The Yocto Project also uses it as the default device manager.
- `mdev`: This offers a simpler solution then `udev`; it is, in fact, a derivation of udev.

Since system objects are also represented as files, it simplifies the method of interaction with them for applications. This would not been possible without the use of device nodes, that are actually files in which normal file interaction functions can be applied, such as `open()`, `read()`, `write()`, and `close()`.

Filesystem options

The root filesystem can be deployed under a very broad form of the filesystem type, and each one does a particular task better than the rest. If some filesystems are optimized for performance, others are better at saving space or even recovering data. Some of the most commonly used and interesting ones will be presented here.

The logical division for a physical device, such as a hard disk or SD card, is called a **partition**. A physical device can have one or more partitions that cover its available storage space. It can be viewed as a logical disk that has a filesystem available for the user's purposes. The management of partitions in Linux is done using the `fdisk` utility. It can be used to `create`, `list`, `destroy`, and other general interactions, with more than 100 partition types. To be more precise, 128 partition types are available on my Ubuntu 14.04 development machine.

One of the most used and well known filesystem partition formats is `ext2`. Also called **second extended filesystem**, it was introduced in 1993 by Rémy Card, a French software developer. It was used as the default filesystem for a large number of Linux distributions, such as Debian and Red Hat Linux, until it was replaced by its younger brothers, `ext3` and `ext4`. It continues to remain the choice of many embedded Linux distributions and flash storage devices.

The `ext2` filesystem splits data into blocks, and the blocks are arranged into block groups. Each block group maintains a copy of a superblock and the descriptor table for that block group. Superblocks are to store configuration information, and hold the information required by the booting process, although there are available multiple copies of it; usually, the first copy that is situated in the first block of the file system is the one used. All the data for a file is usually kept in a single block so that searches can be made faster. Each block group, besides the data it contains, has information about the superblock, descriptor table for the block group, inode bitmap and table information, and the block bitmap. The superblock is the one that holds the information important for the booting process. Its first block is used for the booting process. The last notion presented is in the form of `inodes`, or the index nodes, which represent files and directories by their permission, size, location on disk, and ownership.

There are multiple applications used for interaction with the `ext2` filesystem format. One of them is `mke2fs`, which is used to create an `ext2` filesystem on a `mke2fs /deb/sdb1 -L` partition (`ext2` label partition). The is the `e2fsck` command, which is used to verify the integrity of the filesystem. If no errors are found, these tools give you information about the partition filesystem configuration, `e2fsck /dev/sdb1`. This utility is also able to fix some of the errors that appear after improper utilization of the device, but cannot be used in all scenarios.

Ext3 is another powerful and well known filesystem. It replaced `ext2` and became one of the most used filesystems on Linux distributions. It is in fact similar to `ext2`; the difference being that it has the possibility to journalize the information available to it. The `ext2` file format can be changed in an `ext3` file format using the `tune2fs -j /dev/sdb1` command. It is basically seen as an extension for the `ext2` filesystem format, one that adds the journaling feature. This happens because it was engineered to be both forward and backward compatible.

Journaling is a method that is used to log all the changes made on a filesystem form by making the recovery functionality possible. There are also other features that `ext3` adds besides the ones that are already mentioned; here, I am referring to the possibility of not checking for consistencies in the filesystem, mostly because journalizing the log can be reversed. Another important feature is that it can be mounted without checking whether the shutdown was performed correctly. This takes place because the system does not need to conduct a consistency check at power down.

Ext4 is the successor of `ext3`, and was built with the idea of improving the performance and the storage limit in `ext3`. It is also backward compatible with the `ext3` and `ext2` filesystems and also adds a number of features:

- Persistent preallocation: This defines the `fallocate()` system call that can be used to preallocate space, which is most likely in a contiguous form; it is very useful for databases and streaming of media
- Delayed allocation: This is also called **allocate-on-flush**; it is used to delay the allocation blocks from the moment data from the disk is flushed, to reduce fragmentation and increase performance
- Multi block allocation: This is a side effect of delayed allocation because it allows for data buffering and, at the same time, the allocation of multiple blocks.
- Increase subdirectory limit: This the `ext3` has a limit of 32000 subdirectories, the `ext4` does not have this limitation, that is, the number of subdirectories are unlimited
- Checksum for journal: This is used to improve reliability

Journalling Flash Filesystem version 2 (**JFFS2**) is a filesystem designed for the NAND and NOR flash memory. It was included in the Linux mainline kernel in 2001, the same year as the `ext3` filesystem, although in different months. It was released in November for the Linux version 2.4.15, and the JFFS2 filesystem was released in September with the 2.4.10 kernel release. Since it's especially used to support flash devices, it takes into consideration certain things, such as the need to work with small files, and the fact that these devices have a wear level associated with them, which solves and reduces them by their design. Although JFFS2 is the standard for flash memory, there are also alternatives that try to replace it, such as LogFS, Yet Another Flash File System (YAFFS), and Unsorted Block Image File System (UBIFS).

Besides the previously mentioned filesystems, there are also some pseudo filesystems available, including `proc`, `sysfs`, and `tmpfs`. In the next section, the first two of them will be described, leaving the last one for you to discover by yourself.

The `proc` filesystem is a virtual filesystem available from the first version of Linux. It was defined to allow a kernel to offer information to the user about the processes that are run, but over time, it has evolved and is now able to not only offer statistics about processes that are run, but also offer the possibility to adjust various parameters regarding the management of memory, processes, interrupts, and so on.

With the passing of time, the `proc` virtual filesystem became a necessity for Linux system users since it gathered a very large number of user space functionalities. Commands, such as `top`, `ps`, and `mount` would not work without it. For example, the `mount` example given without a parameter will present `proc` mounted on the `/proc` in the form of `proc` on `/proc type proc (rw,noexec,nosuid,nodev)`. This takes place since it is necessary to have `proc` mounted on the `root` filesystem on par with directories, such as `/etc`, `/home`, and others that are used as the destination of the `/proc` filesystem. To mount the `proc` filesystem, the mount `-t proc nodev/proc` mount command that is similar to the other filesystems available is used. More information on this can be found inside the kernel sources documentation at `Documentation/filesystems/proc.txt`.

The `proc` filesystem has the following structure:

- For each running process, there is an available directory inside `/proc/<pid>`. It contains information about opened files, used memory, CPU usage, and other process-specific information.
- Information on general devices is available inside `/proc/devices`, `/proc/interrupts`, `/proc/ioports`, and `/proc/iomem`.
- The kernel command line is available inside `/proc/cmdline`.
- Files used to change kernel parameters are available inside `/proc/sys`. More information is also available inside `Documentation/sysctl`.

The `sysfs` filesystem is used for the representation of physical devices. It is available since the introduction of the 2.6 Linux kernel versions, and offers the possibility of representing physical devices as kernel objects and associate device drivers with corresponding devices. It is very useful for tools, such as `udev` and other device managers.

The `sysfs` directory structure has a subdirectory for every major system device class, and it also has a system buses subdirectory. There is also `systool` that can be used to browse the `sysfs` directory structure. Similar to the proc filesystem, `systool` also can also be visible if the `sysfs on /sys type sysfs (rw,noexec,nosuid,nodev) mount` command is offered on the console. It can be mounted using the `mount -t sysfs nodev /sys` command.

> More information on available filesystems can be found at `http://en.wikipedia.org/wiki/List_of_file_systems`.

Understanding BusyBox

BusyBox was developed by Bruce Perens in 1999 with the purpose of integrating available Linux tools in a single executable. It has been used with great success as a replacement for a great number of Linux command line utilities. Due to this, and the fact that it is able to fit inside small embedded Linux distributions, it has gained a lot of popularity in the embedded environment. It provides utilities from file interations, such as `cp`, `mkdir`, `touch`, `ls`, and `cat`, as well as general utilities, such as `dmesg`, `kill`, `fdisk`, `mount`, `umount`, and many others.

Not only is it very easy to configure and compile, but it is also very easy to use. The fact that it is very modular and offers a high degree of configuration makes it the perfect choice to use. It may not include all the commands available in a full-blown Linux distribution available on your host PC, but the ones that it does are more than enough. Also, these commands are just simpler versions of the full-blown ones used at implementation level, and are all integrated in one single executable available in `/bin/busybox` as symbolic links of this executable.

A developer interaction with the BusyBox source code package is very simple: just configure, compile, and install it, and there you have it. Here are some detailed steps to explain the following:

- Run the configuration tool and chose the features you want to make available
- Execute make `dep` to construct the dependencies tree
- Build the package using the `make` command

> Install the executable and symbolic links on the target. People who are interested in interacting with the tool on their workstations should note that if the tool is installed for the host system, then the installation should be done in a location that does not overwrite any of the utilities and start up scripts available to the host.

The configuration of the BusyBox package also has a `menuconfig` option available, similar to the one available for the kernel and U-Boot, that is, `make menuconfig`. It is used to show a text menu that can be used for faster configuration and configuration searches. For this menu to be available, first the `ncurses` package needs to be available on the system that calls the make `menuconfig` command.

At the end of the process, the BusyBox executable is available. If it's called without arguments, it will present an output very similar to this:

```
Usage: busybox [function] [arguments]...
   or: [function] [arguments]...

        BusyBox is a multi-call binary that combines many common Unix
        utilities into a single executable.  Most people will create a
        link to busybox for each function they wish to use and BusyBox
        will act like whatever it was invoked as!

Currently defined functions:
        [, [[, arping, ash, awk, basename, bunzip2, busybox, bzcat, cat,
        chgrp, chmod, chown, chroot, clear, cp, crond, crontab, cut,
date,
        dd, df, dirname, dmesg, du, echo, egrep, env, expr, false, fgrep,
        find, free, grep, gunzip, gzip, halt, head, hexdump, hostid,
hostname,
        id, ifconfig, init, insmod, ipcalc, ipkg, kill, killall,
killall5,
        klogd, length, ln, lock, logger, logread, ls, lsmod, md5sum,
mesg,
        mkdir, mkfifo, mktemp, more, mount, mv, nc, "netmsg", netstat,
        nslookup, passwd, pidof, ping, pivot_root, poweroff, printf, ps,
        pwd, rdate, reboot, reset, rm, rmdir, rmmod, route, sed, seq,
        sh, sleep, sort, strings, switch_root, sync, sysctl, syslogd,
        tail, tar, tee, telnet, test, time, top, touch, tr, traceroute,
        true, udhcpc, umount, uname, uniq, uptime, vi, wc, wget, which,
        xargs, yes, zcat
```

It presents the list of the utilities enabled in the configuration stage. To invoke one of the preceding utilities, there are two options. The first option requires the use of the BusyBox binary and the number of utilities called, which are represented as `./busybox ls`, while the second option involves the use of the symbolic link already available in directories, such as `/bin`, `/sbin`, `/usr/bin`, and so on.

Besides the utilities that are already available, BusyBox also offers implementation alternatives for the `init` program. In this case, the `init` does not know about a runlevel, and all its configurations available inside the `/etc/inittab` file. Another factor that differentiates it from the standard `/etc/inittab` file is the fact that this one also has its special syntax. For more information, `examples/inittab` available inside BusyBox can be consulted. There are also other tools and utilities implemented inside the BusyBox package, such as a lightweight version for `vi`, but I will let you discover them for yourself.

Minimal root filesystem

Now that all the information relating to the `root` filesystem has been presented to you, it would be good exercise to describe the must-have components of the minimal `root` filesystem. This would not only help you to understand the `rootfs` structure and its dependencies better, but also help with requirements needed for boot time and the size optimization of the `root` filesystem.

The starting point to describe the components is `/sbin/init`; here, by using the `ldd` command, the runtime dependencies can be found. For the Yocto Project, the `ldd /sbin/init` command returns:

```
linux-gate.so.1 (0xb7785000)
libc.so.6 => /lib/libc.so.6 (0x4273b000)
/lib/ld-linux.so.2 (0x42716000)
```

From this information, the `/lib` directory structure is defined. Its minimal form is:

```
lib
|-- ld-2.3.2.so
|-- ld-linux.so.2 -> ld-2.3.2.so
|-- libc-2.3.2.so
'-- libc.so.6 -> libc-2.3.2.so
```

The following symbolic links to ensure backward compatibility and version immunity for the libraries. The `linux-gate.so.1` file in the preceding code is a **virtual dynamically linked shared object** (**vDSO**), exposed by the kernel at a well established location. The address where it can be found varies from one machine architecture to another.

After this, `init` and its runlevel must be defined. The minimal form for this is available inside the BusyBox package, so it will also be available inside the `/bin` directory. Alongside it, a symbolic link for shell interaction is necessary, so this is how the minimal for the bin directory will look:

```
bin
|-- busybox
'-- sh -> busybox
```

Next, the runlevel needs to be defined. Only one is used in the minimal `root` filesystem, not because it is a strict requirement, but due to the fact that it can suppress some BusyBox warnings. This is how the `/etc` directory will look:

```
etc
'-- init.d
    '-- rcS
```

At the end, the console device needs to be available to the user for input and output operations, so the last piece of the `root` filesystem is inside the `/dev` directory:

```
dev
'-- console
```

Having mentioned all of this, the minimal `root` filesystem seems to have only five directories and eight files. Its minimal size is below 2 MB and around 80 percent of its size is due to the C library package. It is also possible to minimize its size by using the Library Optimizer Tool. You can find more information on this at `http://libraryopt.sourceforge.net/`.

The Yocto Project

Moving to the Yocto Project, we can take a look at the core-image-minimal to identify its content and minimal requirements, as defined inside the Yocto Project. The `core-image-minimal.bb` image is available inside the `meta/recipes-core/images` directory, and this is how it looks:

```
SUMMARY = "A small image just capable of allowing a device to boot."


IMAGE_INSTALL = "packagegroup-core-boot ${ROOTFS_PKGMANAGE_BOOTSTRAP}
${CORE_IMAGE_EXTRA_INSTALL} ldd"


IMAGE_LINGUAS = " "


LICENSE = "MIT"


inherit core-image


IMAGE_ROOTFS_SIZE ?= "8192"
```

You can see here that this is similar to any other recipe. The image defines the `LICENSE` field and inherits a `bbclass` file, which defines its tasks. A short summary is used to describe it, and it is very different from normal package recipes. It does not have `LIC_FILES_CHKSUM` to check for licenses or a `SRC_URI` field, mostly because it does not need them. In return, the file defines the exact packages that should be contained in the `root` filesystem, and a number of them are grouped inside `packagegroup` for easier handling. Also, the `core-image bbclass` file defines a number of other tasks, such as `do_rootfs`, which is only specific for image recipes.

Constructing a `root` filesystem is not an easy task for anyone, but Yocto does it with a bit more success. It starts from the base-files recipe that is used to lay down the directory structure according to the **Filesystem Hierarchy Standard** (**FHS**), and, along with it, a number of other recipes are placed. This information is available inside the `./meta/recipes-core/packagegroups/packagegroup-core-boot.bb` recipe. As can be seen in the previous example, it also inherits a different kind of class, such as `packagegroup.bbclass`, which is a requirement for all the package groups available. However, the most important factor is that it clearly defines the packages that constitute `packagegroup`. In our case, the core boot package group contains packages, such as `base-files`, `base-passwd` (which contains the base system master password and group files), `udev`, `busybox`, and `sysvinit` (a System V similar to init).

As can be seen in the previously shown file, the BusyBox package is a core component of the Yocto Project's generated distributions. Although information was available about the fact that BusyBox can offer an init alternative, the default Yocto generated distributions do not use this. Instead, they choose to move to the System V-like init, which is similar to the one available for Debian-based distributions. Nevertheless, a number of shell interaction tools are made available through the BusyBox recipe available inside the `meta/recipes-core/busybox` location. For users interested in enhancing or removing some of features made available by the `busybox` package, the same concepts that are available for the Linux kernel configuration are used. The `busybox` package uses a `defconfig` file on which a number of configuration fragments are applied. These fragments can add or remove features and, in the end, the final configuration file is obtained. This identifies the final features available inside the `root` filesystem.

Inside the Yocto Project, it is possible to minimize the size of the `root` filesystem by using the `poky-tiny.conf` distribution policies, which are available inside the `meta-yocto/conf/distro` directory. When they're used, these policies reduce not only the boot size, but the boot time as well. The simplest example for this is available using the `qemux86` machine. Here, changes are visible, but they are somewhat different from the ones already mentioned in the *Minimal root filesystem* section. The purpose of the minimization work done on `qemux86` was done around the core-image-minimal image. Its goals is to reduce the size to under 4 MB of the resulting `rootfs` and the boot time to under 2 seconds.

Now, moving to the selected Atmel SAMA5D3 Xplained machine, another `rootfs` is generated and its content is quite big. Not only has it included the `packagegroup-core-boot.bb` package group, but other package groups and separate packages are also included. One such example is the `atmel-xplained-demo-image.bb` image available inside the `meta-atmel` layer in the `recipes-core/images` directory:

```
DESCRIPTION = "An image for network and communication."
LICENSE = "MIT"
PR = "r1"

require atmel-demo-image.inc

IMAGE_INSTALL += "\
    packagegroup-base-3g \
    packagegroup-base-usbhost \
    "
```

Inside this image, there is also another more generic image definition that is inherited. Here, I am referring to the `atmel-demo-image.inc` file, and when opened, you can see that it contains the core of all the `meta-atmel` layer images. Of course, if all the available packages are not enough, a developer could decide to add their own. There has two possibilities in front of a developer: to create a new image, or to add packages to an already available one. The end result is built using the `bitbake atmel-xplained-demo-image` command. The output is available in various forms, and they are highly dependent on the requirements of the defined machine. At the end of the build procedure, the output will be used to boot the root filesystem on the actual board.

Summary

In this chapter, you have learned about the Linux `rootfs` in general, and also about the communication with the organization of the Linux kernel, Linux `rootfs`, its principles, content, and device drivers. Since communication tends to become larger over time, information about how a minimal filesystem should look was also presented to you.

Besides this information, in the next chapter, you will be given an overview of the available components of the Yocto Project, since most of them are outside Poky. You will also be introduced to, and given a brief gist of, each component. After this chapter, a bunch of them will be presented to you and elaborated on.

6
Components of the Yocto Project

In this chapter, you will be given a short introduction to a number of components from the ecosystem of the Yocto Project. This chapter is meant to introduce all of them so that in subsequent chapters they can be presented more elaborately. It also tries to direct readers toward extra readings. For each presented tool, feature, or interesting fact, links are offered to help interested readers search for their own answers to the questions in this book and those that this chapter does not cover.

This chapter is full of guidance and relevant examples for an embedded development process that involves specific Yocto Project tools. The selection of the tools was done in a purely subjective manner. Only the tools that are considered helpful in the development process have been selected. We also considered the fact that some of them could offer new insights into the embedded world and the development for embedded systems in general.

Poky

Poky represents the reference build system for the metadata and tools of the Yocto Project, which are used as starting points for anyone interested in interacting with the Yocto Project. It is platform-independent and provides the tools and mechanisms to build and customize the end result, which is in fact a Linux software stack. Poky is used as the central piece of interaction with the Yocto Project.

When working with the Yocto Project as a developer, it is very important to have information about mailing lists and an **Internet Relay Chat** (**IRC**) channel. Also, Project Bugzilla can be a source of inspiration in terms of a list of available bugs and features. All of these elements would need a short introduction, so the best starting point would be the Yocto Project Bugzilla. It represents a bug tracking application for the users of the Yocto Project and is the place where problems are reported. The next component is represented by the available channels of IRC. There are two available components on a freenode, one used for Poky and the other for discussions related to the Yocto Project, such as **#poky** and **#yocto**, respectively. The third element is represented by the Yocto Project mailing lists, which are used to subscribe to these mailing lists of the Yocto Project:

- `http://lists.yoctoproject.org/listinfo/yocto`: This refers to the mailing list where the Yocto Project discussions take place
- `http://lists.yoctoproject.org/listinfo/poky`: This refers to the mailing list where discussions regarding the Poky build of the Yocto Project system take place
- `http://lists.yoctoproject.org/listinfo/yocto-announce`: This refers to the mailing list where official announcements of the Yocto Project are made, as well as where milestones of the Yocto Project are presented

With the help of `http://lists.yoctoproject.org/listinfo`, more information can be gathered regarding general and project-specific mailing lists. It contains a list of all the mailing lists available at `https://www.yoctoproject.org/tools-resources/community/mailing-lists`.

In order to initiate development using the Yocto Project in general, and Poky in particular, you should not only use the previously mentioned components; some information regarding these tolls should also be made available. A very good explanation of the Yocto Project is available on their documentation page at `https://www.yoctoproject.org/documentation`. Those of you interested in reading a shorter introduction, it may be worth checking out the *Embedded Linux Development with Yocto Project, Otavio Salvador* and *Daiane Angolini*, by *Packt Publishing*.

To use the Yocto Project, a number of specific requirements are needed:

- **A host system**: Let's assume that this is a Linux-based host system. However, it is not just any host system; Yocto has certain requirements. The supported operating systems are available inside the `poky.conf` file, available inside directory `meta-yocto/conf/distro`. The supported operating systems are defined in the `SANITY_TESTED_DISTROS` variable, and a few of these systems are as follows:

  - Ubuntu-12.04
  - Ubuntu-13.10
  - Ubuntu-14.04
  - Fedora-19
  - Fedora-20
  - CentOS-6.4
  - CentOS-6.5
  - Debian-7.0
  - Debian-7.1
  - Debian-7.2
  - Debian-7.3
  - Debian-7.4
  - Debian-7.5
  - Debian-7.6
  - SUSE-LINUX-12.2
  - openSUSE-project-12.3
  - openSUSE-project-13.1
- **Required packages**: This contains a list of the minimum requirements for the packages available on the host system, besides the ones already available. Of course, this is different from one host system to another and the systems vary according to their purposes. However, for the Ubuntu host, we need the following requirements:
  - **Essentials**: This refers to `sudo apt-get install gawk wget git-core diffstat unzip texinfo gcc-multilib build-essential chrpath socat`
  - **Graphical and Eclipse Plug-in extras**: This refers to `sudo apt-get install libsdl1.2-dev xterm`
  - **Documentation**: This refers to `sudo apt-get install make xsltproc docbook-utils fop dblatex xmlto`
  - **ADT Installer Extras**: This refers to `sudo apt-get install autoconf automake libtool libglib2.0-dev`

- **Yocto Project release**: Before staring any work, one of the available Poky releases should be chosen. This book is based on the dizzy branch, which is the Poky 1.7 version, but a developer can chose whatever fits him or her best. Of course, since the interaction with the project is done using the `git` versioning system, the user will first need to clone the Poky repository, and any contributions to the project should be submitted as a patch to the open source community. There is also a possibility of getting a tar archive, but this method has some limitations due to the fact that any changes done on the source are harder to trace, and it also limits the interaction with the community involved in the project.

There are other extra optional requirements that should be taken care of if special requirements are needed, as follows:

- **Custom Yocto Project kernel interaction**: If a developer decides that the kernel source Yocto Projects are maintained and are not suitable for their needs, they could get one of the local copies of the Yocto Project supported by kernel versions, available at `http://git.yoctoproject.org/cgit.cgi` under the Yocto Linux Kernel section, and modify it according to their needs. These changes, of course, along with the rest of the kernel sources, will need to reside in a separate repository, preferably `git`, and it will be introduced to the Yocto world through a kernel recipe.
- **The meta-yocto-kernel-extras git repository**: Here the metadata needed is gathered when building and modifying kernel images. It contains a bunch of `bbappend` files that can be edited to indicate to the local that the source code has changed, which is a more efficient method to use when you are working on the development of features of the Linux kernel. It is available under the **Yocto Metadata Layers** section at `http://git.yoctoproject.org/cgit.cgi`.
- **Supported Board Support Packages (BSPs)**: There are a large number of BSP layers that are available and supported by the Yocto Project. The naming of each BSP layer is very simple, `meta-<bsp-name>`, and can be found at `http://git.yoctoproject.org/cgit.cgi` under the **Yocto Metadata Layers** section. Each BSP layer is, in fact, a collection of recipes that define the behavior and minimum requirements offered by the BSP provider. More information regarding the development of BSP can be found at `http://www.yoctoproject.org/docs/1.7/dev-manual/dev-manual.html#developing-a-board-support-package-bsp`.

- **Eclipse Yocto Plug-ins**: For developers who are interested in writing applications, an Eclipse **Integrated Development Environment** (**IDE**) is available with Yocto-specific plug-ins. You can find more information on this at `http://www.yoctoproject.org/docs/1.7/dev-manual/dev-manual.html#setting-up-the-eclipse-ide`.

The development process inside the Yocto Project has many meanings. It can refer to the various bugs and features that are available inside the Yocto Project Bugzilla. The developer can assign one of them to his or her account and solve it. Various recipes can be upgraded, and this process also requires the developer's involvement; new features can also be added and various recipes need to be written by developers. All these tasks need to have a well defined process in place that also involves `git` interaction.

To send changes added in the recipes back into the community, the available create-pull-request and send-pull request scripts can be used. These scripts are available inside the poky repository in the scripts directory. Also, in this section, there are also a bunch of other interesting scripts available, such as the `create-recipe` script, and others that I will let you discover on your own. The other preferred method to send the changes upstream would be to use the manual method, which involves interaction with `git` commands, such as `git add`, `git commit -s`, `git format-patch`, `git send-email`, and others.

Before moving on to describe the other components presented in this chapter, a review of the existing Yocto Project development models will be made. This process involves these tools made available by the Yocto Project:

- **System development**: This covers the development of the BSP, kernel development, and its configurations. Each of them has a section in the Yocto Project documentation describing respective development processes, as shown at `http://www.yoctoproject.org/docs/1.7/bsp-guide/bsp-guide.html#creating-a-new-bsp-layer-using-the-yocto-bsp-script` and `http://www.yoctoproject.org/docs/1.7/kernel-dev/kernel-dev.html`.
- **User application development**: This covers the development of applications for a targeted hardware device. The information regarding the necessary setup for the application development on the host system is available at `http://www.yoctoproject.org/docs/1.7/adt-manual/adt-manual.html`. This component will also be discussed in the *Eclipse ADT Plug-ins* section of this chapter.

- **Temporary modification of source code**: This covers the temporary modifications that appear in the development process. This involves the solution for various implementation problems that are available in a project's source code. After the problem is solved, the changes need to be available upstream and applied accordingly.
- **Development of a Hob image**: The Hob build system can be used for operating and customizing system images. It is a graphical interface developed in Python as a more efficient interface with the Bitbake build system.
- **Devshell development**: This is a method of development that uses the exact environment of the Bitbake build system's tasks. It is one of the most efficient methods used for debugging or package editing. It is also one of the quickest ways to set up the build environment when writing various components of a project.

For operating systems where the provided components are too old to satisfy the requirements of the Yocto Project, a buildtools toolchain is recommended for providing the required versions of the software. There are two methods used for installing a `buildtools` tarball. The first method implies the use of an already available prebuilt tarball, and the second one involves building it using the Bitbake build system. More information about this option can be found in the subsections under the **Required Git, tar, and Python Versions** section of the Yocto documentation mega manual available at `http://www.yoctoproject.org/docs/1.7/mega-manual/mega-manual.html#required-git-tar-and-python-versions`.

Eclipse ADT plug-ins

The **Application Development Toolkit**, also called ADT, provides a cross-development platform suitable for custom build and user-targeted applications. It is comprised of the following elements:

- **A cross-toolchain**: It is associated with the `sysroot`, both of them being automatically generated using Bitbake, and the target-specific metadata is made available by the target hardware supplier.
- **The Quick Emulator environment (Qemu)**: It is used to simulate the target hardware.
- **User-space tools**: It improves the overall experience of development of an application
- **Eclipse IDE**: It contains Yocto Project-specific plug-ins

In this section, each of the preceding elements will be discussed, and we will start with the cross-development toolchain. It consists of a cross-linker, cross-debugger, and a cross-compiler that are used for the application development of a target. It also needs the associated target `sysroot` because the necessary headers and libraries are required when building an application that will run on the target device. The generated `sysroot` is obtained from the same configuration that generates the `root` filesystem; this refers to the *image* recipe.

The toolchain can be generated using multiple methods. The most common one is to download the toolchain from `http://downloads.yoctoproject.org/releases/yocto/yocto-1.7/toolchain/`, and get the appropriate toolchain installer for your host and target. One such example is the `poky-glibc-x86_64-core-image-sato-armv7a-vfp-neon-toolchain-1.7.sh` script, which when executed will install the toolchain in the default location of the `/opt/poky/1.7/` directory. This location can be changed if proper arguments are offered in the script before starting the execution of the script.

Another method I prefer to use when generating a toolchain involves the use of the Bitbake build system. Here, I am referring to `meta-ide-support`. When running `bitbake meta-ide-support`, the cross-toolchain is generated and it populates the build directory. After this task is finished, the same result is obtained as in the previously mentioned solution, but in this case, a build directory that is already available is used. The only remaining task for both solutions would be to set up the environment using the script that contains the `environment-setup` string and start using it.

The Qemu emulator offers the possibility to simulate one hardware device when this one is not available. There are multiple ways of making it available in the development process:

- Install the ADT using the adt-installer generated script. One of the steps available in this script offers the possibility to enable or disable the use of Qemu in the development process.
- A Yocto Project release is downloaded and in the development process, the environment is set up by default. Then, the Qemu is installed and available for use.
- A `git` clone of the Poky repository is created and the environment is set up. In this case, the Qemu is installed and available also.
- The `cross-toolchain` tarball was downloaded, installed, and the environment was set up. This also, by default, enables the use of Qemu and installs it for later use.

The user-space tools are included into the distribution and are used during the development process. They are very common on a Linux platform and can include the following:

- **Perf**: It is a Linux performance counter that measures certain hardware and software events. More information about this is available at `https://perf.wiki.kernel.org/`, and also on the profiling and tracing manual of Yocto, where a whole section is devoted to this tool.
- **PowerTop**: It is a power measurement tool that is used to determine the amount of power a software consumes. More information about it is available at `https://01.org/powertop/`.
- **LatencyTop**: It is a similar tool to PowerTop, the difference being that this one focuses on the latency measurement from audio skips and stutters on the desktop to server overload; it has measurement for these kind of scenarios and answers for the latency problems. Although it seems that no commit has been done inside this project since 2009, it is still used today due to the fact that it is very useful.
- **OProfile**: It represents a system-wide profiler for the Linux ecosystem with a low overhead. More information about it is available at `http://oprofile.sourceforge.net/about/`. It also has a section available in the profiling and tracing manual of Yocto.
- **SystemTap**: It offers information on the infrastructure of a running Linux system, as well as the performance and functional problems of the system. It is not available though as an Eclipse extension, but only as a tool inside the Linux distribution. More information about it can be found at `http://sourceware.org/systemtap`. It also has a section defined in the profiling and tracing manual of Yocto.
- **Lttng-ust**: It is the user-space tracer for the `lttng` project and offers information related to user-space activities. More information is available at `http://lttng.org/`.

The last element of the ADT platform is represented by the Eclipse IDE. It is, in fact, the most popular development environment, and it offers full support for the development of the Yocto Project. With the installation of the Yocto Project Eclipse Plug-ins into the Eclipse IDE, the Yocto Project experience is complete. These plugins offer the possibility to cross-compile, develop, deploy, and execute the resultant binary in a Qemu emulated environment. Activities, such as cross-debugging, tracing, remote profiling, and power data collection, are also possible. More information about the activities that appear related to working with Eclipse Plug-ins for the Yocto Project can be found at `http://www.yoctoproject.org/docs/1.7/mega-manual/mega-manual.html#adt-eclipse`.

To better understand the workflow of the application development of the ADT toolkit platform and Eclipse, an overview of the whole process is available in the following image:

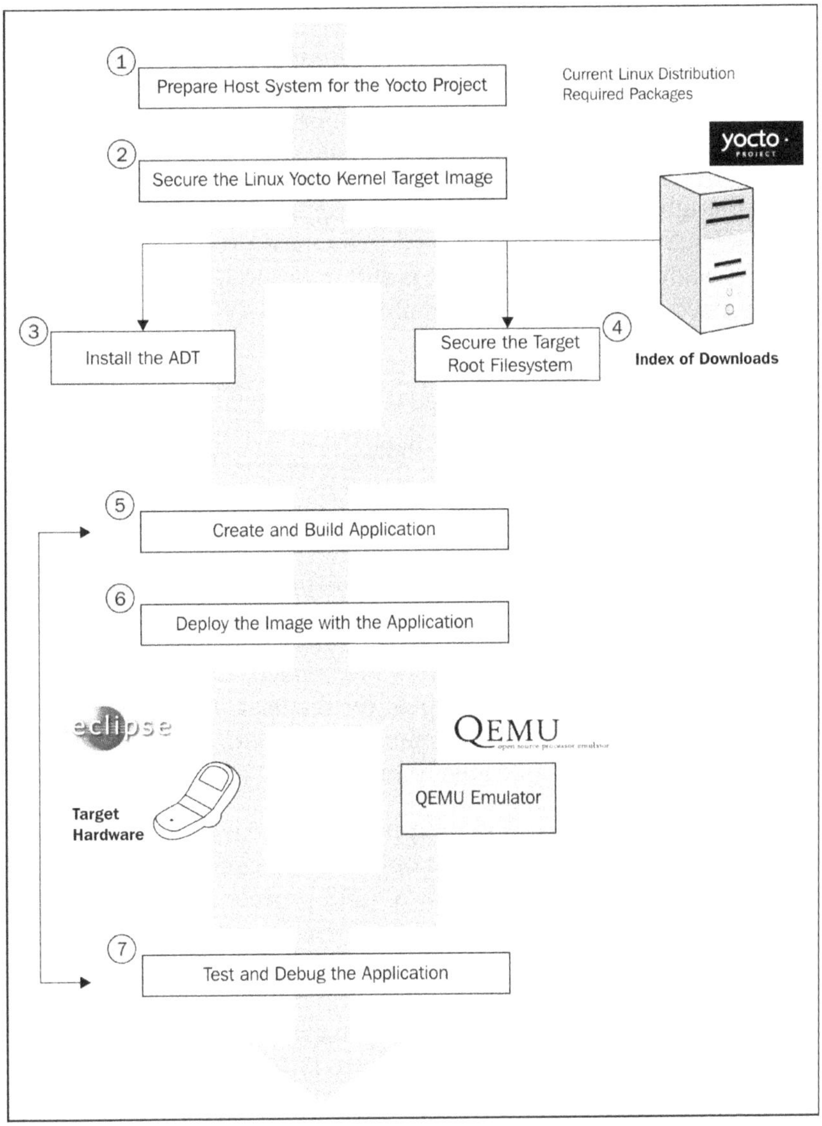

The application development process can also be done with other tools that are different from the ones already presented. However, all these options involve the use of a Yocto Project component, most notably the Poby reference system. Therefore, ADT is the suggested, tested, and recommended option by the open source community.

Hob and Toaster

The project—**Hob**—represents a graphical user interface for the Bitbake build system. Its purpose was to simplify the interaction with the Yocto Project and create a leaner learning curve for the project, allowing users to perform daily tasks in a simpler manner. Its primary focus was the generation of a Linux operating system image. With time, it evolved and can now be considered a tool suitable for both experienced and nonexperienced users. Although I mostly prefer using the command line interaction, this statement does not hold true for all Yocto Project users.

It might seem, though, that Hob development stopped with the release of Daisy 1.6. The development activity somewhat moved to the new project—**Toaster**—, which will be explained shortly; the Hob project is still in use today and its functionalities should be mentioned. So, the current available version of Hob is able to do the following:

- Customize an available base image recipe
- Create a completely customized image
- Build any given image
- Run an image using Qemu
- Deploy an image on a USB disk for the purpose of live-booting it on a target

The Hob project can be started in the same way that Bitbake is executed. After the environment sources and the build directory are created, the `hob` command can be called and the graphical interface will appear for the user. The disadvantage of this is that this tool does not substitute the command-line interaction. If new recipes need to be created, then this tool will not be able to provide any help with the task.

The next project is called Toaster. It is an application programming interface and also a web interface that the Yocto Project builds. In its current state, it is only able to gather and present information relevant to a build process through a web browser. These are some of its functionalities:

- Visibility for the executed and reused tasks during the build process
- Visibility for build components, such as recipes and packages of an image - this is done in a manner similar to Hob
- Offering information about recipes, such as dependencies, licenses, and so on
- Offering performance-related information, such as disk I/O , CPU usage, and so on
- Presenting errors, warnings, and trace reports for the purpose of debugging

Although it might not seem much, this project promises to offer the possibility to build and customize builds the same way that Hob did, along with many other goodies. You can find useful information about this tool at: `https://wiki.yoctoproject.org/wiki/Toaster`.

Autobuilder

Autobuilder is a project that facilitates the build test automation and conducts quality assurance. Through this internal project, the Yocto community tries to set a path on which embedded developers are able to publish their QA tests and testing plans, develop new tools for automatic testing, continuous integration, and develop QA procedures to demonstrate and show them for the benefit of all involved parties.

These points are already achieved by a project that publishes its current status using this Autobuilder platform, which is available at `http://autobuilder.yoctoproject.org/`. This link is accessible to everyone and testing is performed on all the changes related to the Yocto Project, as well as nightly builds for all supported hardware platforms. Although started from the Buildbot project, from which it borrowed components for continuous integration, this project promises to move forward and offer the possibility of performing runtime testing and other must-have functionalities.

You can find some useful information about this project at: `https://wiki.yoctoproject.org/wiki/AutoBuilder` and `https://wiki.yoctoproject.org/wiki/QA`, which offers access to the QA procedures done for every release, as well as some extra information.

Lava

The Lava project is not an internal work of the Yocto Project, but is, in fact, a project developed by Linaro, which is an automated validation architecture aimed towards testing the deployments of Linux systems on devices. Although its primary focus is the ARM architecture, the fact that it is open source does not make it a disincentive. Its actual name is **Linaro Automation and Validation Architecture** (**LAVA**).

This project offers the possibility of deploying an operating system on a hardware or virtual platform, defining, tests, and performing them on the project. The tests can be of various complexities, they can be combined into bigger and more conclusive tests, and the results are tracked in time, after which the resulting data is exported for analysis.

This is developed with the idea of a continuous evolving architecture that allows test performing along with automation and quality control. At the same time, it offers validation for gathered data. Tests can be anything from compiling a boot test to a change on the kernel scheduler that may or may not have reduced power consumption.

Although it is still young, this project has gained quite an audience, so some investigation into the project would not hurt anyone.

> The LAVA manual is available at `https://validation.linaro.org/static/docs/`

Wic

Wic is more of a feature then a project per se. It is the least documented, and if a search is conducted for it, you may find no results. I have decided to mention it here because in the development process, some special requirements could appear, such as generating a custom `root` filesystem from available packages (such as `.deb`, `.rpm`, or `.ipk`). This job is the one that is best suited for the wic tool.

This tool tries to solve some special requirements from devices or bootloaders, such as special formatting or the partitioning of the `root` filesystem. It is a highly customized tool that offers the possibility of extending its features. It has been developed from another tool called **oeic**, which was used to create a certain proprietary formatted image for hardware and was imported into the Yocto Project to serve a broader purposes for developers who did not wanted to touch recipes and had already packaged sources, or required special formatting for their deliverable Linux image.

Unfortunately, there is no documentation available for this tool, but I can direct those who are interested to its location on the Yocto Project. It resides in the Poky repository in the scripts directory under the name of wic. Wic can be used as any script, and it provides a help interface where you can seek more information. Also, its functionalities will be presented in an extended manner in the coming chapters.

A list with all the available projects developed around the Yocto Project can be found at `https://www.yoctoproject.org/tools-resources/projects`. Some of the projects available there were not discussed in the context of this chapter, but I will let you discover each one of them. There are also other external projects that did not make the list. I encourage you to find out and learn about them on your own.

Summary

In this chapter, you were presented with the elements that will be discussed next in this book. In the following chapter, each of the previously mentioned sections will be presented in various chapters, and the information will be presented in-depth and in a more applied manner.

In the next chapter, the previously mentioned process will start with the Application Development Toolkit platform. It will be explained with the steps necessary for the setup of the platform, and some usage scenarios will also be introduced to you. These involve cross-development, debugging using Qemu, and the interaction between specific tools.

7
ADT Eclipse Plug-ins

In this chapter, you will be presented with a new perspective of the available tool in the Yocto Project. This chapter marks the beginning of the introduction to various tools available in the Yocto Project ecosystem, tools that are very useful and different from the Poky reference system. In this chapter, a short presentation to the **Application Development Environment** (**ADE**) is presented with emphasis on the Eclipse project and the Yocto Project's added plug-ins. A number of the plug-ins are shown along with their configurations and use cases.

A broader view of the **Application Development Toolkit** (**ADT**) will also be shown to you. This project's main objective is to offer a software stack that is able to develop, compile, run, debug, and profile software applications. It tries to do this without requiring extra learning from the developer's point of view. Its learning curve is very low, taking into consideration the fact that Eclipse is one of the most used **Integrated Development Environment** (**IDEs**), and over time, it has become very user-friendly, stable, and dependable. The ADT user experience is very similar to the one that any Eclipse or non-Eclipse user has when they use an Eclipse IDE. The available plug-ins try to make this experience as similar as possible so that development is similar to any Eclipse IDE. The only difference is between configuration steps, and this defines the difference between one Eclipse IDE version and another.

The ADT offers the possibility of using a standalone cross-compiler, debugging tool profilers, emulators, and even development board interaction in a platform-independent manner. Although interaction with hardware is the best option for an embedded developer, in most cases, the real hardware is missing due to various reasons. For these scenarios, it is possible to use a QEMU emulator to simulate the necessary hardware.

The Application Development Toolkit

ADT is one of the components of the Yocto Project and provides a cross-development platform, which is perfect for user-specific application development. For the development process to take place in an orderly manner, some components are required:

- Eclipse IDE Yocto plug-ins
- QEMU emulator for specific hardware simulations
- Cross-toolchain alongside its specific `sysroot`, which are both architecture-specific and are generated using the metadata and the build system made available by the Yocto Project
- Userspace tools to enhance a developer's experience with the application development process

The Eclipse plug-ins are available when offering full support to the Yocto Project with the Eclipse IDE and maximizing the Yocto experience. The end result is an environment that is customized for the Yocto developer's needs, with a cross-toolchain, deployment on a real hardware, or QEMU emulation features, and also a number of tools that are available for collecting data, tracing, profiling, and performance reviews.

The QEMU emulator is used to simulate various hardware. It can be obtained with these methods:

- Using the ADT installer script, which offers the possibility of installing it
- Cloning a Poky repository and sourcing the environment, access is granted to a QEMU environment
- Downloading a Yocto release and sourcing the environment offers for the same result
- Installing a cross-toolchain and sourcing the environment to make the QEMU environment available

The toolchain contains a cross-debugger, cross-compiler, and cross-linker, which are very well used in the process of application development. The toolchain also comes with a matching sysroot for the target device because it needs access to various headers and libraries necessary to run on the target architecture. The sysroot is generated from the root filesystem and uses the same metadata configuration.

The userspace tools include the tools already mentioned in the previous chapters, such as SystemTap, PowerTop, LatencyTop, perf, OProfile, and LTTng-UST. They are used for getting information about the system and developed application; information, such as power consumption, desktop stutters, counting of events, performance overviews, and diagnosing software, hardware, or functional problems, and even tracing software activities.

Setting up the environment

Before explaining the ADT Project further, its Eclipse IDE plug-ins, other features, and functionalities of the setup would be required. To install the Eclipse IDE, the first step involves the setup of a host system. There are multiple methods to do this:

- **Using an ADT install script**: This is the recommended method to install the ADT, mostly because the installation process is completely automated. Users are in control of the features that they want available.
- **Using the ADT tarball**: This method involves a section of an appropriate tarball with the architecture-specific toolchain and setting it up using a script. The tarball can be both downloaded and manually built using Bitbake. This method also has limitations due to the fact that not all of its features are available after installation, apart from the cross-toolchain and QEMU emulator.
- **Using a toolchain from the build directory**: This method takes advantage of the fact that a build directory is already available, so the setup of the cross-toolchain is very easy. Also, in this case, it faces the same limitation as the one mentioned in the preceding point.

The ADT install script is the preferred method to install the ADT. Of course, before moving on to the installation step, the necessary dependencies need to be available to make sure that the ADT install script runs smoothly.

These packages were already mentioned in the previous chapters, but they will once again, be explained here to make things easy for you. I advise you to go back to these chapters and refer to the information once again as a memory exercise. To refer to packages that might be of interest to you, take a look at the ADT Installer packages, such as `autoconf automake libtool libglib2.0-dev`, Eclipse Plug-ins, and graphical support offered by the `libsdl1.2-dev xterm` packages.

After the host system is prepared with all the required dependencies, the ADT tarball can be downloaded from `http://downloads.yoctoproject.org/releases/yocto/yocto-1.7/adt-installer/`. At this location, the `adt_installer.tar.bz2` archive is available. It needs to be downloaded and its content extracted.

This tarball can also be generated using the Bitbake build system inside a build directory, and the result will be available inside the `tmp/deploy/sdk/adt_installer.tar.bz2` location. To generate it, the next command needs to be given into the build directory, which is `bitbake adt-installer`. The build directory also needs to be properly configured for the target device.

The archive is unpacked using the `tar -xjf adt_installer.tar.bz2` command. It can be extracted in any directory, and after unpacking the `adt-installer` directory, it is created and contains the ADT installer script called `adt_installer`. It also has a configuration file called `adt_installer.conf`, which is used to define the configurations before running the script. The configuration file defines information, such as the filesystem, kernel, QEMU support, and so on.

These are the variables that the configuration file contains:

- `YOCTOADT_REPO`: This defines the packages and root filesystem on which the installation is dependent. Its reference value is defined at `http://adtrepo.yoctoproject.org//1.7`. Here, the directory structure is defined and its structure is the same between releases.
- `YOCTOADT_TARGETS`: This defines the target architecture for which the cross development environment is set up. There are default values defined that can be associated with this variable, such as `arm`, `ppc`, `mips`, `x86`, and `x86_64`. Also, multiple values can be associated with it and the separation between them being is done using the space separator.
- `YOCTOADT_QEMU`: This variable defines the use of the QEMU emulator. If it is set to `Y`, the emulator will be available after installation; otherwise the value is set to `N`, and hence, the emulator won't be available.
- `YOCTOADT_NFS_UTIL`: This defines if the NFS user-mode that will be installed. The available values are, as defined previously, `Y` and `N`. For the use of the Eclipse IDE plug-ins, it is necessary to define the `Y` value for both `YOCTOADT_QEMU` and `YOCTOADT_NFS_UTIL`.
- `YOCTOADT_ROOTFS_<arch>`: This specifies which architecture root filesystem to use from the repository that is defined in the first mentioned `YOCTOADT_REPO` variable. For the `arch` variable, the default values are the ones already mentioned in the `YOCTOADT_TARGETS` variable. This variable's valid values are represented by the image files available, such as `minimal`, `sato`, `minimal-dev`, `sato-sdk`,`lsb`, `lsb-sdk`, and so on. For multiple arguments to the variable, the space separator can be used.

- YOCTOADT_TARGET_SYSROOT_IMAGE_<arch>: This represents the root filesystem from which the sysroot of the cross-development toolchain will be generated. The valid values for the 'arch' variable are the same as the one mentioned previously. Its value is dependent on what was previously defined as values for the YOCTOADT_ROOTFS_<arch> variable. So, if only one variable is defines as the value for the YOCTOADT_ROOTFS_<arch> variable, the same value will be available for YOCTOADT_TARGET_SYSROOT_IMAGE_<arch>. Also, if multiple variables are defined in the YOCTOADT_ROOTFS_<arch> variable, then one of them needs to define the YOCTOADT_TARGET_SYSROOT_IMAGE_<arch> variable.
- YOCTOADT_TARGET_MACHINE_<arch>: This defines the machine for which the image is downloaded, as there could be compilation option differences between machines of the same architecture. The valid values for this variable are can be mentioned as: qemuarm, qemuppc, ppc1022ds, edgerouter, beaglebone, and so on.
- YOCTOADT_TARGET_SYSROOT_LOC_<arch>: This defines the location where the target sysroot will be available after the installation process.

There are also some variables defined in the configuration files, such as YOCTOADT_BITBAKE and YOCTOADT_METADATA, which are defined for future work references. After all the variables are defined according to the needs of the developer, the installation process can start. This is done by running the adt_installer script:

```
cd adt-installer
./adt_installer
```

Here is an example of the adt_installer.conf file:

```
# Yocto ADT Installer Configuration File
#
# Copyright 2010-2011 by Intel Corp.
#
# Permission is hereby granted, free of charge, to any person obtaining a copy
# of this software and associated documentation files (the "Software"), to deal
# in the Software without restriction, including without limitation the rights
# to use, copy, modify, merge, publish, distribute, sublicense, and/or sell
```

```
# copies of the Software, and to permit persons to whom the Software is
# furnished to do so, subject to the following conditions:

# The above copyright notice and this permission notice shall be included
in
# all copies or substantial portions of the Software.

# THE SOFTWARE IS PROVIDED "AS IS", WITHOUT WARRANTY OF ANY KIND, EXPRESS
OR
# IMPLIED, INCLUDING BUT NOT LIMITED TO THE WARRANTIES OF
MERCHANTABILITY,
# FITNESS FOR A PARTICULAR PURPOSE AND NONINFRINGEMENT. IN NO EVENT SHALL
THE
# AUTHORS OR COPYRIGHT HOLDERS BE LIABLE FOR ANY CLAIM, DAMAGES OR OTHER
# LIABILITY, WHETHER IN AN ACTION OF CONTRACT, TORT OR OTHERWISE, ARISING
FROM,
# OUT OF OR IN CONNECTION WITH THE SOFTWARE OR THE USE OR OTHER DEALINGS
IN
# THE SOFTWARE.


# Your yocto distro repository, this should include IPKG based packages
and root filesystem files where the installation is based on

YOCTOADT_REPO="http://adtrepo.yoctoproject.org//1.7"
YOCTOADT_TARGETS="arm x86"
YOCTOADT_QEMU="Y"
YOCTOADT_NFS_UTIL="Y"

#YOCTOADT_BITBAKE="Y"
#YOCTOADT_METADATA="Y"

YOCTOADT_ROOTFS_arm="minimal sato-sdk"
YOCTOADT_TARGET_SYSROOT_IMAGE_arm="sato-sdk"
YOCTOADT_TARGET_MACHINE_arm="qemuarm"
YOCTOADT_TARGET_SYSROOT_LOC_arm="$HOME/test-yocto/$YOCTOADT_TARGET_
MACHINE_arm"
```

```
#Here's a template for setting up target arch of x86
YOCTOADT_ROOTFS_x86="sato-sdk"
YOCTOADT_TARGET_SYSROOT_IMAGE_x86="sato-sdk"
YOCTOADT_TARGET_MACHINE_x86="qemux86"
YOCTOADT_TARGET_SYSROOT_LOC_x86="$HOME/test-yocto/$YOCTOADT_TARGET_
MACHINE_x86"

#Here's some template of other arches, which you need to change the value
in ""
YOCTOADT_ROOTFS_x86_64="sato-sdk"
YOCTOADT_TARGET_SYSROOT_IMAGE_x86_64="sato-sdk"
YOCTOADT_TARGET_MACHINE_x86_64="qemux86-64"
YOCTOADT_TARGET_SYSROOT_LOC_x86_64="$HOME/test-yocto/$YOCTOADT_TARGET_
MACHINE_x86_64"

YOCTOADT_ROOTFS_ppc="sato-sdk"
YOCTOADT_TARGET_SYSROOT_IMAGE_ppc="sato-sdk"
YOCTOADT_TARGET_MACHINE_ppc="qemuppc"
YOCTOADT_TARGET_SYSROOT_LOC_ppc="$HOME/test-yocto/$YOCTOADT_TARGET_
MACHINE_ppc"

YOCTOADT_ROOTFS_mips="sato-sdk"
YOCTOADT_TARGET_SYSROOT_IMAGE_mips="sato-sdk"
YOCTOADT_TARGET_MACHINE_mips="qemumips"
YOCTOADT_TARGET_SYSROOT_LOC_mips="$HOME/test-yocto/$YOCTOADT_TARGET_
MACHINE_mips"
```

After the installation has started, the user is asked the location of the cross-toolchain. If no alternative is offered, the default path is selected and the cross-toolchain is installed in the `/opt/poky/<release>` directory. The installation process can be visualized both in a silent or interactive way. By using the `I` option, the installation is done in an interactive mode, while the silent mode is enabled using the `S` option.

At the end of the install procedure, the cross-toolchain will be found in its defined location. An environment setup script will be available for later usage, and the image tarball in the `adt-installer` directory, and the `sysroot` directory is defined in the location of the `YOCTOADT_TARGET_SYSROOT_LOC_<arch>` variable.

As shown previously, there is more than one method to prepare the ADT environment. The second method involves only the installation of the toolchain installer—although it offers the possibility of having a prebuilt cross-tooolchain, support files and scripts, such as the `runqemu` script to start something similar to a kernel or Linux image in an emulator—which does not offer the same possibilities as the first option. Also, this option has its limitations regarding the `sysroot` directory. Although it's been generated, the `sysroot` directory might still need to be extracted and installed in a separate location. This can happened for various reasons, such as the need to boot a root filesystem over NFS or develop the application using the root filesystem as the target `sysroot`.

The root filesystem can be extracted from an already generated cross-toolchain using the `runqemu-extract-sdk` script, which should be called only after the cross-development environment script was set up using source command.

There are two methods to obtain the toolchain installed for this second option. The first method involves the use of the toolchain installer available at `http://downloads.yoctoproject.org/releases/yocto/yocto-1.7/toolchain/`. Open the folder that matches your development host machine. In this folder, multiple install scripts are available. Each one matches a target architecture, so the right one should be selected for the target you have. One such example can be seen from `http://downloads.yoctoproject.org/releases/yocto/yocto-1.7/toolchain/x86_64/poky-glibc-x86_64-core-image-sato-armv7a-vfp-neon-toolchain-1.7.sh`, which is, in fact, the installer script for the `armv7a` target and the `x86_64` host machine.

If your target machine is not one of the ones that are made available by the Yocto community, or if you prefer an alternative to this method, then building the toolchain installer script is the method for you. In this case, you will require a build directory, and you will be presented with two alternatives, both of them are equally good:

- The first one involves the use of the `bitbake meta-toolchain` command, and the end result is an installer script that requires the installation and set up of the cross-toolchain in a separate location.
- The second alternative involves the use of the `bitbake -c populate_sdk <image-name>` task, which offers the toolchain installer script and the matching `sysroot` for the target. The advantage here is that the binaries are linked with only one and the same `libc`, making the toolchain self-contained. There is, of course, a limitation that each architecture can create only one specific build. However, target-specific options are passed through the `gcc` options. Using variables, such as `CC` or `LD`, makes the process easier to maintain and also saves some space in the build directory.

After the installer is downloaded, make sure that the install script has set the execution correctly, and start the installation with the `./poky-glibc-x86_64-core-image-sato-armv7a-vfp-neon-toolchain-1.7.sh` command.

Some of the information you require includes the place where the installation should be made, the default location being the `/opt/poky/1.7` directory. To avoid this, the script can be called with the `-d <install-location>` argument and the installation can be made in the `<install-location>` location, as mentioned.

> Make sure that the `MACHINE` variable is set accordingly in the `local.conf` file. Also, if the build is done for a different host machine, then `SDKMACHINE` should also be set. More than one `MACHINE` cross-toolchain can be generated in the same build directory, but these variables need to be properly configured.

After the installation process is finished, the cross-toolchain will be available in the selected location, and the environment script will also be available for sourcing when needed.

The third option involves the use of the build directory and the execution of the `bitbake meta-ide-support` command. Inside the build directory, the proper environment needs to be set using one of the two available build environment setup scripts, which include the `oe-init-build-env` script or `oe-init-build-env-memres`. The local configuration from the `local.conf` file also needs to be set accordingly for the target architecture. After these steps are fulfilled by the developer, the `bitbake meta-ide-support` command could be used to start the generation of the cross-toolchain. At the end of the process, an environment setup script will be available inside the `<build-dir-path>/tmp` directory, but in this case, the toolchain is tightly linked into the build directory in which it was built.

With the environment set up, writing of an application can start, but the developer would still need to complete some steps before finishing the activity, such as testing the application on the real root filesystem, debugging, and many others. For the kernel module and driver implementation, the kernel source code will be required, so the activity is just starting.

Eclipse IDE

The plug-ins available for Eclipse from the Yocto Project include the functionalities for the ADT Project and toolchain. They allow developers to use a cross-compiler, debugger, and all the available tools generated with the Yocto Project, Poky, and additional meta layers. Not only can these components be used within the Eclipse IDE, but they also offer a familiar environment for application development.

The Eclipse IDE is an alternative for developers who are not interested in interacting with editors, such as `vim`, although, in my opinion, `vim` can be used for all kinds of projects. Even if their dimensions or complexities are not a problem, the overhead for using `vim` might not suit all tastes. The Eclipse IDE is the best alternative available for all developers. It has a lot of useful features and functionalities that can make your life a little easier and it is pretty easy to grasp.

The Yocto Project offers support for two versions of Eclipse, Kepler and Juno. The Kepler version is the one recommended with the latest Poky release. I also recommend the Kepler 4.3.2 version of Eclipse, the one downloaded from the official download site of Eclipse, `http://www.eclipse.org/downloads`.

From this site, the Eclipse Standard 4.3.2 version containing the **Java Development Tools (JDT)**, the Eclipse Platform, and the Development Environment Plug-ins for the host machine should be downloaded. After the download is finished, the received archive content should be extracted using the tar command:

```
tar xzf eclipse-standard-kepler-SR2-linux-gtk-x86_64.tar.gzls
```

The next step is represented by the configuration. With the content extracted, the Eclipse IDE needs to be configured before installing the Yocto Project-specific plug-ins. The configuration starts with initializing the Eclipse IDE:

The Eclipse IDE is started after executing the `./eclipse` executable and setting the `Workspace` location. This is how the starting windows looks:

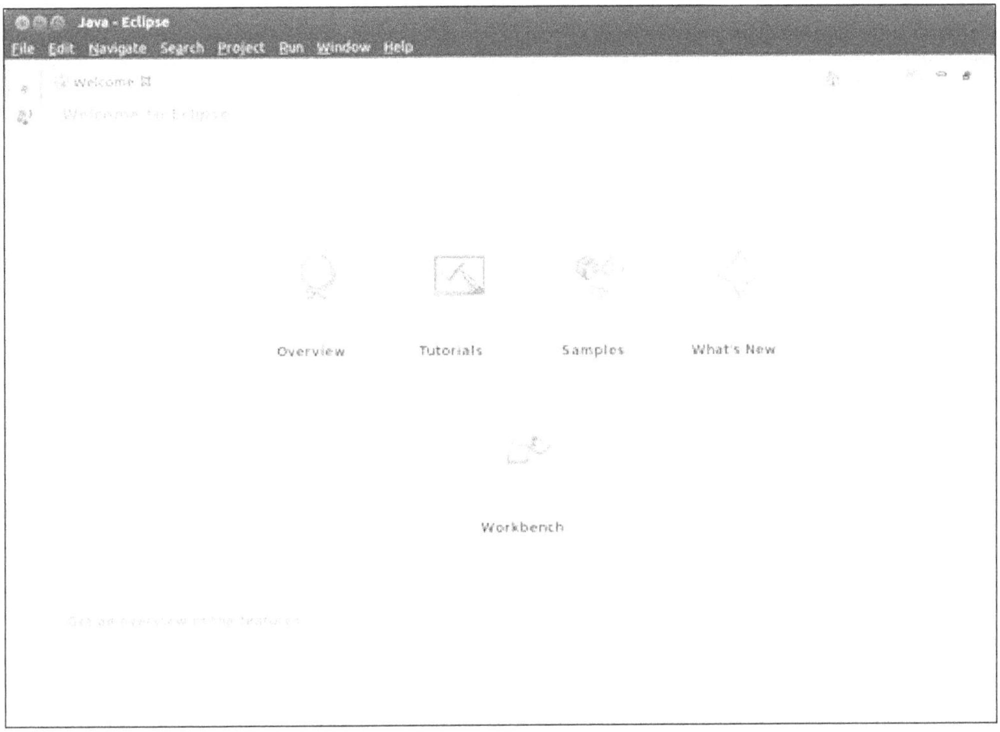

Eclipse window

To initialize the Eclipse IDE perform the following steps:

1. Select **Workbench**, and you will be moved into the empty workbench where the projects source code will be written.

2. Now, navigate through the **Help** menu and select **Install New Software**.

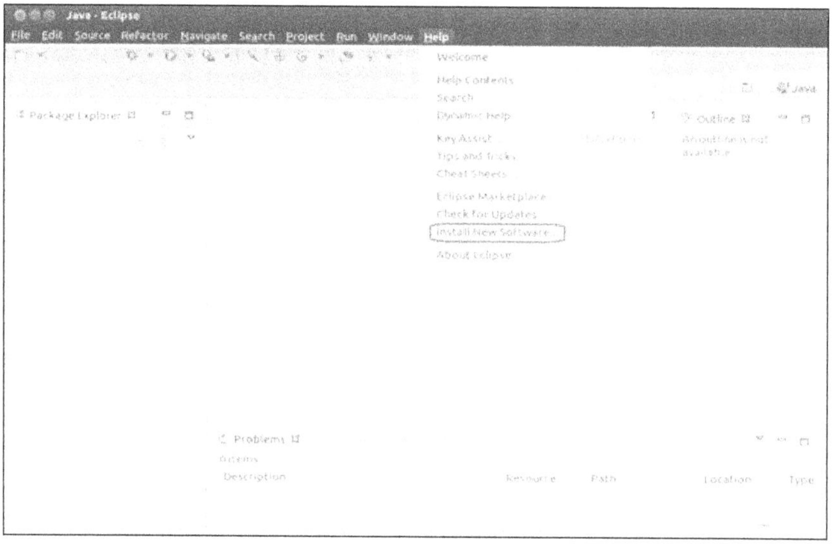

Help menu

3. A new window will open, and in the **Work with:** drop-down menu, select **Kepler - http://download.eclipse.org/releases/kepler**, as shown in the following screenshot:

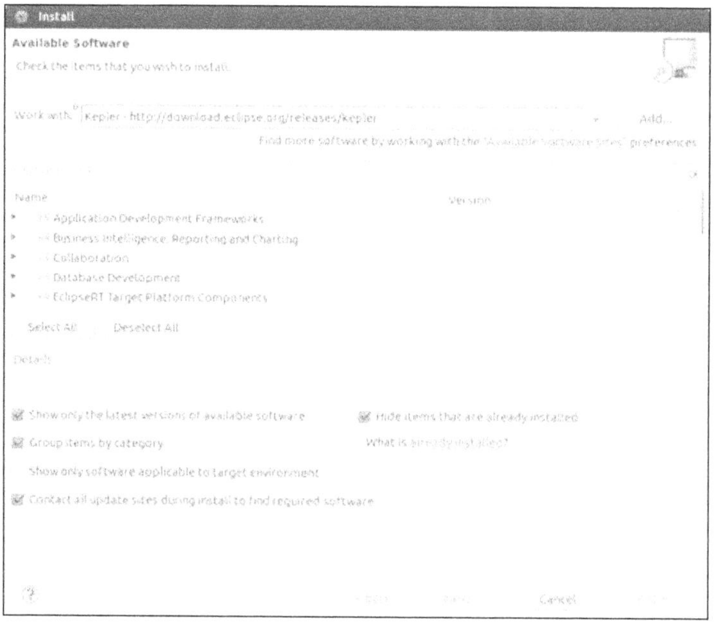

Install window

4. Expand the **Linux Tools** section and select **LTTng - Linux Tracing Toolkit** box, as shown in the following screenshot:

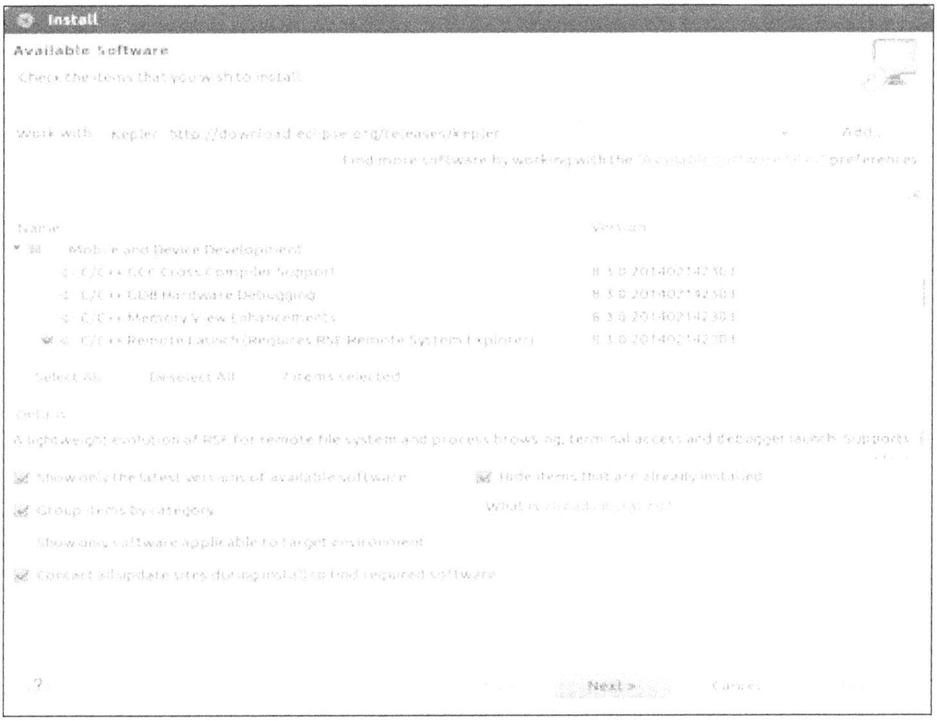

Install—LTTng - Linux Tracing Toolkit box

5. Expand the **Moble and Device Development** section and select the following:
    - **C/C++ Remote Launch (Requires RSE Remote System Explorer)**
    - **Remote System Explorer End-user Runtime**
    - **Remote System Explorer User Actions**
    - **Target Management Terminal**

- **TCF Remote System Explorer add-in**
- **TCF Target Explorer**

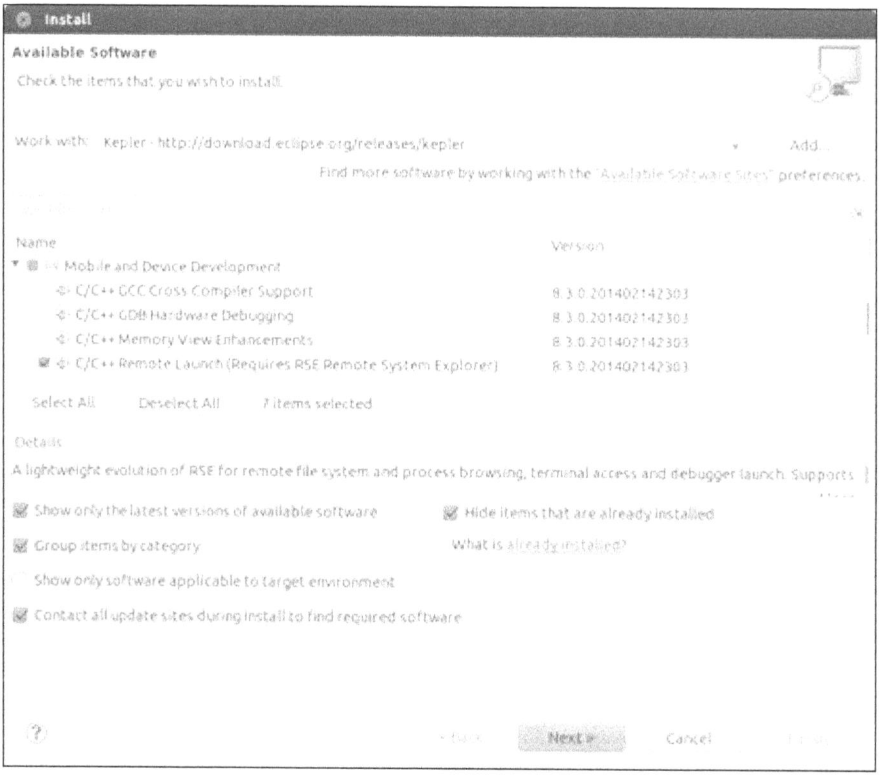

6. Expand the **Programming Languages** section and select the following:
    - **C/C++ Autotools Support**
    - **C/C++ Development Tools**

This is shown in the following screenshot:

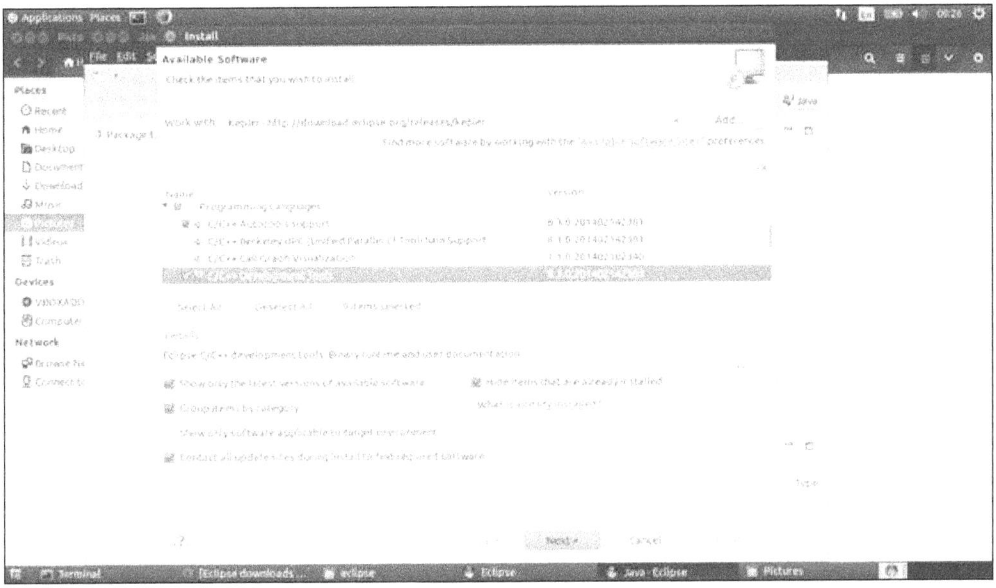

Available software list window

7. Finish the installation after taking a quick look at the **Install Details** menu and enabling the license agreement:

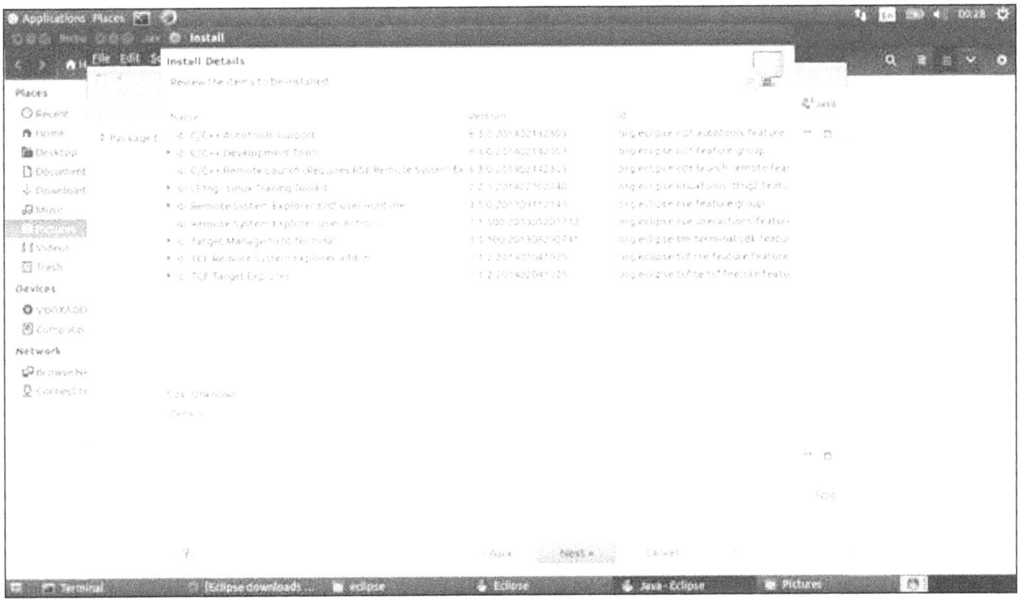

Install details window

After these steps, the Yocto Project Eclipse plug-ins can be installed into the IDE, but not before restarting the Eclipse IDE to make sure that the preceding changes take effect. The result after the configuration phase is visible here:

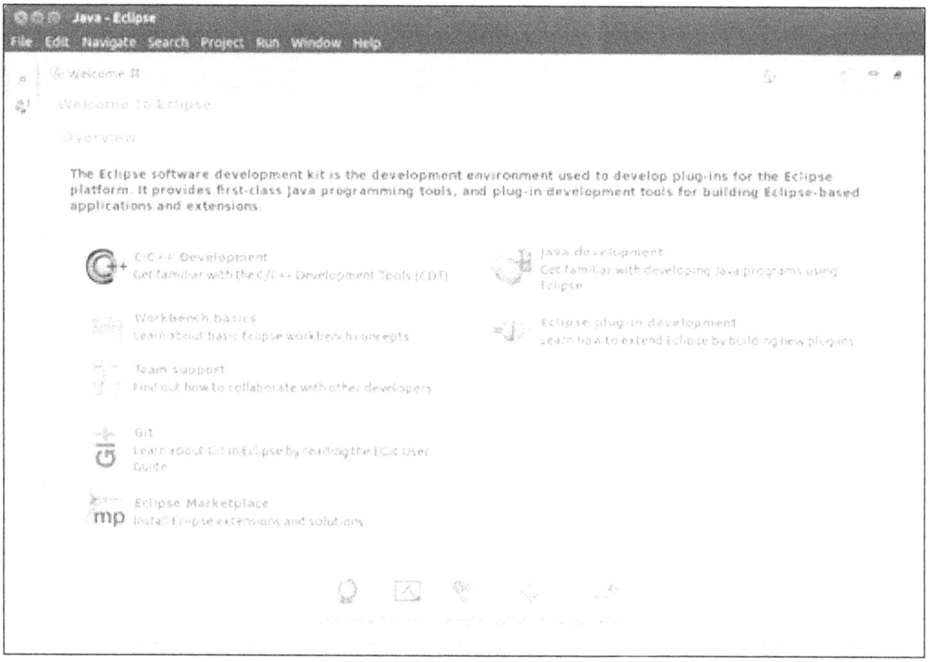

Eclipse – Configuring phase results

To install the Eclipse plug-ins for the Yocto Project, these steps are required:

1. Start the Eclipse IDE as mentioned previously.
2. As shown in the previous configuration, select the **Install New Software** option from the **Help** menu.
3. Click on the **Add** button and insert `downloads.yoctoproject.org/releases/eclipse-plugin/1.7/kepler/` in the URL section. Give a proper name to the new **Work with:** site as indicated here:

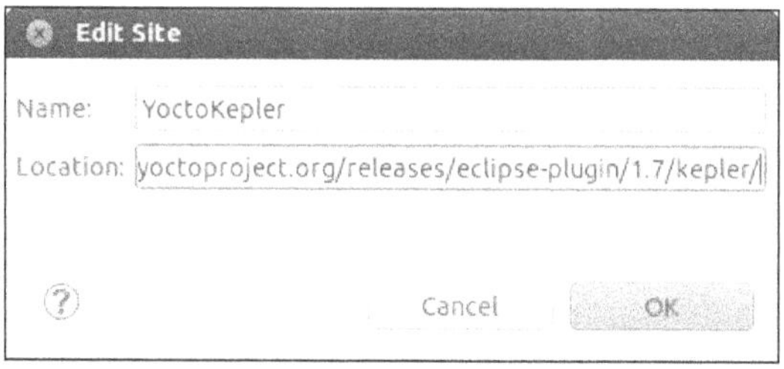

Edit site window

4. After the **OK** button is pressed, and the **Work with** site is updated, new boxes appear. Select all of them, as shown in this image, and click on the **Next** button:

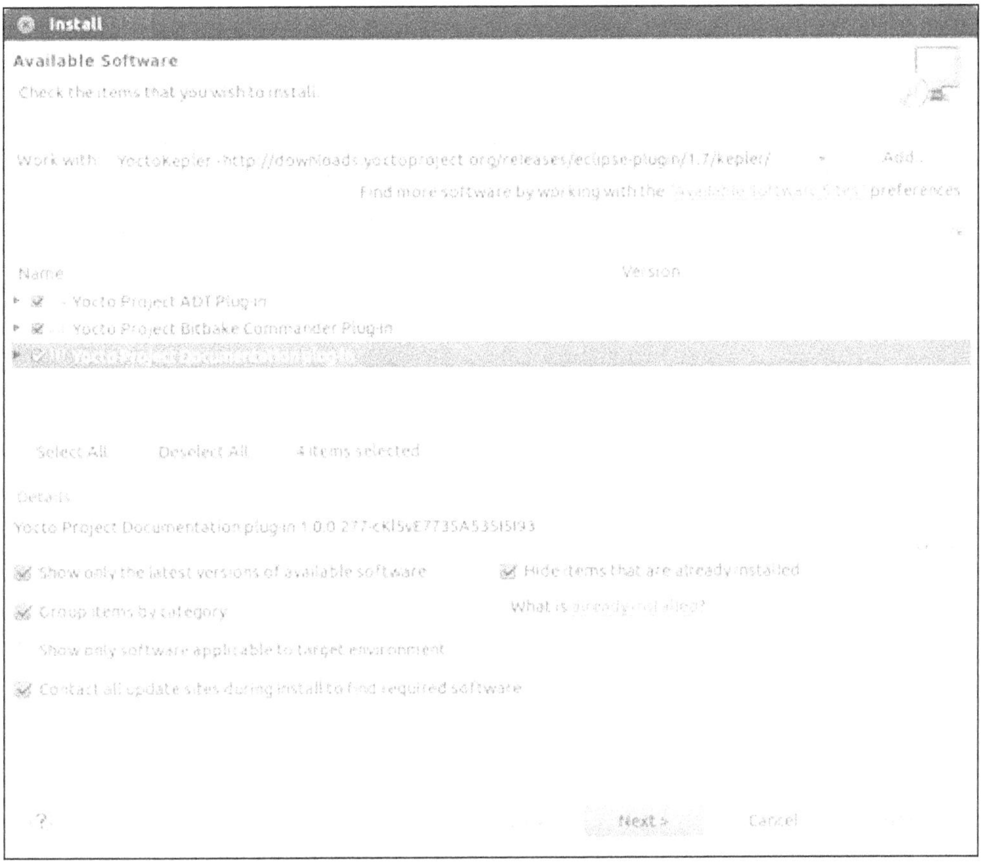

Install details window

5. One final pick at the installed components and the installation is approaching its end.

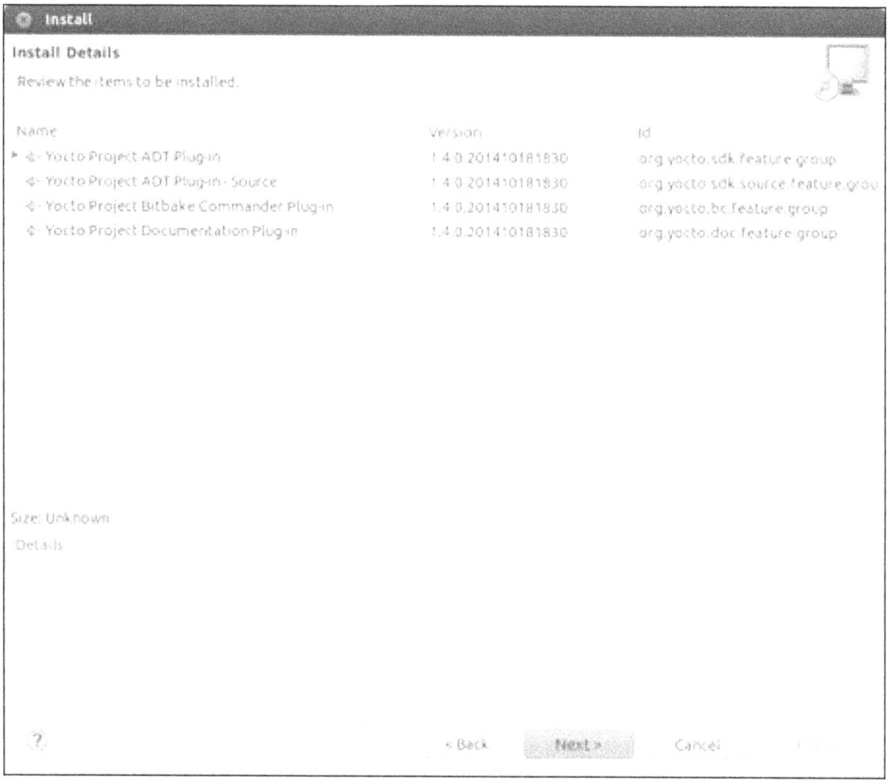

Install details window

6. If this warning message appears, press **OK** and move further. It only lets you know that the installed packages have unsigned content.

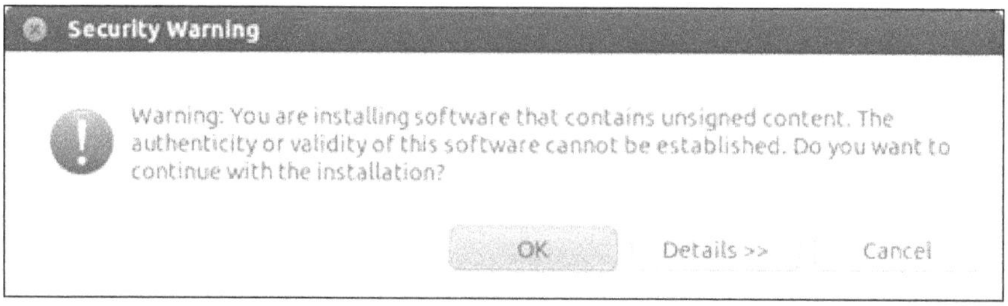

Security warning window

The installation finishes only after the Eclipse IDE is restarted for the changes to take effect.

After the installation, the Yocto plug-ins are available and ready to be configured. The configuration process involves the setup of the target-specific option and cross-compiler. For each specific target, the preceding configurations steps need to be performed accordingly.

The configuration process is done by selecting the **Preferences** option from the **Window** menu. A new window will open, and from there, the **Yocto Project ADT** option should be selected. More details are available, as shown in the following screenshot:

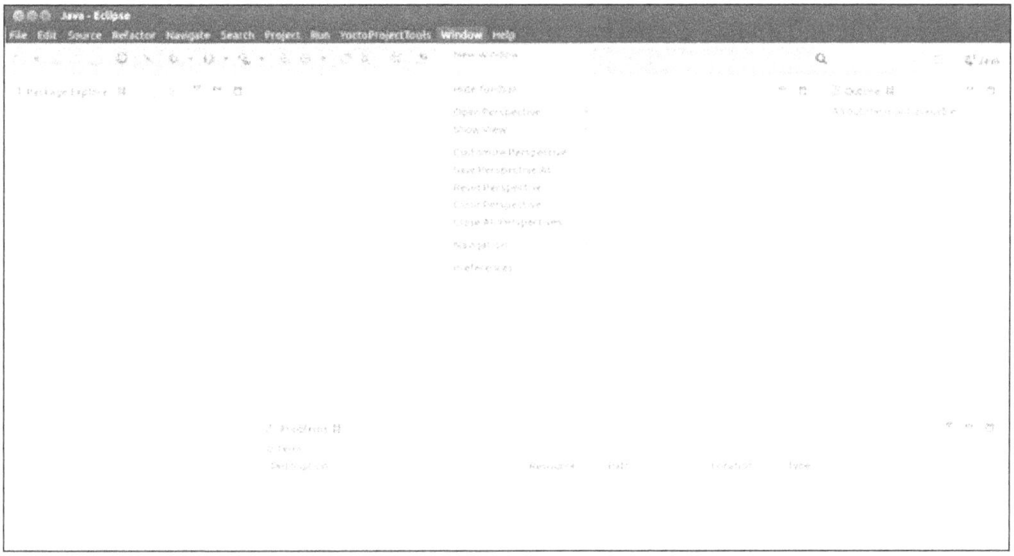

Eclipse IDE – Preferences

The next thing to do involves the configuration of the available options of the cross-compiler. The first option refers to the toolchain type, and there are two options available, **Standalone prebuilt toolchain** and **Build system derived toolchain**, which is the default selected option. The former refers to a toolchain specific for an architecture that already has an existing kernel and root filesystem, so the developed application will be made available in the image manually. However, this step is not a requirement since all the components are separated. The latter option refers to a toolchain built inside a Yocto Project build directory.

The next elements that need to be configured are the toolchain location, `sysroot` location, and the target architecture. The **Toolchain Root Location** is used to define the toolchain install location. For an installation done with the `adt_installer` script, for example, the toolchain will be available in the `/opt/poky/<release>` directory. The second argument, **Sysroot Location**, represents the location of the target device root filesystem. It can be found in the `/opt/poky/<release>` directory, as seen the preceding example, or even inside the build directory if other method to generate it were used. The third and last option from this section is represented by the **Target Architecture** and it indicates the type of hardware used or emulated. As it can be seen on the window, it is a pull-down menu where the required option is selected, and a user will find all the supported architectures listed. In a situation where the necessary architecture is not available inside the pull-down menu, the corresponding image for the architecture will need to be built.

The last remaining section is represented by the target specific option. This refers to the possibility of emulating an architecture using QEMU or running the image on the externally available hardware. For external hardware, use the **External HW** option that needs to be selected for the work to be finished, but for the QEMU emulation, there are still things to do besides selecting the **QEMU** option. In this scenario, the user will also need to indicate the **Kernel** and **Custom Option**. For the kernel selection, the process is simple. It is available in the prebuilt image location in case the **Standalone pre-built toolchain** option was selected or in the `tmp/deploy/images/<machine-name>` directory if the **Build system derived toolchain** option was selected. For the second option, the **Custom Option** argument, the process for adding it will not be as simple as the preceding options.

The **Custom Option** field needs to be filled with various options, such as `kvm`, nographic, `publicvnc`, or `serial`, which indicate major options for the emulated architecture or their parameters. These are kept inside angled brackets, and include parameters, such as the memory used (`-m 256`), networking support (`-net`), and full screen support (`-full-screen`). More information regarding the available options and parameters can be found using the `man qemu` command. All of the preceding configurations can be overwritten using the **Change Yocto Project Settings** option from the **Project** menu after a project is defined.

To define a project, these steps need to be taken:

1. Select the **Project...** option from the **File** | **New** menu option, as shown here:

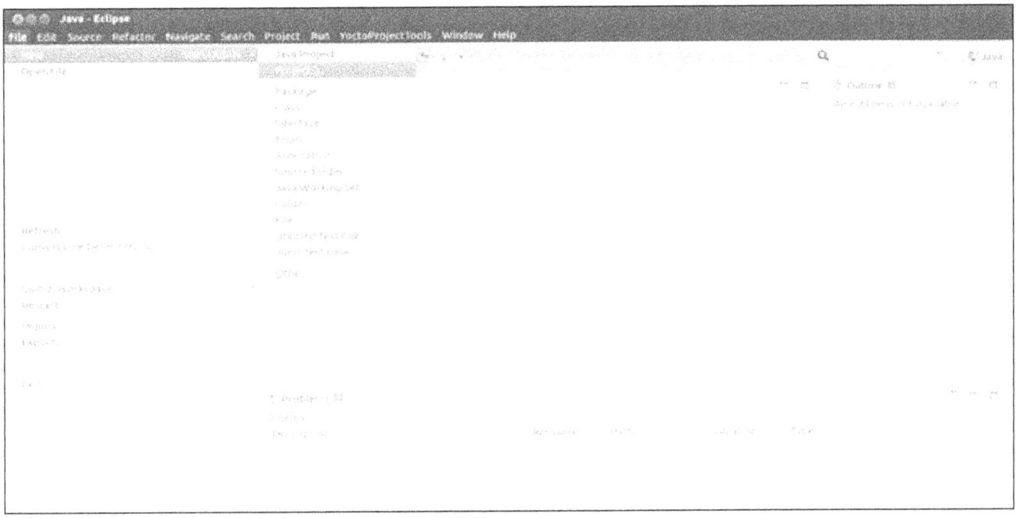

Eclipse IDE – Project

2. Select **C project** from the **C/C++** option. This will open a **C Project** window:

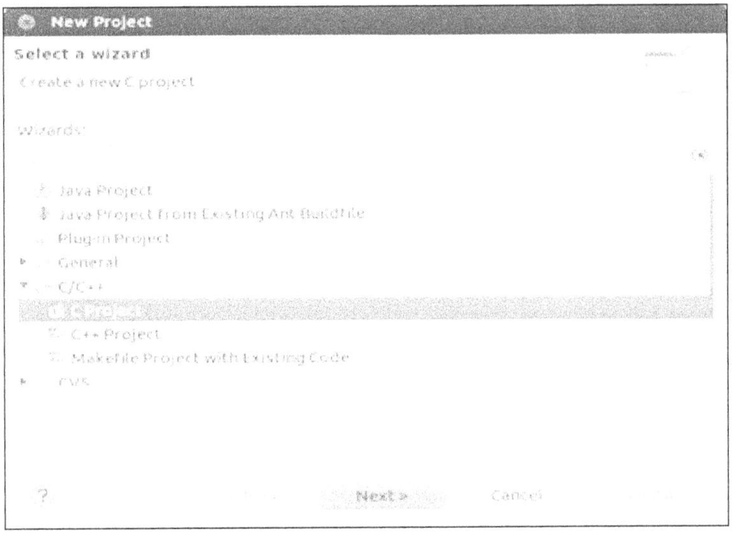

Eclipse IDE – New project window

3. In the **C Project** window, there are multiple options available. Let's select **Yocto Project ADT Autotools Project**, and from there, the **Hello World ANSI C Autotools Project** option. Add a name for the new project, and we are ready to move to the next steps:

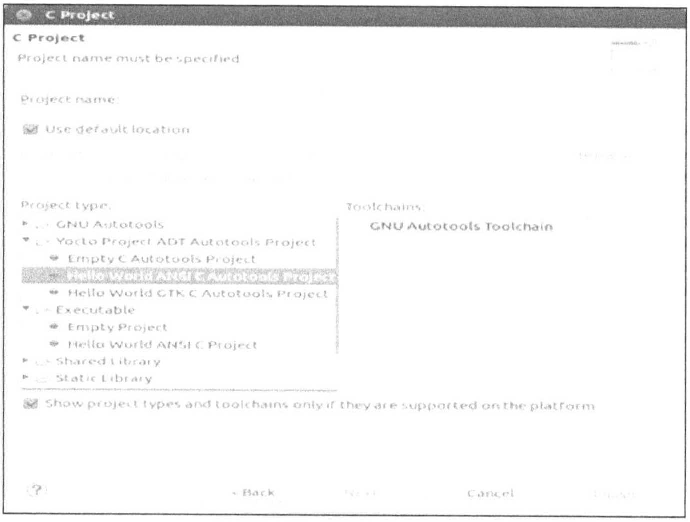

C project window

4. In the **C Project** window we you be prompted to add information regarding the **Author**, **Copyright notice**, **Hello world greetings**, **Source**, and **License** fields accordingly:

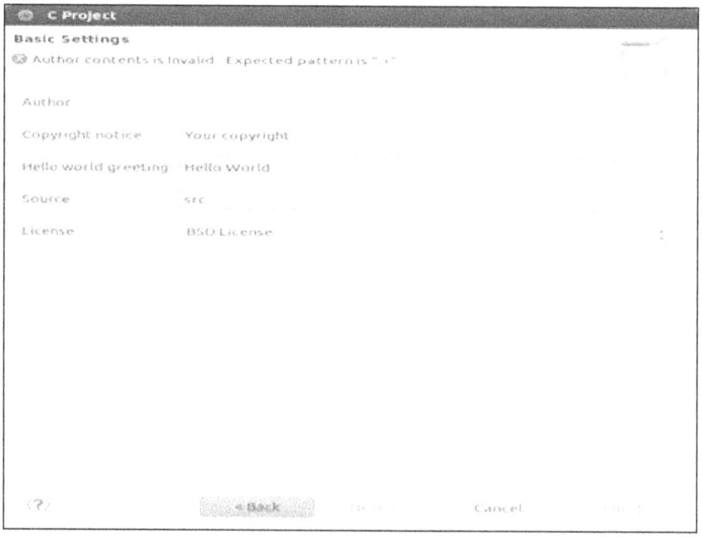

C project—basic settings window

5. After all the information is added, the **Finish** button can be clicked on. The user will be prompted in the new **C/C++** perspective that is specific for the opened project, with the newly created project appearing on the left-hand side of the menu.
6. After the project is created and the source code is written, to build the project, select the **Build Project** option from the **Project...** menu.

QEMU emulator

QEMU is used in the Yocto Project as a virtualization machine and emulator for various target architectures. It is very useful to run and test various Yocto generated applications and images, apart from fulfilling other purposes. Its primary use outside of the Yocto world is its selling point for the Yocto Project too, making it the default tool to be used to emulate hardware.

> More information about the use case of QEMU can be found by accessing http://www.yoctoproject.org/docs/1.7/adt-manual/adt-manual.html#the-qemu-emulator.

Interaction with the QEMU emulation is done within Eclipse, as shown previously. For this to happen, the proper configuration would be required, as instructed in the preceding section. Starting the QEMU emulation here is done using the **External Tools** option from the **Run** menu. A new window will be opened for the emulator, and after the corresponding login information is passed to the prompt, the shell will be available for user interaction. An application can be deployed and debugged on the emulator also.

> More information regarding QEMU interaction is available at http://www.yoctoproject.org/docs/1.7/dev-manual/dev-manual.html#dev-manual-qemu.

Debugging

Debugging an application can also be done using the QEMU emulator or the actual target hardware, if it exists. When the project was configured, a run/debug Eclipse configuration was generated as a **C/C+ Remote Application** instance, and it can be found on the basis of its name, which is according to the <project-name>_gdb_-<suffix> syntax. For example, TestProject_gdb_armv5te-poky-linux-gnueabi could be an example of this.

To connect to the Eclipse GDB interface and start the remote target debugging process, the user is required to perform a few steps:

1. Select **C/C++ Remote application** from the **Run** | **Debug configuration** menu and choose the run/debug configuration from the **C/C++ Remote Application** available in the left panel.
2. Select the suitable connection from the drop-down list.
3. Select the binary application to deploy. If multiple executables are available in your project, by pushing the **Search Project** button, Eclipse will parse the project and provide a list with all the available binaries.
4. Enter the absolute path in which the application will be deployed by setting the **Remote Absolute File Path for C/C++ Application:** field accordingly.
5. Selecting the debugger option is available in the **Debugger** tab. To debug shared libraries, a few extra steps are necessary:
    - Select the **Add** | **Path Mapping** option from the **Source** tab to make sure a path mapping is available for the debug configuration.
    - Select **Load shared libraries symbols automatically** from the **Debug/Shared Library** tab and indicate the path of the shared libraries accordingly. This path is highly dependent on the architecture of the processor, so be very careful which library file you indicate. Usually, for the 32-bit architecture, the `lib` directory is selected, and for the 64-bit architecture, the `lib64` directory is chosen.
    - On the **Arguments** tab, there is a possibility of passing various arguments to the application binary during the time of execution.
6. Once all the debug configurations are finished, click on the **Apply** and **Debug** buttons. A new GDB session will be launched and **Debug perspective** will open. When the debugger is being initialized, Eclipse will open three consoles:
    - A GDB console named after the GDB binary described previously, used for command-line interaction
    - A remote shell used to run an application display results
    - A local machine console that is named after the binary path, which in most of cases, is not used. It remains as an artefact.
7. After the setup of the debug configuration, the application can be rebuilt and executed again using the available **Debug** icon in the toolbar. If, in fact, you want only to run and deploy the application, the **Run** icon can be used.

Profiling and tracing

Inside the **Yocto Tools** menu, you can see the supported tools that are used for the tracing and profiling of developed applications. These tools are used for enhancing various properties of the application and, in general, the development process and experience. The tools that will be presented are LTTng, Perf, LatencyTop, PerfTop, SystemTap, and KGDB.

The first one we'll take a look at is the LTTng Eclipse Plug-in, which offers the possibility of tracing a target session and analyzing the results. To start working with the tool, a quick configuration is necessary first, as follows:

1. Start the tracing perspective by selecting **Open Perspective** from the **Window** menu.
2. Create a new tracing project by selecting **Project** from the **File** | **New** menu.
3. Select **Control View** from the **Window** | **Show view** | **Other...** | **Lttng** menu. This will enable you to access all these desired operations:
    - Creating a new connection
    - Creating a session
    - Starting/stopping tracing
    - Enabling events

Next, we'll introduce the user space performance analyzing tool called **Perf**. It offers statistical profiling of the application code and a simple CPU for multiple threads and kernel. To do this, it uses a number of performance counters, dynamic probes, or trace points. To use the Eclipse Plug-in, a remote connection to the target is required. It can be done by the Perf wizard or by using the **Remote System Explorer** | **Connection** option from the **File** | **New** | **Other** menu. After the remote connection is set up, interaction with the tool is the same as in the case of the command line support available for the tool.

LatencyTop is an application that is used to identify the latencies available within the kernel and also their root cause. This tool is not available for ARM kernels that have **Symmetric multiprocessing** (**SMP**) support enabled due to the limitation of the ARM kernels. This application also requires a remote connection. After the remote connection is set up, the interaction is the same as in the case of the command line support available for the tool. This application is run from the Eclipse Plug-in using `sudo`.

PowerTop is used to measure the consumption of electrical power. It analyzes the applications, kernel options, and device drivers that run on a Linux system and estimates their power consumption. It is very useful to identify components that use the most amount of power. This application requires a remote connection. After the remote connection is set up, the interaction with the application is the same as for the command line available support for the tool. This application is run from the Eclipse Plug-in using the -d option to display the output in the Eclipse window.

SystemTap is a tool that enables the use of scripts to get results from a running Linux. SystemTap provides free software (GPL) infrastructure to simplify the gathering of information about the running Linux system via the tracing of all kernel calls. It's very similar to dtrace from Solaris, but it is still not suited for production systems, unlike dtrace. It uses a language similar to `awk` and its scripts have the `.stp` extension. The monitored data can be extracted and various filters and complex processing can be done on them. The Eclipse Plug-in uses the `crosstap` script to translate the `.stp` scripts to a C language to create a `Makefile`, run a C compiler to create a kernel module for the target architecture that is inserted into the target kernel, and later, collect the tracing data from the kernel. To start the SystemTap plug-in in Eclipse, there are a number of steps to be followed:

1. Select the **systemtap** option from the **Yocto Project Tools** menu.
2. In the opened windows, the crosstap argument needs to be passed:
    - Set the **Metadata Location** variable to the corresponding `poky` directory
    - Set **Remote User ID** by entering the root (the default option) because it has `ssh` access to the target-any other user that has the same privileges is also a good choice
    - Set in the **Remote Host** variable to the corresponding IP address for the target
    - Use the **Systemtap Scripts** variable for the full path to the `.stp` scripts
    - Set additional cross options using the **Systemtap Args** field

The output of the `.stp` script should be available in the console view from Eclipse.

The last tool we'll take a look at is **KGDB**. This tool is used specifically for the debugging of Linux kernel, and is useful only if development on the Linux kernel source code is done inside the Eclipse IDE. To use this tool, a number of necessary configuration setups are required:

- Disable the C/C++ indexing:
    - Select the **C/C++ Indexer** option from the **Window** | **Preferences** menu
    - Unselect the **Enable indexer** checkbox
- Create a project where the kernel source code can be imported:
    - Select the **C/C++** | **C Project** option from the **File** | **New** menu
    - Select the **Makefile project** | **Empty project** option and give a proper name to the project
    - Unselect the **Use default location** option
    - Click on the **Browse** button and identify the kernel source code local git repository location
    - Press the **Finish** button and the project should be created

After the prerequisites are fulfilled, the actual configuration can start:

- Select the **Debug Configuration** option from the **Run** menu.
- Double-click on the **GDB Hardware Debugging** option to create a default configuration named **<project name> Default**.
- From the **Main** tab, browse to the location of the `vmlinux` built image, select the **Disable auto build** radio button, as well as the **GDB (DFS) Hardware Debugging Launcher** option.
- For the **C/C++ Application** option available in the **Debugger** tab, browse for the location of the GDB binary available inside the toolchain (if ADT installer script is available, its default location should be `/opt/poky/1.7/sysroots/x86_64-pokysdk-linux/usr/bin/arm-poky-linux-gnueabi/arm-poky-linux-gnueabi-gdb`). Select **Generic serial option** from the **JTAG Device** menu. The **Use remote target** option is a requirement.
- From the **Startup** tab, select the **Load symbols** option. Make sure that the **Use Project binary** option indicates the correct `vmlinux` image and that the **Load image** option is not selected.

- Press the **Apply** button to make sure the previous configuration is enabled.
- Prepare the target for the serial communication debugging:
    - Set the `echo ttyS0,115200 | /sys/module/kgdboc/parameters/kgdboc` option to make sure the appropriate device is used for debugging
    - Start KGDB on the `echo g | /proc/sysrq-trigger` target
    - Close the terminal with the target but keep the serial connectivity
- Select the **Debug Configuration** option from the **Run** menu
- Select the previously created configuration and click on the **Debug** button

After the **Debug** button is pressed, the debug session should start and the target will be halted in the `kgdb_breakpoint()` function. From there, all the commands specific to GDB are available and ready to be used.

The Yocto Project bitbake commander

The bitbake commander offers the possibility of editing recipes and creating a metadata project in a manner similar to the one available in the command line. The difference between the two is that the Eclipse IDE is used to do the metadata interaction.

To make sure that a user is able to do these sort of actions, a number of steps are required:

- Select the **Project** option from the **File** | **New** menu
- Select the **Yocto Project BitBake Commander** wizard from the opened window
- Select the **New Yocto Project** option and a new window will be opened tp define properties of the new project
- Using **Project Location**, identify the parent of the `poky` directory
- Use the **Project Name** option to define the project name. Its default value is poky
- For the **Remote service provider** variable, select the **Local** choice and make use of the same choice for the **Connection name** drop-down list
- Make sure that the **Clone** checkbox is not selected for an installed `poky` source directory

By using the Eclipse IDE, its features are available to be used. One of the most useful features is the quick search option that could prove to be very useful for some developers. Other benefits include the possibility of creating recipes using templates, editing them with syntax highlighting, auto completion, error reports on the fly, and many more.

> The use of bitbake commander is restricted to local connections only. The remote connection causes the IDE to freeze due to a bug available upstream.

Summary

In this chapter, you were presented with information about the functionalities of the ADE offered by the Yocto Project, and the numerous Eclipse Plug-ins available for application development not only as an alternative, but also as a solution for developers who are connected to their IDEs. Although the chapter started with an introduction to the application development options for the command-line enthusiast, it shortly became more about IDE interaction than anything else. This happened because alternative solutions need to be available so that developers could choose what fits their needs best.

In the next chapter, a number of Yocto Project components will be presented. This time, they are not related to application development, but involve metadata interaction, quality assurance, and continuous integration services. I will try to present yet another face of the Yocto Project that I believe will help readers get a better picture of the Yocto Project, and eventually, interact with and contribute to the components that suit them and their needs best.

8

Hob, Toaster, and Autobuilder

In this chapter, you will be introduced to new tools and components used in the Yocto community. As the title suggests, this chapter is dedicated to another category of tools. I will start with **Hob** as a graphical interface, which is slowly dying, and in time, will be replaced by a new web interface called **Toaster**. A new point of discussion will also be introduced in this chapter. Here, I am referring to the QA and testing component that is, in most cases, absent or lacking from most of the projects. Yocto takes this problem very seriously and offers a solution for it. This solution will be presented in the last section of the chapter.

You will also be offered a more detailed presentation to components, such as Hob, Toaster, and Autobuilder. Each of these components will be assessed separately and their benefits and use cases are looked at in detail. For the first two components, (that is, Hob and Toaster) information regarding the build process is offered alongside the various setup scenarios. Hob is similar to BitBake and is tightly integrated with Poky and the Build Directory. Toaster, on the other hand, is a looser alternative that offers multiple configuration alternatives and setups, and a performance section that can be very useful for any developer interested in improving the build system's overall performance. The chapter ends with section on Autobuilder. This project is the cornerstone of the Yocto project that is dedicated to making embedded development and open source more user-friendly, in general, but also offers more secure and error-free projects. I hope that you enjoy this chapter; let's proceed to the first section.

Hob

The Hob project represents a GUI alternative to the BitBake build system. Its purpose is to execute the most common tasks in an easier and faster manner, but it does not make command-line interactions go away. This is because most parts of recipes and configurations still need to be done manually. In the previous chapter, the BitBake Commander extension was introduced as an alternative solution for the editing of recipes, but in this project, it has its limitations.

Hob's primary purpose is to allow interaction with the build system made easier for users. Of course, there are users who do not prefer the graphical user interface alternatives to command-line options, and I kind of agree with them, but this is another discussion altogether. Hob can be an option for them also; it is an alternative not only for people who prefer having an interface in front of them, but also for those who are attached to their command-line interaction.

Hob may not be able to a lot of tasks apart from most common ones, such as building an image, modifying its existing recipes, running an image through a QEMU emulator, or even deploying it on a USB device for some live-booting operations on a target device. Having all these functionalities is not much, but is a lot of fun. Your experience with the tools in Yocto Project do not matter here. The previously mentioned tasks can be done very easily and in an intuitive manner, and this is the most interesting thing about Hob. It offers its users what they need in a very easy fashion. People who interact with it can learn from the lessons it has to offer, whether they're graphic interface enthusiasts or command-line savvy.

In this chapter, I will show you how to use the Hob project to build a Linux operating system image. To demonstrate this, I will use the Atmel SAMA5D3 Xplained machine, which is what I also used for other demonstrations in previous chapters.

First of all, let's see what Hob looks like when you start it for the first time. The result is shown in the following screenshot:

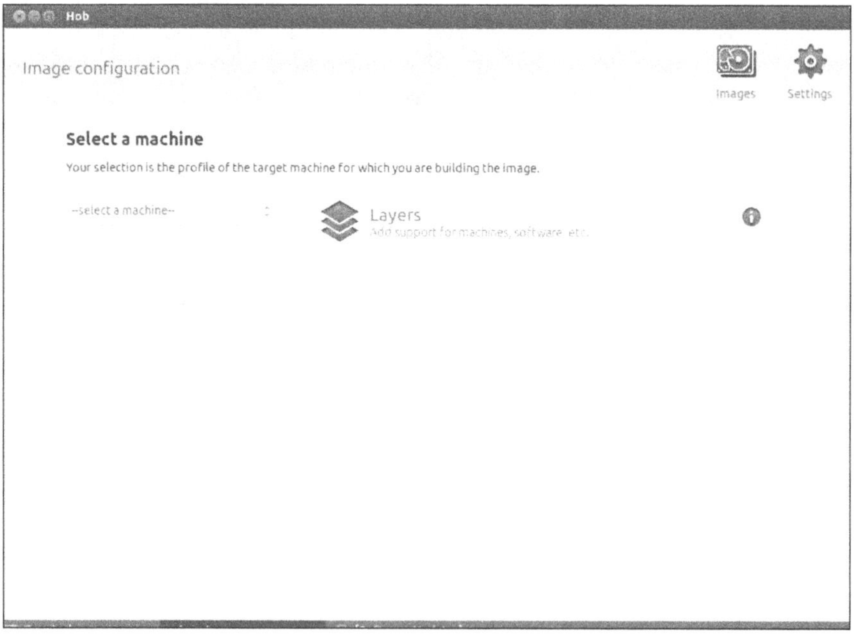

To retrieve the graphical interface, the user needs perform the given steps required for the BitBake command-line interaction. Firstly, it needs to create a build directory and from this build directory, the user needs to start the Hob graphical interface, using the Hob commands, given as follows:

```
source poky/oe-init-build-env ../build-test
hob
```

The next step is to establish the layers that are required for your build. You can do this by selecting them in the **Layers** window. The first thing to do for the `meta-atmel` layer is to add it to the build. Although you may start work in an already existing build directory, Hob will not be able to retrieve the existing configurations and will create a new one over the `bblayers.conf` and `local.conf` configuration files. It will mark the added lines using the next `#added by hob` message.

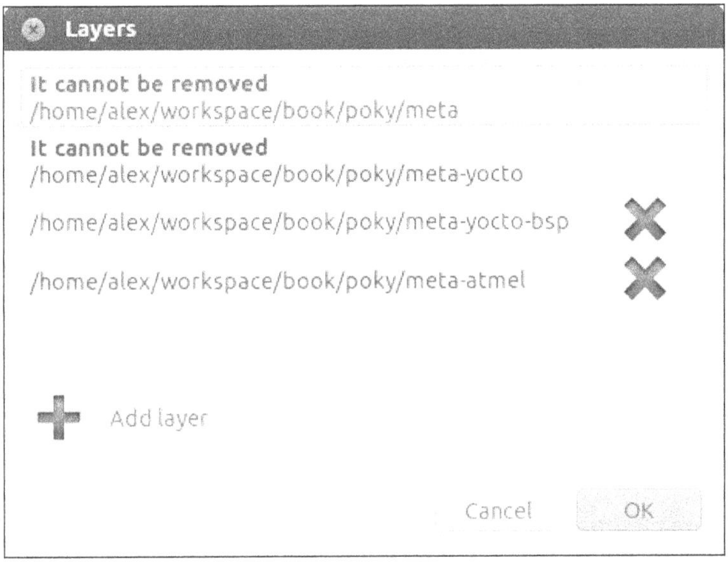

After the corresponding `meta-atmel` layer is added to the build directory, all the supported machines are available in the **Select a machine** drop-down, including those that are added by the `meta-atmel` layer. From the available options, the **sama5d3-xplained** machine needs to be selected:

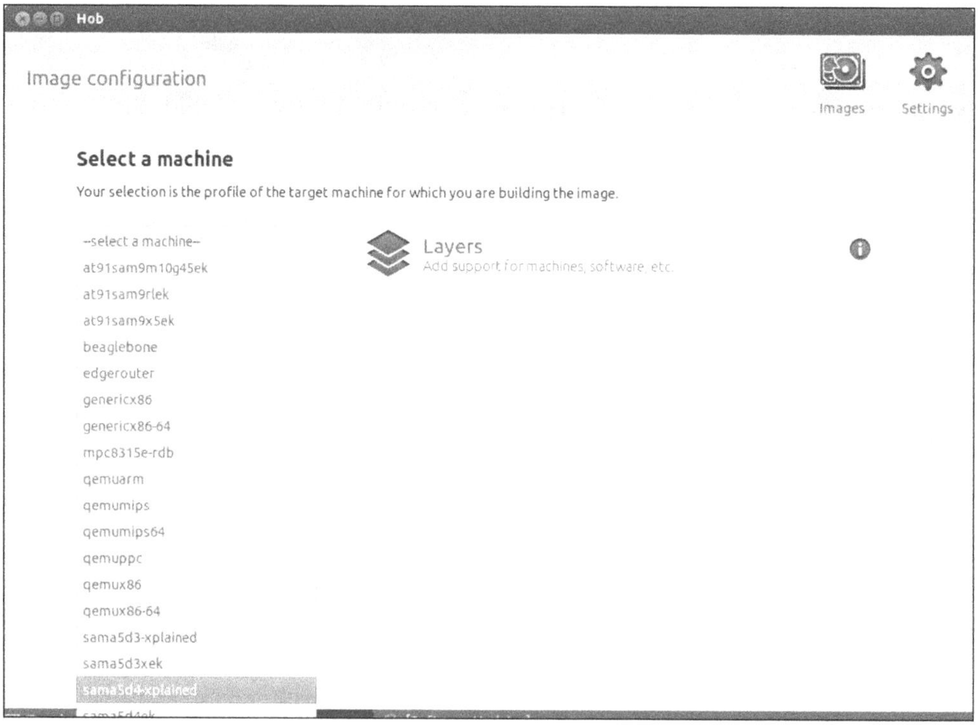

When the Atmel **sama5d3-xplained** machine is selected, an error, shown in the following screenshot, appears:

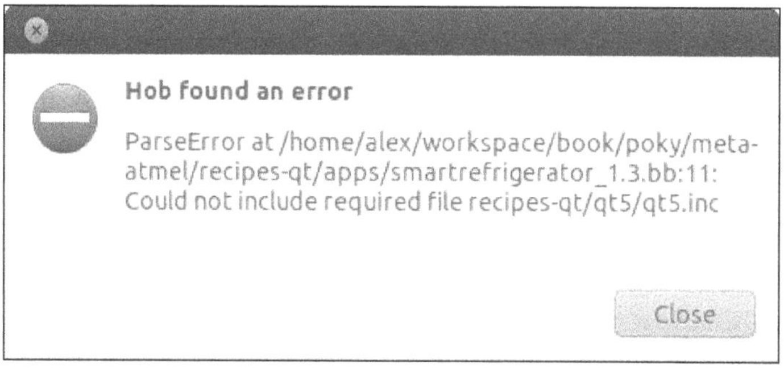

After adding the `meta-qt5` layer to the layers section, this error disappears and the build process can continue. To retrieve the `meta-qt5` layer, the following `git` command is necessary:

```
git clone -b dizzy https://github.com/meta-qt5/meta-qt5.git
```

Since all the available configuration files and recipes are parsed, the parsing process takes a while, and after this, you will see an error, as shown in the following screenshot:

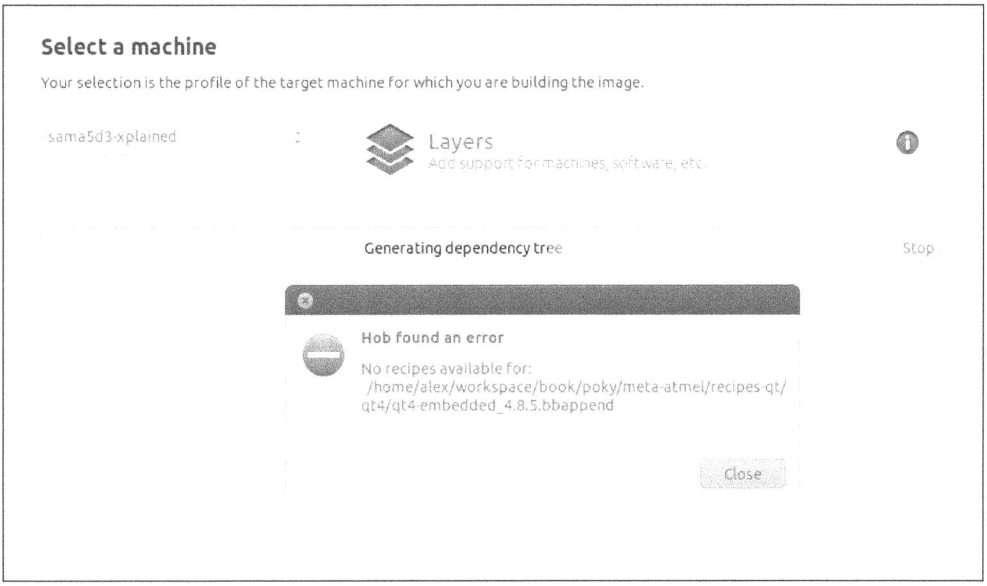

After another quick inspection, you will see the following code:

```
find ../ -name "qt4-embedded*"
./meta/recipes-qt/qt4/qt4-embedded_4.8.6.bb
./meta/recipes-qt/qt4/qt4-embedded.inc
./meta-atmel/recipes-qt/qt4/qt4-embedded-4.8.5
./meta-atmel/recipes-qt/qt4/qt4-embedded_4.8.5.bbappend
```

The only explanation is the fact the `meta-atmel` layer does not update its recipes but appends them. This can be overcome in two ways. The simplest one would be to update the recipe the `.bbappend` file and make sure that the new available recipe is transformed into a patch for the upstream community. A patch with the required changes inside the `meta-atmel` layer will be explained to you shortly, but first, I will present the available options and the necessary changes that are needed to resolve the problems existing in the build process.

The other solution would be to include the required recipes that `meta-atmel` needs for the build process. The best place for it to be available would be also in `meta-atmel`. However, in this case, the `.bbappend` configuration file should be merged with the recipe, since having a recipe and its appended file in the same place does not make much sense.

After this problem is fixed, new options will be available to the user, as depicted in the following screenshot:

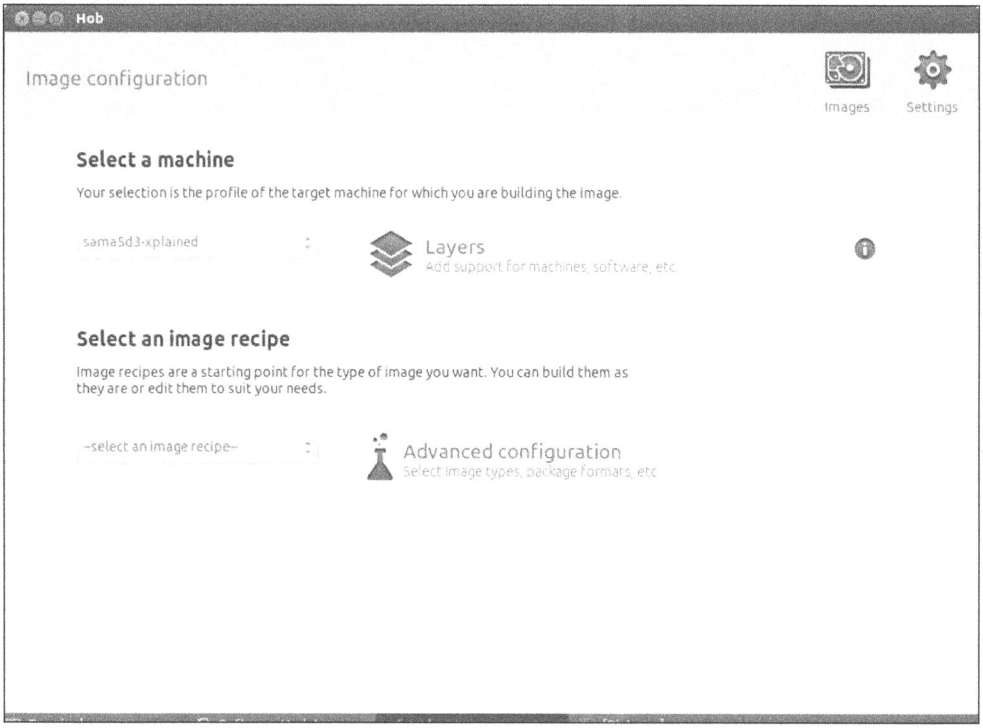

Now, the user has the chance to select the image that needs to be built, as well as the extra configurations that need to be added. These configurations include:

- Selection of the distribution type
- Selection of the image types
- A packaging format
- Other small tweaks around the root filesystem

Some of these are depicted in the following screenshot:

I've chosen to change the distribution type from **poky-tiny** to **poky**, and the resulting root filesystem output format is visible in the following screenshot:

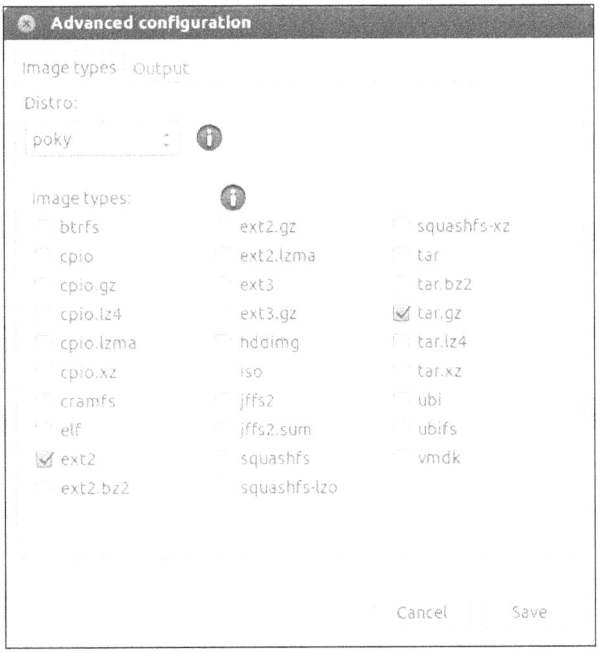

With the tweaks made, the recipes are reparsed, and when this process is finished, the resulting image can be selected so that the build process can start. The image that is selected for this demonstration is the **atmel-xplained-demo-image** image, which corresponds to the recipes with the same name. This information is also displayed in the following screenshot:

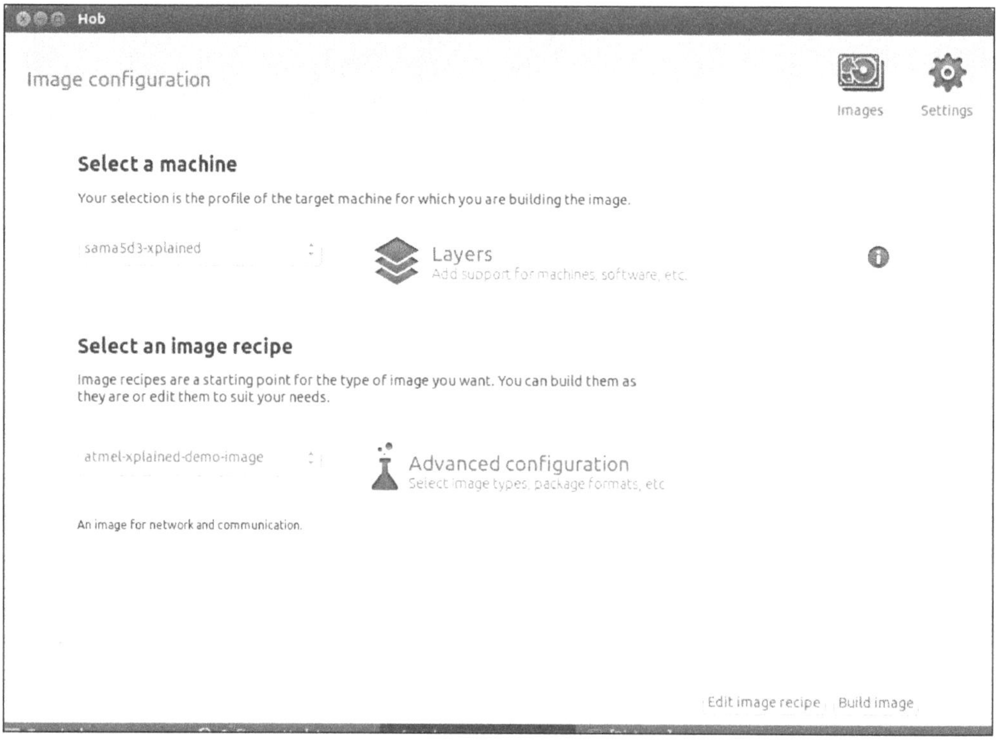

The build process is started by clicking on the **Build image** button. A while after the build starts, an error will show up, which tells us that the **meta-atmel** BSP layer requires more of the dependencies that need to be defined by us:

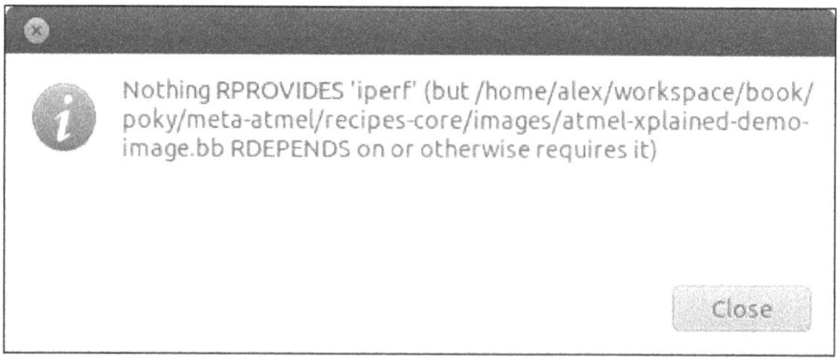

This information is gathered from the iperf recipe, which is not available in the included layers; it is available inside the meta-openembedded/meta-oe layer. After a more detailed search and update process, there have been a few revelations. There are more layer dependencies than required for the meta-atmel BSP layer, which are given as follows:

- The meta-openembedded/meta-oe layer
- The meta-openembedded/meta-networking layer
- The meta-openembedded/meta-ruby layer
- The meta-openembedded/meta-python layer
- The meta-qt5 layer

The end result is available in the BBLAYERS variable that is be found in the bblayers.conf file, shown as follows:

```
#added by hob
BBFILES += "${TOPDIR}/recipes/images/custom/*.bb"
#added by hob
BBFILES += "${TOPDIR}/recipes/images/*.bb"

#added by hob
BBLAYERS = "/home/alex/workspace/book/poky/meta /home/alex/workspace/
book/poky/meta-yocto /home/alex/workspace/book/poky/meta-yocto-bsp /
home/alex/workspace/book/poky/meta-atmel /home/alex/workspace/book/
poky/meta-qt5 /home/alex/workspace/book/poky/meta-openembedded/meta-
oe /home/alex/workspace/book/poky/meta-openembedded/meta-networking /
home/alex/workspace/book/poky/meta-openembedded/meta-ruby /home/alex/
workspace/book/poky/meta-openembedded/meta-python"
```

There are some required changes in the meta-atmel layer that needs to be made before starting a complete build, given as follows:

- Replace packagegroup-core-basic with packagegroup-core-full-cmdline because the latest Poky has updated the packagegroup names.
- Delete python-setuptools because it is not available in the meta-openembedded/meta-oe layer anymore, as well as in the new meta-openembedded/meta-python layer, which is the new placeholder for all Python-related recipes. The python-setuptools tool was removed because it had the ability to download, build, install, upgrade, and uninstall extra Python packages, and is not a mandatory requirement for Yocto. This is its general purpose.
- The preceding change regarding the update to qt4-embedded-4.8.6 for qt4-embedded-4.8.5, as shown earlier, presented errors.

All the changes made to the `meta-atmel` layer are available in following patch:

```
From 35ccf73396da33a641f307f85e6b92d5451dc255 Mon Sep 17 00:00:00
2001
From: "Alexandru.Vaduva" <vaduva.jan.alexandru@gmail.com>
Date: Sat, 31 Jan 2015 23:07:49 +0200
Subject: [meta-atmel][PATCH] Update suppport for
atmel-xplained-demo-image
 image.

The latest poky contains updates regarding the qt4 version support
and also the packagegroup naming.
Removed packages which are no longer available.

Signed-off-by: Alexandru.Vaduva <vaduva.jan.alexandru@gmail.com>
---
 recipes-core/images/atmel-demo-image.inc           |  3 +--
 ...qt-embedded-linux-4.8.4-phonon-colors-fix.patch | 26
----------------------
 ...qt-embedded-linux-4.8.4-phonon-colors-fix.patch | 26
++++++++++++++++++++++
 recipes-qt/qt4/qt4-embedded_4.8.5.bbappend          |  2 --
 recipes-qt/qt4/qt4-embedded_4.8.6.bbappend          |  2 ++
 5 files changed, 29 insertions(+), 30 deletions(-)
 delete mode 100644 recipes-qt/qt4/qt4-embedded-4.8.5/qt-embedded-
linux-4.8.4-phonon-colors-fix.patch
 create mode 100644 recipes-qt/qt4/qt4-embedded-4.8.6/qt-embedded-
linux-4.8.4-phonon-colors-fix.patch
 delete mode 100644 recipes-qt/qt4/qt4-embedded_4.8.5.bbappend
 create mode 100644 recipes-qt/qt4/qt4-embedded_4.8.6.bbappend

diff --git a/recipes-core/images/atmel-demo-image.inc b/recipes-
core/images/atmel-demo-image.inc
index fe13303..a019586 100644
--- a/recipes-core/images/atmel-demo-image.inc
+++ b/recipes-core/images/atmel-demo-image.inc
@@ -2,7 +2,7 @@ IMAGE_FEATURES += "ssh-server-openssh package-
management"

 IMAGE_INSTALL = "\
     packagegroup-core-boot \
-    packagegroup-core-basic \
+    packagegroup-core-full-cmdline \
     packagegroup-base-wifi \
     packagegroup-base-bluetooth \
```

```
     packagegroup-base-usbgadget \
@@ -23,7 +23,6 @@ IMAGE_INSTALL = "\
     python-smbus \
     python-ctypes \
     python-pip \
-    python-setuptools \
     python-pycurl \
     gdbserver \
     usbutils \
diff --git a/recipes-qt/qt4/qt4-embedded-4.8.5/qt-embedded-linux-
4.8.4-phonon-colors-fix.patch b/recipes-qt/qt4/qt4-embedded-
4.8.5/qt-embedded-linux-4.8.4-phonon-colors-fix.patch
deleted file mode 100644
index 0624eef..0000000
--- a/recipes-qt/qt4/qt4-embedded-4.8.5/qt-embedded-linux-4.8.4-
phonon-colors-fix.patch
+++ /dev/null
@@ -1,26 +0,0 @@
-diff --git a/src/3rdparty/phonon/gstreamer/qwidgetvideosink.cpp
b/src/3rdparty/phonon/gstreamer/qwidgetvideosink.cpp
-index 89d5a9d..8508001 100644
---- a/src/3rdparty/phonon/gstreamer/qwidgetvideosink.cpp
-+++ b/src/3rdparty/phonon/gstreamer/qwidgetvideosink.cpp
-@@ -18,6 +18,7 @@
- #include <QApplication>
- #include "videowidget.h"
- #include "qwidgetvideosink.h"
-+#include <gst/video/video.h>
-
- QT_BEGIN_NAMESPACE
-
-@@ -106,11 +107,7 @@ static GstStaticPadTemplate
template_factory_rgb =-     GST_STATIC_PAD_TEMPLATE("sink",-
                            GST_PAD_SINK,
-                             GST_PAD_ALWAYS,
--                            GST_STATIC_CAPS("video/x-raw-rgb, "
--                                            "framerate =
(fraction) [ 0, MAX ], "
--                                            "width = (int) [ 1,
MAX ], "
--                                            "height = (int) [ 1,
MAX ],"
--                                            "bpp = (int) 32"));
-+                            GST_STATIC_CAPS(GST_VIDEO_CAPS_xRGB_
HOST_ENDIAN));
```

```
-
- template <VideoFormat FMT>
- struct template_factory;
-
diff --git a/recipes-qt/qt4/qt4-embedded-4.8.6/qt-embedded-linux-
4.8.4-phonon-colors-fix.patch b/recipes-qt/qt4/qt4-embedded-
4.8.6/qt-embedded-linux-4.8.4-phonon-colors-fix.patch
new file mode 100644
index 0000000..0624eef
--- /dev/null
+++ b/recipes-qt/qt4/qt4-embedded-4.8.6/qt-embedded-linux-4.8.4-
phonon-colors-fix.patch
@@ -0,0 +1,26 @@
+diff --git a/src/3rdparty/phonon/gstreamer/qwidgetvideosink.cpp
b/src/3rdparty/phonon/gstreamer/qwidgetvideosink.cpp
+index 89d5a9d..8508001 100644
+--- a/src/3rdparty/phonon/gstreamer/qwidgetvideosink.cpp
++++ b/src/3rdparty/phonon/gstreamer/qwidgetvideosink.cpp
+@@ -18,6 +18,7 @@
+ #include <QApplication>
+ #include "videowidget.h"
+ #include "qwidgetvideosink.h"
++#include <gst/video/video.h>
+
+ QT_BEGIN_NAMESPACE
+
+@@ -106,11 +107,7 @@ static GstStaticPadTemplate
template_factory_rgb =+     GST_STATIC_PAD_TEMPLATE("sink",+
                            GST_PAD_SINK,+
                            GST_PAD_ALWAYS,+-
                           GST_STATIC_CAPS("video/x-raw-rgb, "
+-                                             "framerate = (fraction)
[ 0, MAX ], "
+-                                             "width = (int) [ 1,
MAX ], "
+-                                             "height = (int) [ 1,
MAX ],"
+-                                             "bpp = (int) 32"));
++                             GST_STATIC_CAPS(GST_VIDEO_CAPS_xRGB_
HOST_ENDIAN));
+
+ template <VideoFormat FMT>
+ struct template_factory;
+
```

```
diff --git a/recipes-qt/qt4/qt4-embedded_4.8.5.bbappend b/recipes-
qt/qt4/qt4-embedded_4.8.5.bbappend
deleted file mode 100644
index bbb4d26..0000000
--- a/recipes-qt/qt4/qt4-embedded_4.8.5.bbappend
+++ /dev/null
@@ -1,2 +0,0 @@
-FILESEXTRAPATHS_prepend := "${THISDIR}/${PN}-${PV}:"
-SRC_URI += "file://qt-embedded-linux-4.8.4-phonon-colors-
fix.patch"
diff --git a/recipes-qt/qt4/qt4-embedded_4.8.6.bbappend b/recipes-
qt/qt4/qt4-embedded_4.8.6.bbappend
new file mode 100644
index 0000000..bbb4d26
--- /dev/null
+++ b/recipes-qt/qt4/qt4-embedded_4.8.6.bbappend
@@ -0,0 +1,2 @@
+FILESEXTRAPATHS_prepend := "${THISDIR}/${PN}-${PV}:"
+SRC_URI += "file://qt-embedded-linux-4.8.4-phonon-colors-
fix.patch"
--
1.9.1
```

This patch has been given in the chapter as an example for Git interaction and is a necessity when creating a patch that needs to be upstream to the community. At the time of writing this chapter, this patch had not yet been released to the upstream community, so this could be a gift for anyone interested in adding a contribution to the meta-atmel community in particular and the Yocto community in general.

The steps necessary to obtain this patch after the changes have been made, are described shortly. They define the steps needed to generate the patch, as shown in the following command, and is `0001-Update-suppport-for-atmel-xplained-demo-image-image.patch`. It can be upstream to the community or directly to the maintainer of the `meta-atmel` layer using the information available in the `README` file and the `git send-email` command:

```
git status
git add --all .
git commit -s
git fetch -a
git rebase -i origin/master
git format-patch -s --subject-prefix='meta-atmel][PATCH' origin/master
vim 0001-Update-suppport-for-atmel-xplained-demo-image-image.patch
```

Toaster

Toaster represents an alternative to Hob, which at a given point in time, will replace it completely. It is also a web-based interface for the BitBake command line. This tool is much more effective than Hob; it is not only able to do the most common tasks in a similar manner as Hob, but it also incorporates a build analysis component that collects data regarding the build process and the resultant outcome. These results are presented in a very easy-to-grasp manner, offering the chance to search, browse, and query the information.

From the collected information, we can mention the following:

- Structure of the image directory
- The available build configurations
- The outcome of a build along with the errors and registered warnings
- The packages present in an image recipe
- Recipes and packages that are built
- Tasks that are executed
- Performance data regarding executed tasks, such as CPU usage, time, and disk I/O usage
- Dependency and reverse dependencies for recipes

There are also some drawbacks to the Hob solution. Toaster does not yet offer the ability to configure and launch a build. However, there are initiatives taken to include these functionalities that Hob has inside Toaster, which will be implemented in the near future.

The current status of the Toaster Project permits the execution in various setups and running modes. Each of them will be presented and accordingly defined as follows:

- **Interactive mode**: This is the mode available and released with the Yocto Project 1.6 release version. It is based on a `toasterui` build recording component and a `toastergui` build inspection and statistics user interface.
- **Managed mode**: In addition to the Yocto Project 1.6 release version, this is the mode that handles build configurations, scheduling, and executions that are triggered from the web interface.
    - **Remote managed mode**: This is a hosted Toaster mode and is defined for production because it offers support for multiple users and customized installations.

    - **Local managed mode or _local_ is**: This is the mode available after a Poky checkout and permits running builds using the local machine code and build directory. It is the also used by anyone who interacts with a Toaster project for the first time.

- For the **interactive mode**, building with tools, such as AutoBuilder, BuildBot, or Jenkins, a set up separated from the hardware on which the Yocto Project builds are running will be required. Behind a normal instance of Toaster, there are three things that happen:
    - A BitBake server is started
    - A Toaster UI is started and connected to the BitBake server as well as to an SQL database
    - A web server is started for the purpose of reading information related to a database and displaying it on the web interface

There are scenarios when multiple Toaster instances are running on multiple remote machines, or when a single Toaster instance is shared among multiple users and build servers. All of them can be resolved by modifying the mode that the Toaster starts in and changing the SQL database and location of the web server accordingly. By having a common SQL database, a web server, and multiple BitBake servers with the Toaster user interface for each separate build directory, you can solve problems involved in the previously mentioned scenarios. So, each component in a Toaster instance can be run on a different machine, as long as communication is done appropriately and the components know about each other.

To set up an SQL server on a Ubuntu machine, a package needs to be installed, using the following command:

```
apt-get install mysgl-server
```

Having the necessary packages is not enough; setting them up is also required. Therefore, the proper username and password for the access web server is necessary, along with the proper administration rights for the MySQL account. Also, a clone of the Toaster master branch would be necessary for the web server, and after the sources are available, make sure that inside the `bitbake/lib/toaster/toastermain/settings.py` file, the `DATABASES` variable indicates the previous setup of the database. Make sure that you use the username and password defined for it.

With the set up done, the database synchronization can begin in the following way:

```
python bitbake/lib/toaster/manage.py syncdb
python bitbake/lib/toaster/manage.py migrate orm
python bitbake/lib/toaster/manage.py migrate bldcontrol
```

Now, the web server can be started using the `python bitbake/lib/toaster/manage.py runserver` command. For background execution, you can use the `nohup python bitbake/lib/toaster/manage.py runserver 2>toaster_web.log >toaster_web.log &` command.

This may be enough for starters, but as case logs are required for the builds, some extra setup is necessary. Inside the `bitbake/lib/toaster/toastermain/settings.py` file, the `DATABASES` variable indicates the SQL database for the logging server. Inside the build directory, call the `source toaster start` command and make sure that the `conf/toaster.conf` file is available. Inside this file, make sure that the Toaster and build history `bbclasses` are enabled to record information about the package:

```
INHERIT += "toaster"
INHERIT += "buildhistory"
BUILDHISTORY_COMMIT = "1"
```

After this set up is available, start the BitBake server and the logging interface with these commands:

```
bitbake --postread conf/toaster.conf --server-only -t xmlrpc -B
localhost:0 && export BBSERVER=localhost:-1
nohup bitbake --observe-only -u toasterui >toaster_ui.log &
```

After this is done, the normal build process can be started and builds can begin while the build is running inside the web interface logs and data is available to be examined. One quick mention, though: do not forget to kill the BitBake server after you have finished working inside the build directory using the `bitbake -m` command.

The local is very similar to the builds of the Yocto Project presented until now. This is the best mode for individual usage and learning to interact with the tool. Before starting the setup process, a few packages are required to be installed, using the following command lines:

```
sudo apt-get install python-pip python-dev build-essential
sudo pip install --upgrade pip
sudo pip install --upgrade virtualenv
```

After these packages are installed, make sure that you install the components required by Toaster; here, I am referring to the Django and South packages:

```
sudo pip install django==1.6
sudo pip install South==0.8.4
```

For interaction with the web server, the `8000` and `8200` ports are necessary, so make sure that they are not already reserved for other interactions. With this in mind, we can start the interaction with Toaster. Using the Poky build directory available from the downloads in the previous chapters, call the `oe-init-build-env script` to create a new build directory. This can be done on an already existing build directory, but having a new one will help identify the extra configuration files available for interaction with Toaster.

After the build directory is set according to your needs, the `source toaster start` command should be called, as mentioned previously, to start Toaster. At `http://localhost:8000`, you will see the following screenshot if no build is executed:

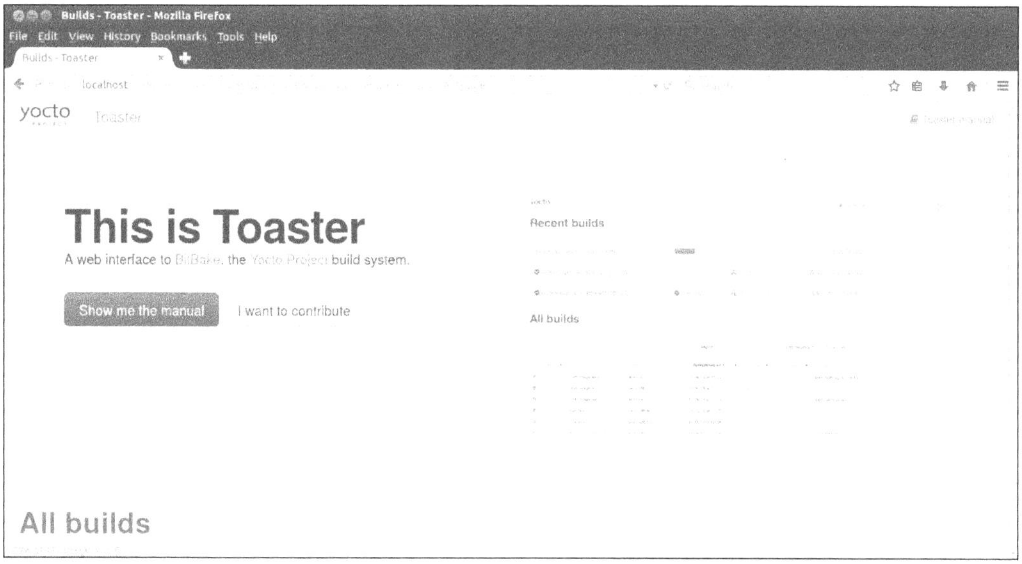

Run a build in the console, and it will be automatically updated in the web interface, as shown in the following screenshot:

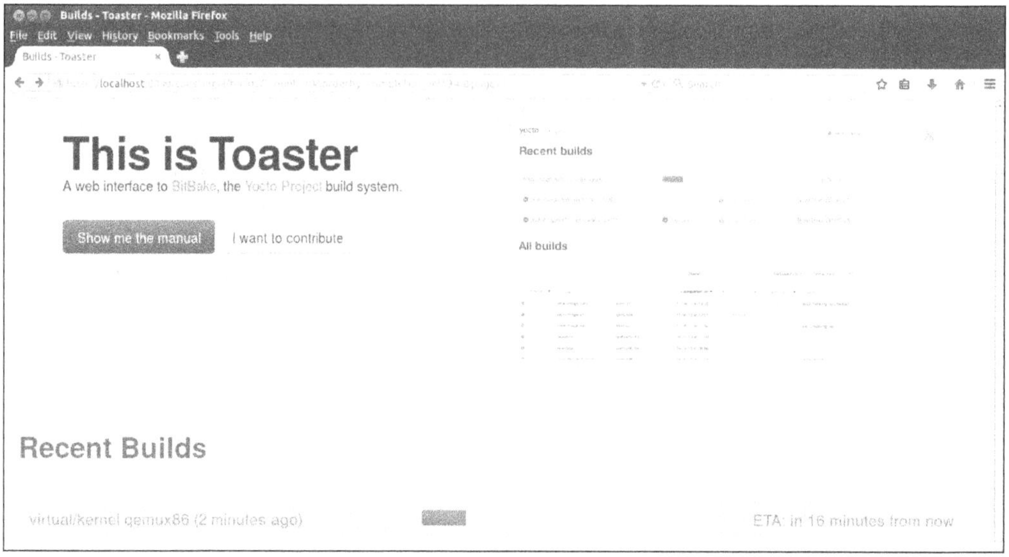

After the build is finished, the web interface will be updated accordingly. I closed the header image and information to make sure that only the builds are visible in the web page.

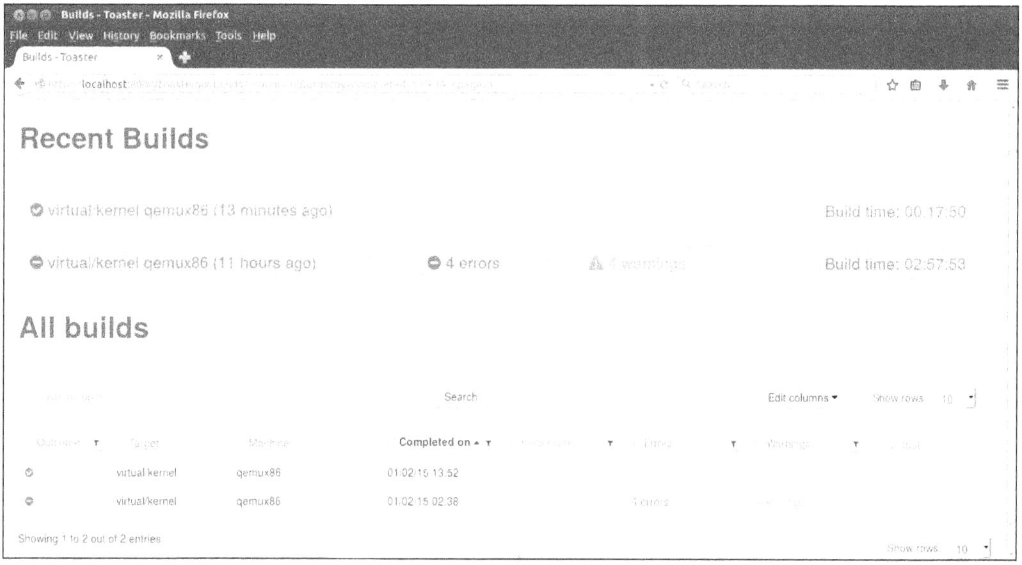

As seen in the preceding example, there are two builds that have finished in the preceding screenshot. Both of them are kernel builds. The first one finished with success, while the second has some errors and warnings. I did this as an example to present the user with alternative outputs for their build.

The build that failed took place due to lack of memory and space on the host machine, as seen in the following screenshot:

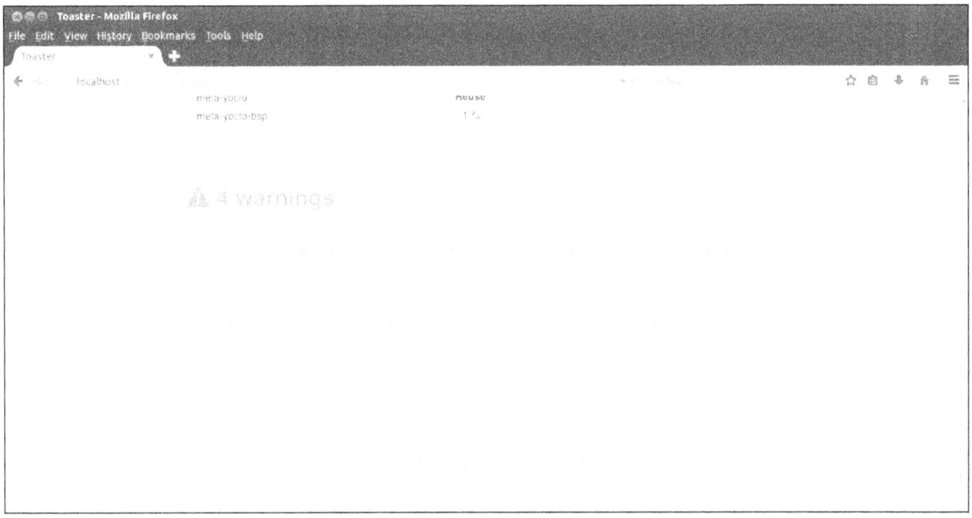

For the failing build, a detailed fail report is available, as displayed in the following screenshot:

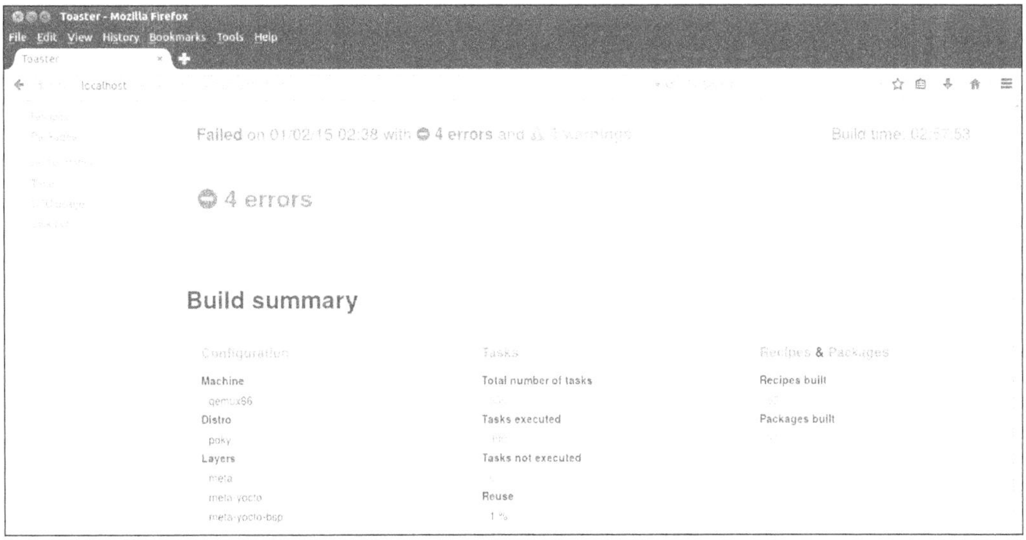

The build that finished successfully offers access to a lot of information. The following screenshot shows interesting features that a build should have. It shows, for the kernel build, all the BitBake variables used, their values, their location, and a short description. This information is very useful for all developers, not only because it offers all of this at a single location, but also because it offers a search option that reduces the search time spent looking for a troublesome variable to a minimum:

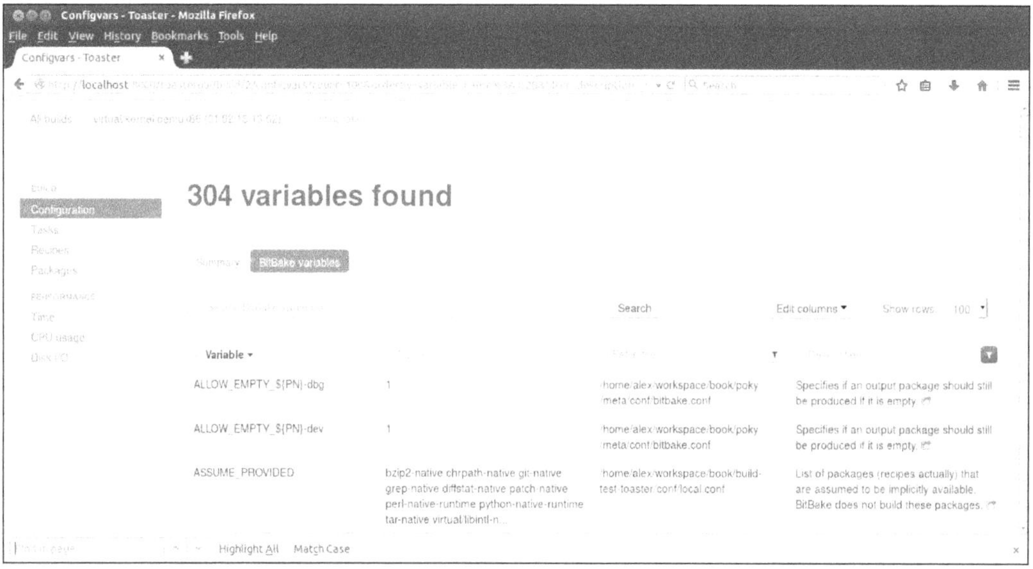

To stop Toaster, the `source toaster stop` command can be used after the execution activities are finished.

Inside a build directory, Toaster creates a number of files; their naming and purpose are presented in the following lines:

- `bitbake-cookerdaemon.log`: This log file is necessary for the BitBake server
- `.toastermain.pid`: This is the file that contains `pid` of the web server
- `.toasterui.pid`: It contains the DSI data bridge, `pid`
- `toaster.sqlite`: This is the database file
- `toaster_web.log`: This is the web server log file
- `toaster_ui.log`: This is the log file used for components of the user interface

With all of these factors mentioned, let's move to the next component, but not before offering a link to some interesting videos about Toaster.

> Information about Toaster Manual 1.7 can be accessed at https://www.yoctoproject.org/documentation/toaster-manual-17.

Autobuilder

Autobuilder is the project responsible for QA, and a testing build is available inside the Yocto Project. It is based on the BuildBot project. Although this topic isn't dealt with in this book, for those of you interested in the BuildBot project, you can find more information about it in the following information box.

> The starting page of Buildbot can be accssed at http://trac.buildbot.net/. You can find a guide on quick starting BuildBot at http://docs.buildbot.net/0.8.5/tutorial/tour.html, and its concepts can be found at http://docs.buildbot.net/latest/manual/concepts.html.

We are now going to address a software area that is very poorly treated by developers in general. Here, I am referring to the testing and quality assurance of a development process. This is, in fact, an area that requires more attention from us, including me as well. The Yocto Project through the AutoBuilder initiative tries to bring more attention to this area. Also, in the past few years, there has been a shift toward QA and **Continuous Integration** (**CI**) of available open source projects, and this can primarily be seen in the Linux Foundation umbrella projects.

The Yocto Project is actively involved in the following activities as part of the AutoBuilder project:

- Publishing the testing and QA plans using Bugzilla test cases and plans (https://bugzilla.yoctoproject.org).
- Demonstrating these plans and making them accessible for everyone to see. Of course, for this, you will need a corresponding account.
- Developing tools, tests, and QA procedures for everyone to use.

Having the preceding activities as a foundation, they offer access to a public AutoBuilder that shows the current status of the Poky master branch. Nightly builds and test sets are executed for all the supported targets and architectures and are all available for everyone at http://autobuilder.yoctoproject.org/.

> If you do not have a Bugzilla account to access the QA activities done within the Yocto Project, refer to `https://wiki.yoctoproject.org/wiki/QA`.

To interact with the AutoBuilder Project, the setup is defined in the `README-QUICKSTART` file as a four-step procedure:

```
cat README-QUICKSTART
Setting up yocto-autobuilder in four easy steps:
------------------------------------------------
git clone git://git.yoctoproject.org/yocto-autobuilder
cd yocto-autobuilder
. ./yocto-autobuilder-setup
yocto-start-autobuilder both
```

The configuration files for this project are available inside the `config` directory. The `autobuilder.conf` file is used to define the parameters for the project, such as `DL_DIR`, `SSTATE_DIR`, and other build artifacts are very useful for a production setup, though not so useful for a local one. The next configuration file to inspect is `yoctoABConfig.py`, available in the `yocto-controller` directory where it defines the properties for the executed builds.

At this point, the AutoBuilder should be running. If it is started inside a web interface, the result should look similar to the following screenshot:

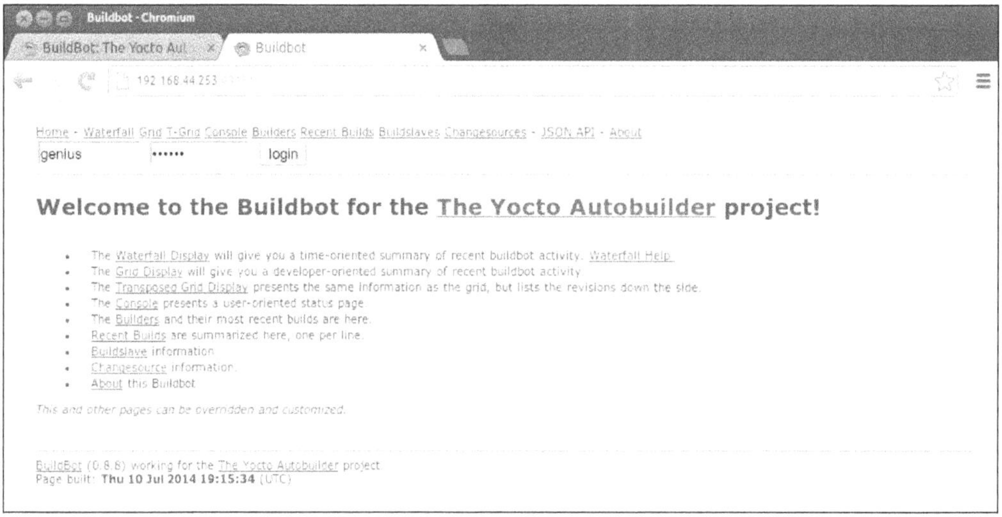

As it can be visible from the header of the web page, there are multiple options available not only for the executed builds, but also for a different view and perspective of them. Here is one of the visualization perspectives:

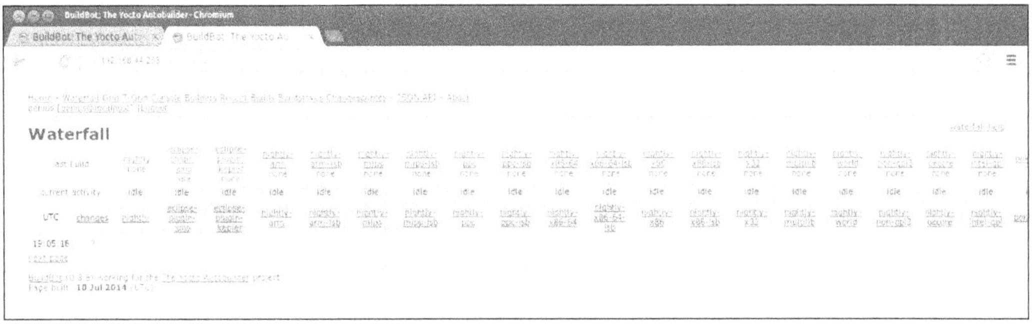

This project has more to offer to its users, but I will let the rest be discovered through trial and error and a reading of the README file. Keep in mind that this project was built with Buildbot, so the workflow is very similar to it.

Summary

In this chapter, you were presented with a new set of components that are available in the Yocto Project. Here, I am referring to the Hob, Toaster, and AutoBuilder projects. The chapter first introduced Hob as a BitBake alternative. It was followed by the Toaster alternative to Hob, which also comes with a lot of interesting features, and although it is not at its best now, over time, it will become a real solution for developers who are not interested in learning a new technology. Instead, they only interact with a tool to get what they want in a quick and easy manner. This chapter finished with the AutoBuilder project that offers a QA and testing platform for the Yocto Project community and can be transformed in a continuous integration tool.

In the next chapter, some of the other tools will be presented, but this time, the focus will move a little towards the exterior of the community and also its small tools. We will also cover projects and tools, such as Swabber, a project that is continuously in a developing stage. We will also take a look at Wic, a little tool with great personality, and the new sensation from Linaro called LAVA. I hope you enjoy learning all of them.

9
Wic and Other Tools

In this chapter, you will be given a brief introduction to a number of tools that address various problems and solves them in ingenious ways. This chapter can be thought of as an appetizer for you. If any of the tools presented here seem to interest you, I encourage you to feed your curiosity and try to find more about that particular tool. Of course, this piece of advice applies to any information presented in this book. However, this bit of advice holds true particularly for this chapter because I've chosen a more general description for the tools I've presented. I've done this as I've assumed that some of you may not be interested in lengthy descriptions and would only want to focus your interest in the development process, rather than in other areas. For the rest of you who are interested in finding out more about other key areas, please feel free to go through the extensions of information available throughout the chapter.

In this chapter, a more detailed explanation of components, such as Swabber, Wic, and LAVA, will be offered. These tools are not the ones, which an embedded developer will encounter on everyday jobs, though interaction with such tools could make life a little easier. The first thing I should mention about these tools is that they have nothing in common with each other, and are very different from each other and address different requests. If Swabber, the first tool presented here, is used for access detection on a host development machine, the second tool represents a solution to the limitations that BitBake has with complex packaging options. Here, I am referring to the wic tool. The last element presented in this chapter is the automation testing framework called LAVA. It is an initiative from Linaro, a project that, in my opinion, is very interesting to watch. They are also combined with a continuous integration tool, like Jenkins, and this could make it a killer combination for every taste.

Swabber

Swabber is a project, which although is presented on Yocto Project's official page, is said to be a work in progress; no activity has been done on it since September 18, 2011. It does not have a maintainers file where you can find more information about its creators. However, the committers list should be enough for anyone interested in taking a deeper look at this project.

This tool was selected for a short introduction in this chapter because it constitutes another point of view of the Yocto Project's ecosystem. Of course, a mechanism for access detection into the host system is not a bad idea and is very useful to detect accesses that could be problematic for your system, but it is not the first tool that comes to mind when developing software. When you have the possibility of redoing your build and inspecting your host ecosystem manually, you tend to lose sight of the fact that tools could be available for this task too, and that they could make your life easier.

For interaction with Swabber, the repository needs to be cloned first. The following command can be used for this purpose:

```
git clone http://git.yoctoproject.org/git/swabber
```

After the source code is available on the host, the content of the repository should look as follows:

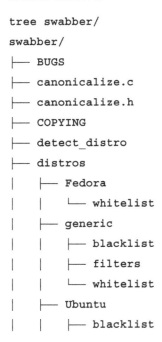

```
tree swabber/
swabber/
├── BUGS
├── canonicalize.c
├── canonicalize.h
├── COPYING
├── detect_distro
├── distros
│   ├── Fedora
│   │   └── whitelist
│   ├── generic
│   │   ├── blacklist
│   │   ├── filters
│   │   └── whitelist
│   ├── Ubuntu
│   │   ├── blacklist
```

```
│   │   ├── filters
│   │   └── whitelist
│   └── Windriver
│       └── whitelist
├── dump_blob.c
├── lists.c
├── lists.h
├── load_distro.c
├── Makefile
├── packages.h
├── README
├── swabber.c
├── swabber.h
├── swabprof.c
├── swabprof.in
├── swab_testf.c
├── update_distro
├── wandering.c
└── wandering.h

5 directories, 28 files
```

As you can see, this project is not a major one, but consists of a number of tools made available by a passionate few. This includes two guys from **Windriver**: Alex deVries and David Borman. They worked on their own on the previously presented tools and made them available for the open source community to use. Swabber is written using the C language, which is a big shift from the usual Python/Bash tools and other projects that are offered by the Yocto Project community. Every tool has its own purpose, the similitude being that all the tools are built using the same Makefile. Of course, this isn't restricted only to the usage of binaries; there are also two bash scripts available for distribution detect and update.

> More information about the tool can be found from its creators. Their e-mail addresses, which are available in the commits for the project, are `alex.devries@windriver.com` and `david.borman@windriver.com`. However, please note that these are the workplace e-mail IDs and the people that worked on Swabber may not have the same e-mail address at the moment.

The interaction with the Swabber tools is well described in the `README` file. Here, information regarding the setup and running of Swabber is available, though, for your sake, this will also be presented in the next few lines, so that you can understand quicker and in an easier manner.

The first required step is the compilation of sources. This is done by invoking the `make` command. After the source code is built and the executables are available, the host distribution can be profiled using the `update_distro` command, followed by the location of the distribution directory. The name we've chosen for it is `Ubuntu-distro-test`, and it is specific for the host distribution on which the tool is executed. This generation process can take some time at first, but after this, any changes to the host system will be detected and the process will take lesser time. At the end of the profiling process, this is how the content of the `Ubuntu-distro-test` directory looks:

```
Ubuntu-distro-test/
├── distro
├── distro.blob
├── md5
└── packages
```

After the host distribution is profiled, a Swabber report can be generated based on the profile created. Also, before creating the report, a profile log can be created for later use along with the reporting process. To generate the report, we will create a log file location with some specific log information. After the logs are available, the reports can be generated:

```
strace -o logs/Ubuntu-distro-test-logs.log -e trace=open,execve -f pwd
./swabber -v -v -c all -l logs/ -o required.txt -r extra.txt -d Ubuntu-distro-test/ ~ /tmp/
```

This information was required by the tool, as shown in its help information:

```
Usage: swabber [-v] [-v] [-a] [-e]
       -l <logpath> ] -o <outputfile> <filter dir 1> <filter dir 2> ...

 Options:
    -v: verbose, use -v -v for more detail
    -a: print progress (not implemented)
    -l <logfile>: strace logfile or directory of log files to read
```

```
    -d <distro_dir>: distro directory
    -n <distro_name>: force the name of the distribution
    -r <report filename>: where to dump extra data (leave empty for
stdout)
    -t <global_tag>: use one tag for all packages
    -o <outputfile>: file to write output to
    -p <project_dir>: directory were the build is being done
    -f <filter_dir>: directory where to find filters for whitelist,
           blacklist, filters
    -c <task1>,<task2>...: perform various tasks, choose from:
           error_codes: show report of files whose access returned an
error
           whitelist: remove packages that are in the whitelist
           blacklist: highlight packages that are in the blacklist as
                    being dangerous
           file_detail: add file-level detail when listing packages
           not_in_distro: list host files that are not in the package
                    database
           wandering: check for the case where the build searches for a
                    file on the host, then finds it in the project.
           all: all the above
```

From the help information attached in the preceding code, the role of the arguments selected for the test command can be investigated. Also, an inspection of the tool's source code is recommended due to the fact that there are no more than 1550 lines in a C file, the biggest one being the `swabber.c` file.

The `required.txt` file contains the information about the packages used and also about the packages specific files. More information regarding configurations is also available inside the `extra.txt` file. Such information includes files and packages that can be accessed, various warnings and files that are not available in the host database, and various errors and files that are considered dangerous.

For the command on which the tracing is done, the output information is not much. It has only been offered as an example; I encourage you to try various scenarios and familiarize yourselves with the tool. It could prove helpful to you later.

Wic

Wic is a command line tool that can be also seen as an extension of the BitBake build system. It was developed due to the need of having a partitioning mechanism and a description language. As it can be concluded easily, BitBake lacks in these areas and although initiatives were taken to make sure that such a functionality would be available inside the BitBake build system, this was only possible to an extent; for more complex tasks, Wic can be an alternative solution.

In the following lines, I will try to describe the problem associated with BitBake's lack of functionality and how Wic can solve this problem in an easy manner. I will also show you how this tool was born and what source of inspiration source was.

When an image is being built using BitBake, the work is done inside an image recipe that inherits `image.bbclass` for a description of its functionality. Inside this class, the `do_rootfs()` task is the one that the OS responsible for the creation of the root filesystem directory that will be later be included in the final package and includes all the sources necessary to boot a Linux image on various boards. With the `do_rootf()` task finished, a number of commands are interrogated to generate an output for each one of the image defined types. The definition of the image type is done through the `IMAGE_FSTYPE` variable and for each image output type, there is an `IMAGE_CMD_type` variable defined as an extra type that is inherited from an external layer or a base type described in the `image_types.bbclass` file.

The commands behind every one of these types are, in fact, a shell command-specific for a defined root filesystem format. The best example of this is the `ext3` format. For this, the `IMAGE_CMD_ext3` variable is defined and these commands are invoked, shown as follows:

```
genext2fs -b $ROOTFS_SIZE ... ${IMAGE_NAME}.rootfs.ext3

tune2fs -j ${DEPLOY_DIR_IMAGE}/${IMAGE_NAME}.rootfs.ext3
```

After the commands are called, the output is in the form of a `image-*.ext3` file. It is a newly created EXT3 filesystem according to the `FSTYPES` defined variable value, and it incorporates the root filesystem content. This example presents a very common and basic filesystem creation of commands. Of course, more complex options could be required in an industry environment, options that incorporate more than the root filesystem and add an extra kernel or even the bootloader alongside it, for instance. For these complex options, extensive mechanisms or tools are necessary.

The available mechanism implemented in the Yocto Project is visible inside the `image_types.bbclass` file through the `IMAGE_CMD_type` variable and has this form:

```
image_types_foo.bbclass:
  IMAGE_CMD_bar = "some shell commands"
  IMAGE_CMD_baz = "some more shell commands"
```

To use the newly defined image formats, the machine configuration needs to be updated accordingly, using the following commands:

```
foo-default-settings.inc
  IMAGE_CLASSES += "image_types_foo"
```

By using the `inherit ${IMAGE_CLASSES}` command inside the `image.bbclass` file, the newly defined `image_types_foo.bbclass` file's functionality is visible and ready to be used and added to the `IMAGE_FSTYPE` variable.

The preceding implementation implies that for each implemented filesystem, a series of commands are invoked. This is a good and simple method for a very simple filesystem format. However, for more complex ones, a language would be required to define the format, its state, and in general, the properties of the image format. Various other complex image format options, such as **vmdk**, **live**, and **directdisk** file types, are available inside Poky. They all define a multistage image formatting process.

To use the `vmdk` image format, a `vmdk` value needs to be defined in the `IMAGE_FSTYPE` variable. However, for this image format to be generated and recognized, the `image-vmdk.bbclass` file's functionalities should be available and inherited. With the functionalities available, three things can happen:

- An EXT3 image format dependency is created on the `do_rootfs()` task to make sure the `ext3` image format is generated first. The `vmdk` image format depends on this.
- The `ROOTFS` variable is set for the `boot-directdisk` functionality.
- The `boot-directdisk.bbclass` is inherited.

This functionality offers the possibility of generating images that can be copied onto a hard disk. At the base of it, the `syslinux` configuration file can be generated, and two partitions are also required for the boot up process. The end result consists of an MBR and partition table section followed by a FAT16 partition containing the boot files, SYSLINUX and the Linux kernel, and an EXT3 partition for the root filesystem location. This image format is also responsible for moving the Linux kernel, the `syslinux.cfg`, and `ldlinux.sys` configurations on the first partition, and copying using the `dd` command the EXT3 image format onto the second partition. At the end of this process, space is reserved for the root with the `tune2fs` command.

Historically, the usage of `directdisk` was hardcoded in its first versions. For every image recipe, there was a similar implementation that mirrored the basic one and hardcoded the heritage inside the recipe for the `image.bbclass` functionality. In the case of the `vmdk` image format, the `inherit boot-directdisk` line is added.

With regard to custom-defined image filesystem types, one such example can be found inside the `meta-fsl-arm` layer; this example is available inside the `imx23evk.conf` machine definition. This machine adds the next two image filesystem types: `uboot.mxsboot-sdcard` and `sdcard`.

```
meta-fsl-arm/imx23evk.conf
  include conf/machine/include/mxs-base.inc
  SDCARD_ROOTFS ?= "${DEPLOY_DIR_IMAGE}/${IMAGE_NAME}.rootfs.ext3"
  IMAGE_FSTYPES ?= "tar.bz2 ext3 uboot.mxsboot-sdcard sdcard"
```

The `mxs-base.inc` file included in the preceding lines is in return including the `conf/machine/include/fsl-default-settings.inc` file, which in return adds the `IMAGE_CLASSES +="image_types_fsl"` line as presented in the general case. Using the preceding lines offers the possibility for the `IMAGE_CMD` commands to be first executed for the commands available for the `uboot.mxsboot-sdcard` format, followed by the `sdcard IMAGE_CMD` commands-specific image format.

The `image_types_fsl.bbclass` file defines the `IMAGE_CMD` commands, as follows:

```
inherit image_types
  IMAGE_CMD_uboot.mxsboot-sdcard = "mxsboot sd ${DEPLOY_DIR_IMAGE}/u-
boot-${MACHINE}.${UBOOT_SUFFIX} \
${DEPLOY_DIR_IMAGE}/${IMAGE_NAME}.rootfs.uboot.mxsboot-sdcard"
```

At the end of the execution process, the `uboot.mxsboot-sdcard` command is called using the `mxsboot` command. Following the execution of this command, the `IMAGE_CMD_sdcard` specific commands are called to calculate the SD card size and alignment, as well as to initialize the deploy space and set the appropriate partition type to the `0x53` value and copy the root filesystem onto it. At the end of the process, several partitions are available and they have corresponding twiddles that are used to package bootable images.

There are multiple methods to create various filesystems and they are spread over a large number of existing Yocto layers with some documentation available for the general public. There are even a number of scripts used to create a suitable filesystem for a developer's needs. One such example is the `scripts/contrib/mkefidisk.sh` script. It is used to create an EFI-bootable direct disk image from another image format, that is, a `live.hddimg` one. However, a main idea remains: this kind of activity should be done without any middle image filesystem that is generated in intermediary phases and with something other than a partition language that is unable to handle complicated scenarios.

Keeping this information in mind, it seems that in the preceding example, we should have used another script. Considering the fact that it is possible to build an image from within the build system and also outside of it, the search for a number of tools that fit our needs was started. This search ended at the Fedora kickstart project. Although it has a syntax that is also suitable for areas involving deployment efforts, it is often considered to be of most help to developers.

> You can find more information about the Fedora Kickstart project at `http://fedoraproject.org/wiki/Anaconda/Kickstart`.

From this project, the most used and interesting components were `clearpart`, `part`, and `bootloader`, and these are useful for our purposes as well. When you take a look at the Yocto Project's Wic tool, it is also available inside the configuration files. If the configuration file for Wic is defined as `.wks` inside the Fedora kickstart project, the configuration file read uses the `.yks` extension. One such configuration file is defined as follows:

```
def pre():
    free-form python or named 'plugin' commands

  clearpart commands
  part commands
  bootloader commands
  named 'plugin' commands

  def post():
    free-form python or named 'plugin' commands
```

The idea behind the preceding script is very simple: the `clearpart` component is used to clear the disk of any partitions while the `part` component is used for the reverse, that is, the components used for creating and installing the filesystem. The third too that is defined is the `bootloader` component, which is used for installation of the bootloader, and also handles the corresponding information received from the `part` component. It also makes sure that the boot process is done as described inside the configuration file. The functions defined as `pre()` and `post()` are used for pre and post calculus for creation of the image, stage image artefacts, or other complex tasks.

As shown in the preceding description, the interaction with the Fedora kickstarter project was very productive and interesting, but the source code is written using Python inside the Wic project. This is due to the fact that a Python implementation for a similar tool was searched for and it was found under the form of the `pykickstarted` library. This is not all that the preceding library was used for by the Meego project inside its **Meego Image Creator** (**MIC**) tool. This tool was used for a Meego-specific image creation process. Later, this project was inherited by the Tizen project.

> For more about MIC, refer to `https://github.com/01org/mic`.

Wic, the tool that I promised to present in this section is derived from the MIC project and both of them use the kickstarter project, so all three are based on plugins that define the behavior of the process of creating various image formats. In the first implementation of Wic, it was mostly a functionality of the MIC project. Here, I am referring to the Python classes it defines that were almost entirely copied inside Poky. However, over time, the project started to have its own implementations, and also its own personality. From version 1.7 of the Poky repository, no direct reference to MIC Python defined classes remained, making Wic a standalone project that had its own defined plugins and implementations. Here is how you can inspect the various configuration of formats accessible inside Wic:

```
tree scripts/lib/image/canned-wks/
scripts/lib/image/canned-wks/
├── directdisk.wks
├── mkefidisk.wks
├── mkgummidisk.wks
└── sdimage-bootpart.wks
```

There are configurations defined inside Wic. However, considering the fact that the interest in this tool has grown in the last few years, we can only hope that the number of supported configurations will increase.

I mentioned previously that the MIC and Fedora kickstarter project dependencies were removed, but a quick search inside the Poky `scripts/lib/wic` directory will reveal otherwise. This is because Wic and MIC are both have the same foundation, the `pykickstarted` library. Though Wic is now heavily based on MIC and both have the same parent, the kickstarter project, their implementations, functionalities, and various configurations make them different entities, which although related have taken different paths of development.

LAVA

LAVA (**Linaro Automation and Validation Architecture**) is a continuous integration system that concentrates on a physical target or virtual hardware deployment where a series of tests are executed. The executed tests are of a large variety from the simplest ones which only requires booting a target to some very complex scenarios that require external hardware interaction.

LAVA represents a collection of components that are used for automated validation. The main idea behind the LAVA stack is to create a quality controlled testing and automation environment that is suitable for projects of all sizes. For a closer look at a LAVA instance, the reader could inspect an already created one, the official production instance of which is hosted by Linaro in Cambridge. You can access it at `https://validation.linaro.org/`. I hope you enjoy working with it.

The LAVA framework offers support for the following functionalities:

- It supports scheduled automatic testing for multiple packages on various hardware packages
- It makes sure that after a device crashes, the system restarts automatically
- It conducts regression testing
- It conducts continuous integration testing
- It conducts platform enablement testing
- It provides support for both local and cloud solutions
- It provides support for result bundles
- It provides measurements for performance and power consumption

LAVA is primarily written using Python, which is no different from what the Yocto Project offers us. As seen in the Toaster Project, LAVA also uses the Django framework for a web interface and the project is hosted using the Git versioning system. This is no surprise since we are talking about Linaro, a not-for-profit organization that works on free and open source projects. Therefore, the thumb rule applied to all the changes made to the project should return in the upstream project, making the project a little easier to maintain. However, it is also more robust and has better performance.

> For those of you interested in more details about how this project can be used, refer to `https://validation.linaro.org/static/docs/overview.html`.

For testing with the LAVA framework, the first step would be to understand its architecture. Knowing this helps not only with test definitions, but also with extending them, as well as the development of the overall project. The major components of this project are as follows:

```
                     +-------------+
                     |web interface|
                     +-------------+
                            |
                            v
                        +--------+
                   +---->|database|
                   |     +--------+
                   |
+----------+------[worker]------------+
|          |                          |
|  +----------------+    +----------+ |
|  |scheduler daemon|--->|dispatcher| |
|  +----------------+    +----------+ |
|                             |       |
+-----------------------------+-------+
                              |
                              v
                  +------------------+
                  | device under test |
                  +------------------+
```

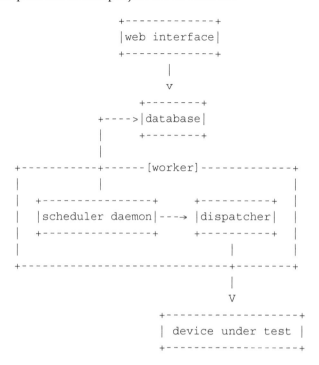

The first component, the **web interface**, is responsible for user interaction. It is used to store data and submitted jobs using RDBMS, and is also responsible to display the results, device navigation, or as job submission receiver activities that are done through the XMLRPC API. Another important component is represented by **the scheduler daemon**, which is responsible for the allocation of jobs. Its activity is quite simple. It is responsible for pooling the data from a database and reserving devices for jobs that are offered to them by the dispatcher, another important component. The **dispatcher** is the component responsible for running actual jobs on the devices. It also manages the communication with a device, download images, and collects results.

There are scenarios when only the dispatcher can be used; these scenarios involve the usage of a local test or a testing feature development. There are also scenarios where all the components run on the same machine, such as a single deployment server. Of course, the desired scenario is to have components decoupled, the server on one machine, database on another one, and the scheduler daemon and dispatcher on a separate machine.

For the development process with LAVA, the recommended host machines are Debian and Ubuntu. The Linaro development team working with LAVA prefer the Debian distribution, but it can work well on an Ubuntu machine as well. There are a few things that need to be mentioned: for the Ubuntu machine, make sure that the universe repositories are available and visible by your package manager.

The first package that is necessary is `lava-dev`; it also has scripts that indicate the necessary package dependencies to assure the LAVA working environment. Here are the necessary commands required to do this:

```
sudo apt-get install lava-dev
git clone http://git.linaro.org/git/lava/lava-server.git
cd lava-server
/usr/share/lava-server/debian-dev-build.sh lava-server

git clone http://git.linaro.org/git/lava/lava-dispatcher.git
cd lava-dispatcher
/usr/share/lava-server/debian-dev-build.sh lava-dispatcher
```

Taking into consideration the location of the changes, various actions are required. For example, for a change in the `templates` directory's HTML content, refreshing the browser will suffice, but any changes made in the `*_app` directory's Python implementation will require a restart of the `apache2ctl` HTTP server. Also, any change made in the `*_daemon` directory's Python sources will require a restart of `lava-server` altogether.

> For all of you interested in acquiring more information about LAVA development, the development guide constitutes a good resource of documentation, which is available at `https://validation.linaro.org/static/docs/#developer-guides`.

To install LAVA or any LAVA-related packages on a 64-bit Ubuntu 14.04 machine, new package dependencies are required in addition to the enabled support for universal repositories `deb http://people.linaro.org/~neil.williams/lava jessie main`, besides the installation process described previously for the Debian distribution. I must mention that when the `lava-dev` package is installed, the user will be prompted to a menu that indicates `nullmailer mailname`. I've chosen to let the default one remain, which is actually the host name of the computer running the `nullmailer` service. I've also kept the same configuration defined by default for `smarthost` and the installation process has continued. The following are the commands necessary to install LAVA on a Ubuntu 14.04 machine:

```
sudo add-apt-repository "deb http://archive.ubuntu.com/ubuntu $(lsb_
release -sc) universe"
sudo apt-get update
sudo add-apt-repository "deb http://people.linaro.org/~neil.williams/lava
jessie main"
sudo apt-get update

sudo apt-get install postgresql
sudo apt-get install lava
sudo a2dissite 000-default
sudo a2ensite lava-server.conf
sudo service apache2 restart
```

> Information about the LAVA installation process is available at `https://validation.linaro.org/static/docs/installing_on_debian.html#`. Here, you also find the installation processes for bot Debian and Ubuntu distributions.

Summary

In this chapter, you were presented a new set of tools. I will honestly admit that these tools are not the ones used most often in an embedded environment, but they've been introduced in order to offer another point of view to the embedded development environment. This chapter tried to explain to developers that there is more to the embedded world then just development and the tools that help with these tasks. In most cases, the adjacent components are the ones that could inspire and influence the development process the most.

In the next chapter, a short presentation of the Linux real-time requirements and solutions will be presented. We will emphasize the various features that work alongside Linux in this area. A short presentation of the meta-realtime layer will be offered, and features, such as Preempt-RT and NOHZ, will be discussed. Without further ado, let's proceed to the next chapter. I hope you will enjoy its content.

10
Real-time

In this chapter, you will be presented with information on the real-time component of the Yocto Project. Also, in the same context, a short discussion regarding the general purpose of an operating system and a real-time operating system will be explained. We will then move toward the PREEMPT_RT patches that try to change normal Linux into a full powered real-time operating system; we will try to look at it from more angles and at the end, sum it up and draw a conclusion out of it. This is not all, any real-time operation needs its applications, so a short presentation on the do's and don'ts of application writing that is suitable in the context of a real-time operating system, will also be presented. Keeping all of this in mind, I believe it's time to proceed with this chapter content; I hope you enjoy it.

You will find a more detailed explanation of real-time components in this chapter. Also, the relation between Linux and real-time will be shown to you. As everyone knows already, the Linux operation system was designed as a general purpose OS very similar to the already available UNIX. It is very easy to see the fact that a multiuser system, such as Linux, and a real-time one are somewhat in conflict. The main reason for this is that for a general purpose, multiple user operating systems, such as Linux, are configured to obtain a maximal average throughput. This sacrifices latencies that offer exactly the opposite requirements for a real-time operating system.

The definition for real time is fairly easy to understand. The main idea behind it in computing is that a computer or any embedded device is able to offer feedback to its environment in time. This is very different from being fast; it is, in fact, fast enough in the context of a system and fast enough is different for the automobile industry or nuclear power plants. Also, this kind of a system will offer reliable responses to take decisions that don't not affect any exterior system. For example, in a nuclear power plant, it should detect and prevent any abnormal conditions to ensure that a catastrophe is avoided.

Understanding GPOS and RTOS

When Linux is mentioned, usually **General Purpose Operating System** (**GPOS**) is related to it, but over time, the need to have the same benefits as **Real-Time Operating System** (**RTOS**) for Linux has become more stringent. The challenge for any real-time system is to meet the given timing constrains in spite of the number and type of random asynchronous events. This is no simple task and an extensive number of papers and researches were done on theory of the real-time systems. Another challenge for a real-time system would be to have an upper limit on latency, called a scheduling deadline. Depending on how systems meet this challenge, they can be split into hard, firm, and soft:

- **Hard real-time system**: This represents system for which a deadline miss will result in a complete system failure.
- **Firm real-time system**: This represents systems for which a deadline miss is acceptable but the system quality can be degraded. Also, after the deadline is missed, the result that is offered is not useful anymore.
- **Soft real-time system**: This represents systems for which missing of deadlines degrades the usefulness of the received result and consequently, of the quality of the system. In these kind of systems, the meeting of the deadline is seen as a goal than as a strict requirement.

There are multiple reasons for Linux not being suitable as a RTOS:

- **Paging**: The page swap process through virtual memory is without limits. There is no method in place to know the time that will pass until you can get a page from a disk, and this implies that there is no upper limit to the delay caused by the fault in a page.
- **Coarsed-grained synchronization**: Here, the definition of the Linux kernel is not preemptible. This means that once a process is inside the kernel context, it cannot be preempted until it exits the context. At an event occurrence, the new event needs to wait for scheduling until the already available one exits the kernel context.
- **Batching**: An operation can be batched for a more efficient use of resources. The simplest example of this is the page freeing process. Instead of freeing each separate page, Linux is able to pass multiple pages and clean as many as possible.
- **Request reordering**: The I/O requests can be reordered for processes, making the process of using hardware more efficient.

- **Fairness in scheduling**: This is a UNIX heritage and refers to the fact that a scheduler tries to be fair with all running processes. This property offers the possibility of lower priority processes that have been waiting for a long time to be scheduled before higher priority ones.

All the preceding characteristics constitute the reason why an upper boundary cannot be applied to the latency of a task or process, and also why Linux cannot become a hard real-time operating system. Let's take a look at the following diagram which illustrates the approaches of Linux OS to offer real-time characteristics:

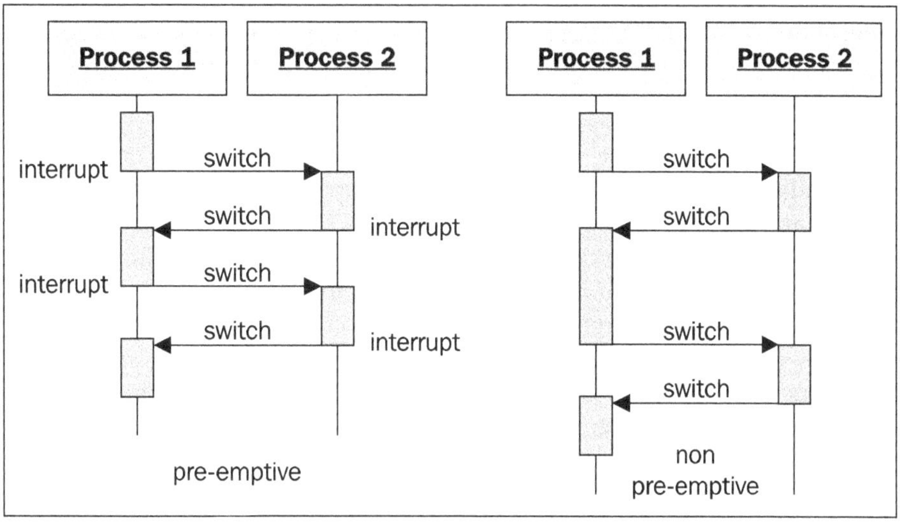

The first thing anyone can do to improve the latency of the standard Linux operating system would be to try and make a change to the scheduling policies. The default Linux time sharing scheduling policies are called **SCHED_OTHER**, and they use a fairness algorithm, giving all processes zero priority, the lowest one available. Other such scheduling policies are **SCHED_BATCH** for batch scheduling of the processes and the **SCHED_IDLE**, which is suitable for the scheduling of extremely low priority jobs. The alternatives to this scheduling policy are **SCHED_FIFO** and **SCHED_RR**. Both of them are intended as real-time policies and are time-critical applications that require precise control processes and their latencies.

To offer more real-time characteristics to a Linux operating system, there are also two more approaches that can be presented. The first one refers to a more preemptive implementation of the Linux kernel. This approach can take advantage of the already available spinlock mechanism used for SMP support, making sure that multiple processes are prevented from executing simultaneously, though in the context of a single processor, the spinlocks are no ops. The interrupt handling also requires modifications this rescheduling to make possible if another higher priority process appears; in this situation, a new scheduler might also be required. This approach offers the advantage of not changing the interaction of a user space and the advantage of using APIs, such as POSIX or others. The drawback of this is that the kernel changes are very serious and every time a kernel version changes, these changes need to be adapted accordingly. If this work was not enough already, the end result is not fully real-time operating system, but one that reduces the latency of the operating system.

The other available implementation is interrupt abstraction. This approach is based on the fact that not all systems require a hard real-time determinism and most of them only require a section of their task to be executed in a real-time context. The idea behind this approach is to run Linux with the priority of an idle task under a real-time kernel and non-real-time tasks to continue to execute them as they normally do. This implementation fakes the disabling of an interrupt for the real-time kernel, but in fact, it is passed to the real-time kernel. For this type of implementation, there are three available solutions:

- **RTLinux**: It represents the original implementation of the interrupt abstraction approach and was developed at the Institute of Mining and Technology, New Mexico. Although it still has an open source implementation, most of the development is now done through FSMLabs engineers, later required by the Wind River System on the commercial version of it. The commercial support for RTLinux ended in August 2011.
- **RTAI**: It is an enhancement made to the RTLinux solution developed in the department of Aerospace Engineering from the Politecnico di Milano. This project is a very active with a high number of developers and has current releases available.
- **Xenomai**: It represents the third implementation. It's history is a bit twisted: it appeared in August 2001, only to be merged with RTAI in 2013 to generate a real-time operating system that was fit for production. However, the fusion was dispersed in 2005 and it became an independent project again.

The following diagram presents a basic RTLinux architecture.

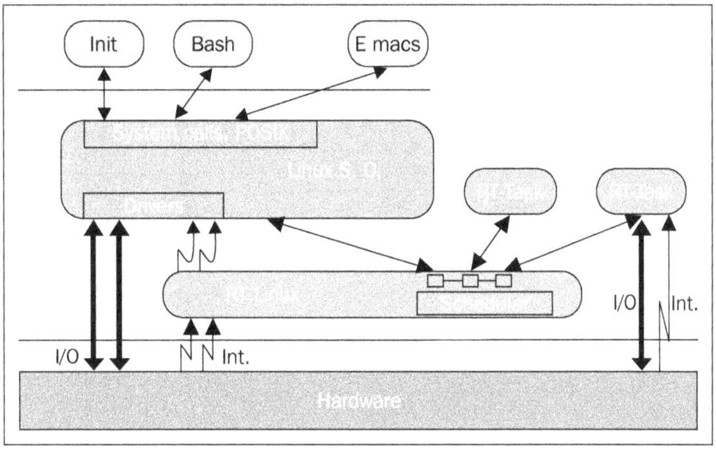

A similar architecture, as shown in the preceding diagram, applies to the two other solutions since both of them were born from the RTLinux implementation. The difference between them is at the implementation level and each offers various benefits.

PREEMPT_RT

The PREEMPT_RT patches are the first option for every developer when a real-time solution is required. For some developers, the PREEMPT_RT patches transform Linux into a real-time solution suitable for their needs. This solution could not replace a real-time operation system, but is, in fact, suitable for a large number of systems.

The biggest advantage that PREEMPT_RT has over other real-time solutions for Linux is that it actually transforms Linux into a real-time operating system. All the other alternatives usually create a microkernel that is executed as a hypervisor and Linux is only executed as a task of it, so the communication of real-time tasks with the non-real-time ones is done through this microkernel. For the PREEMPT_RT patch, this problem is no more.

The standard version of the Linux kernel is only able to offer soft real-time requirements, such as basic POSIX user space operations where no deadline is guaranteed. Adding patches, such as Ingo Molnar's PREEMPT_RT patch, and also Thomas Gheixner's patch with regards to a generic clock event layer that offers a high resolution support, you can say that you have a Linux kernel that offers high real-time capabilities.

With the presence of the real-time preemption patch in the industry, a number of interesting opportunities have appeared, making it an option for firm and hard real-time applications in areas, such as industrial control or professional audio. This is mainly because of the design of the PREEMPT_RT patch and its aim toward integration inside the mainline kernel. We will learn about its usage further in the chapter. The following diagram shows the working of the Preemptible Linux Kernel:

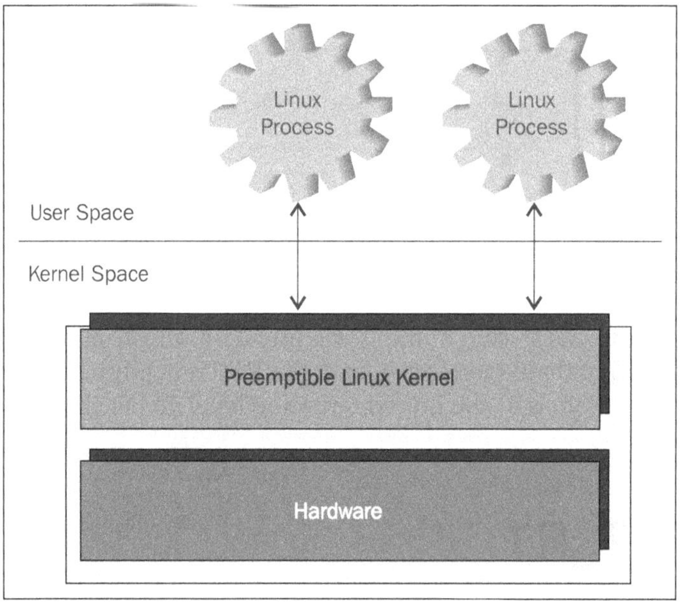

The PREEMPT_RT patch transforms Linux from a general purpose operating system into a preemptible one using the following tricks:

- Protecting critical sections with the preemptible `rwlock_t preemptible` and `spinlock_t`. The use of the old solutions is still available using `raw_spinlock_t`, which shares the same API as `spinlock_t`.
- The kernel locking mechanisms is preempted by using `rtmutexes`.
- A priority inversion and priority inheritance mechanism is implemented for `mutexes`, `spinlocks` and `rw_semaphores`.
- Converting the available Linux timer API into one with a high resolution timer that offers the possibility of having timeouts.
- Implementing the usage of kernel threads for interrupt handlers. The real-time preemption patch treats soft interrupt handlers into the kernel thread context using a `task_struct` like structure for every user space process. There is also the possibility of registering an IRQ into the kernel context.

> For more information on priority inversion, `http://www.embedded.com/electronics-blogs/beginner-s-corner/4023947/Introduction-to-Priority-Inversion` is a good starting point.

Applying the PREEMPT_RT patch

Before moving to the actual configuration part, you should download a suitable version for the kernel. The best inspiration source is `https://www.kernel.org/`, which should be the starting point because it does not contain any extra patches. After the source code is received, the corresponding `rt` patches version can be downloaded from `https://www.kernel.org/pub/linux/kernel/projects/rt/`. The kernel version chosen for this demonstration is the 3.12 kernel version, but if any other kernel version is required, the same steps can be taken with a similar end result. The development of the real-time preemption patches is very active, so any missing version support is covered very fast. Also, for other sublevel versions, the patches can be found in the `incr` or older subdirectories of that particular kernel version. The following is the example for sublevel versions:

```
wget https://www.kernel.org/pub/linux/kernel/v3.x/linux-
3.12.38.tar.xz
wget https://www.kernel.org/pub/linux/kernel/projects/rt/3.12/patch-
3.12.38-rt52.patch.gz
```

After the source code is received, the sources need to be unpacked and the patches applied:

```
tar xf linux-3.12.38.tar.xz
cd linux-3.12.38/
gzip -cd ../patch-3.12.38-rt52.patch.gz | patch -p1
```

The next step involves the configuration of the kernel sources. The configuration differs from one architecture to another, but the general idea remains. The following configurations are required for a QEMU ARM machine supported inside Poky. To enable the PREEMPT_RT support for a machine, there are multiple options available. You can implement a low-latency support version, which is most suitable for a desktop computer using a kernel configuration fragment similar to this:

```
CONFIG_GENERIC_LOCKBREAK=y
CONFIG_TREE_PREEMPT_RCU=y
CONFIG_PREEMPT_RCU=y
CONFIG_UNINLINE_SPIN_UNLOCK=y
CONFIG_PREEMPT=y
```

```
CONFIG_PREEMPT__LL=y
CONFIG_PREEMPT_COUNT=y
CONFIG_DEBUG_PREEMPT=y
CONFIG_RCU_CPU_STALL_VERBOSE=y
```

This option is one of the most often used and it also constitutes the primary source of usage of the PREEMPT_RT patches. The alternative of this would be to enable the fully preemptive support for the PREEMPT_RT patches using a configuration similar to this:

```
CONFIG_PREEMPT_RT_FULL=y
CONFIG_HZ_1000=y
CONFIG_HZ=1000
```

If you're interested in configuring the kernel manually, it can use the `menuconfig` option. The following `CONFIG_PREEMPT*` configurations are available for easier access to the required options. The first image mainly contains the `CONFIG_PREEMPT` and `CONFIG_PREEMPT_COUNT` variables, which should be the first ones to enable. There is also a configuration option called `CONFIG_PREEMPT_NONE` that is used for no forced preemptive actions.

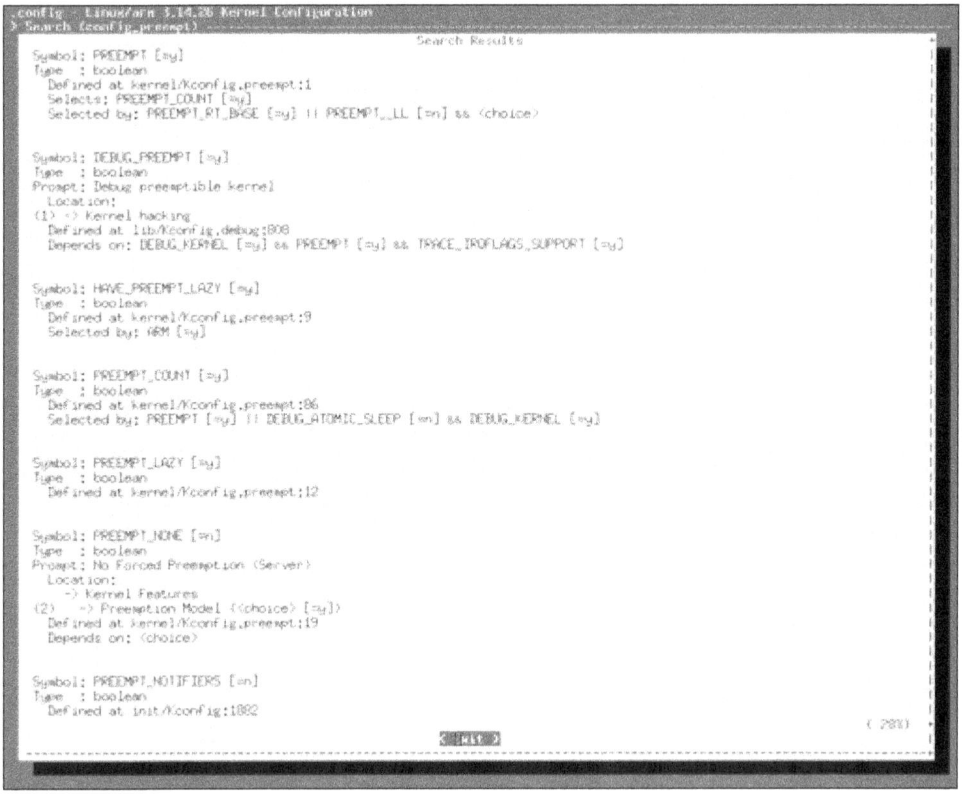

In the following image, the `CONFIG_PREEMPT_RCU` and `CONFIG_PREEMPT_RT_FULL` configurations are available. More information related to `RCU` is available at `https://lwn.net/Articles/262464/`.

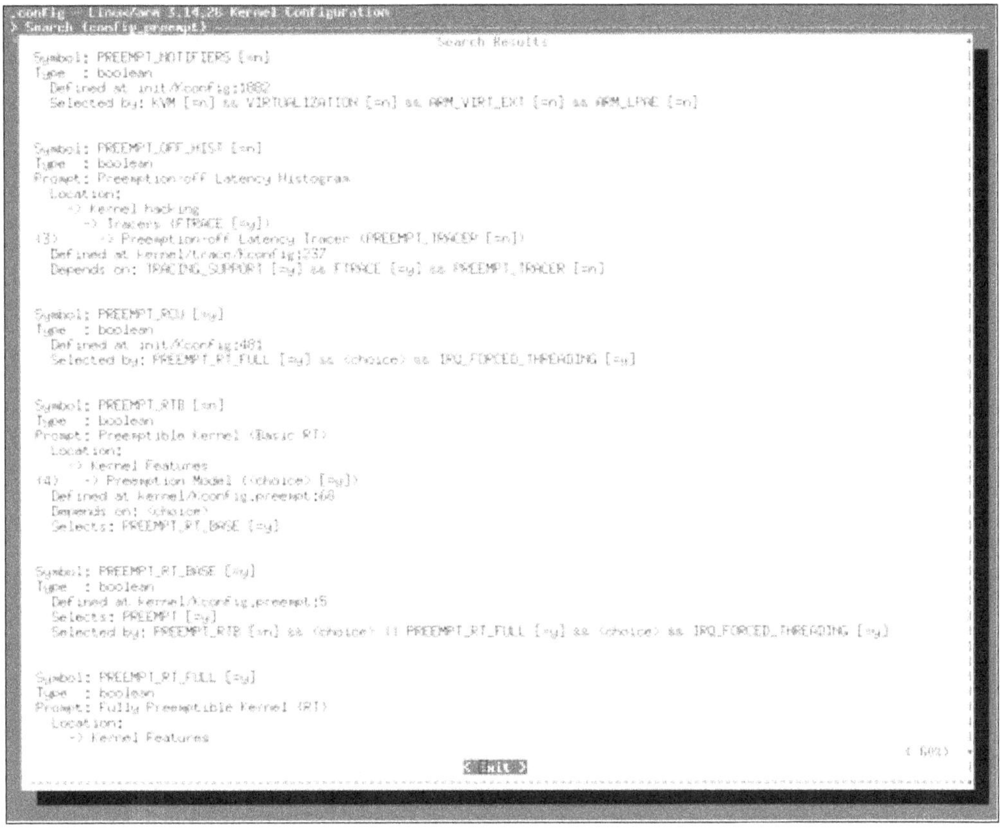

The third image contains the `CONFIG_PREEMPT__LL` configuration. Another interesting configuration is `CONFIG_PREEMPT_VOLUNTARY`, which also reduces the latency along with the `CONFIG_PREEMPT__LL` configuration, for a desktop computer.

One interesting argument against the *low-latency desktop* option is available at `https://sevencapitalsins.wordpress.com/2007/08/10/low-latency-kernel-wtf/`.

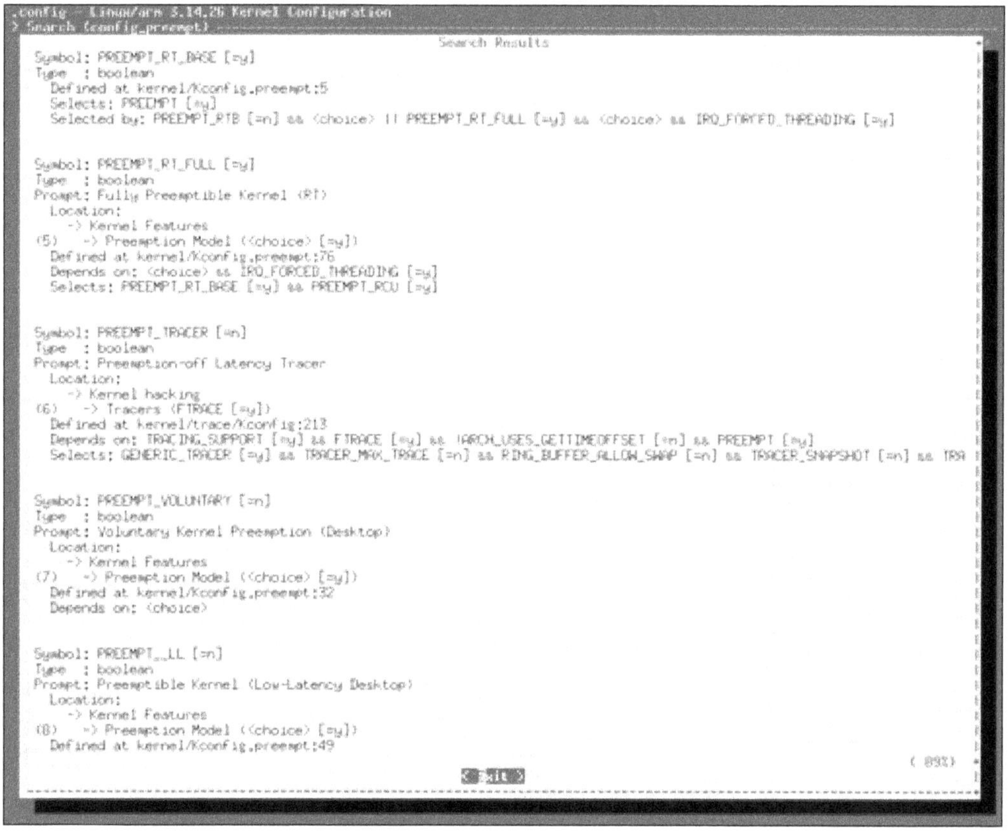

The last one contains the `CONFIG_TREE_PREEMPT_RCU` configuration used to change the `RCU` implementation. The same process can be used to search and enable the other configurations that do not contain the search word in their name.

For more information regarding the PREEMPT_RT patch, refer to `http://varun-anand.com/preempt.html` and `http://www.versalogic.com/mediacenter/whitepapers/wp_linux_rt.asp`.

After the kernel image is obtained with the newly applied and configured real-time preemptible kernel patch, it needs to be booted to make sure the activity is done appropriately so that the end result can be usable. Using the `uname -a` command, the `patch rt*` revision number is visible and should be applied to the kernel version. Of course, there are other methods that can used to identify this information. An alternative for the `uname -a` command is the `dmesg` command on its output the string real-time preemption support should be visible, but only one method should be enough. The following image offers a representation of how the `uname -a` command output should look:

Taking a look at the list of processes, it can be seen, as mentioned earlier, that the IRQ handler is treated using kernel threads. This information is visible in the next `ps` command output due to the fact that it is put between square brackets. Single IRQ handlers are represented by the `task_struct` structures that are similar to the user space ones, making them easily controllable from the user space:

```
ps ax
PID TTY       STAT   TIME COMMAND
1 ?          S       0:00 init [2]
2 ?          S       0:00 [softirq-high/0]
3 ?          S       0:00 [softirq-timer/0]
4 ?          S       0:00 [softirq-net-tx/]
5 ?          S       0:00 [softirq-net-rx/]
6 ?          S       0:00 [softirq-block/0]
7 ?          S       0:00 [softirq-tasklet]
8 ?          S       0:00 [softirq-hrtreal]
9 ?          S       0:00 [softirq-hrtmono]
10 ?          S<      0:00 [desched/0]
11 ?          S<      0:00 [events/0]
12 ?          S<      0:00 [khelper]
13 ?          S<      0:00 [kthread]
15 ?          S<      0:00 [kblockd/0]
58 ?          S       0:00 [pdflush]
59 ?          S       0:00 [pdflush]
61 ?          S<      0:00 [aio/0]
60 ?          S       0:00 [kswapd0]
647 ?          S<      0:00 [IRQ 7]
648 ?          S<      0:00 [kseriod]
651 ?          S<      0:00 [IRQ 12]
654 ?          S<      0:00 [IRQ 6]
675 ?          S<      0:09 [IRQ 14]
687 ?          S<      0:00 [kpsmoused]
689 ?          S       0:00 [kjournald]
691 ?          S<      0:00 [IRQ 1]
769 ?          S<s     0:00 udevd --daemon
871 ?          S<      0:00 [khubd]
```

```
882 ?        S<     0:00 [IRQ 10]
2433 ?        S<     0:00 [IRQ 11]
[...]
```

The next bit of information that needs to be gathered involves the formatting of the interrupt process entries, which are a bit different than the ones used for a vanilla kernel. This output is visible by inspecting the `/proc/interrupts` file:

```
cat /proc/interrupts
CPU0
0:     497464  XT-PIC          [........N/  0]  pit
2:          0  XT-PIC          [........N/  0]  cascade
7:          0  XT-PIC          [........N/  0]  lpptest
10:          0  XT-PIC          [........./  0]  uhci_hcd:usb1
11:      12069  XT-PIC          [........./  0]  eth0
14:       4754  XT-PIC          [........./  0]  ide0
NMI:          0
LOC:       1701
ERR:          0
MIS:          0
```

Then, information available in the fourth column provides the IRQ line notifications, such as: `[........N/  0]`. Here, each dot represents an attribute and each attribute is a value, as described in the following points. Here is the order of their presence:

- `I (IRQ_INPROGRESS)`: This refers to the IRQ handler that is active
- `D (IRQ_DISABLED)`: This represents the IRQ as being disabled
- `P (IRQ_PENDING)`: The IRQ here is presented as being in a pending state
- `R (IRQ_REPLAY)`: In this state, the IRQ has been replied to, but no ACK is received yet
- `A (IRQ_AUTODETECT)`: This represents the IRQ as being in an autodetect state
- `W (IRQ_WAITING)`: This refers to the IRQ being in an autodetect state, but not seen yet
- `L (IRQ_LEVEL)`: The IRQ is in a level-triggered state
- `M (IRQ_MASKED)`: This represents the state in which the IRQ is not visible as being masked anymore
- `N (IRQ_NODELAY)`: This is the state in which the IRQ must be executed immediately

In the preceding example, you can see that multiple IRQs are marked as visible and hard IRQs that are run in the kernel context. When an IRQ status is marked as `IRQ_NODELAY`, it shows the user that the handler of the IRQ is a kernel thread and it will be executed as one. The description of an IRQ can be changed manually, but this is not an activity that will be described here.

> For more information on how to change the real-time attributes for a process, a good starting point is the `chrt` tool, available at `http://linux.die.net/man/1/chrt`.

The Yocto Project -rt kernel

Inside Yocto, kernel recipes with PREEMPT_RT patches are applied. For the moment, there are only two recipes that incorporate the PREEMPT_RT patch; both are available inside the meta layer. The recipes that refer to kernel versions 3.10 and 3.14 and their naming are `linux-yocto-rt_3.10.bb` and `linux-yocto-rt_3.14.bb`. The `-rt` ending in the naming indicates that these recipes fetch the PREEMPT_RT branches of the Linux kernel versions maintained by the Yocto community.

The format for the 3.14 kernel recipe is presented here:

```
cat ./meta/recipes-kernel/linux/linux-yocto-rt_3.14.bb
KBRANCH ?= "standard/preempt-rt/base"
KBRANCH_qemuppc ?= "standard/preempt-rt/qemuppc"

require recipes-kernel/linux/linux-yocto.inc

SRCREV_machine ?= "0a875ce52aa7a42ddabdb87038074381bb268e77"
SRCREV_machine_qemuppc ?=
"b993661d41f08846daa28b14f89c8ae3e94225bd"
SRCREV_meta ?= "fb6271a942b57bdc40c6e49f0203be153699f81c"

SRC_URI = "git://git.yoctoproject.org/linux-yocto-3.14.git;
bareclone=1;branch=${KBRANCH},meta;name=machine,meta"

LINUX_VERSION ?= "3.14.19"

PV = "${LINUX_VERSION}+git${SRCPV}"

KMETA = "meta"
```

```
LINUX_KERNEL_TYPE = "preempt-rt"

COMPATIBLE_MACHINE = "(qemux86|qemux86-
64|qemuarm|qemuppc|qemumips)"

# Functionality flags
KERNEL_EXTRA_FEATURES ?= "features/netfilter/netfilter.scc
features/taskstats/taskstats.scc"
KERNEL_FEATURES_append = " ${KERNEL_EXTRA_FEATURES}"
KERNEL_FEATURES_append_qemux86=" cfg/sound.scc
cfg/paravirt_kvm.scc"
KERNEL_FEATURES_append_qemux86=" cfg/sound.scc
cfg/paravirt_kvm.scc"
KERNEL_FEATURES_append_qemux86-64=" cfg/sound.scc"
```

As shown, one of the recipes seemed to have a duplicated line and a patch is necessary to remove it:

```
commit e799588ba389ad3f319afd1a61e14c43fb78a845
Author: Alexandru.Vaduva <Alexandru.Vaduva@enea.com>
Date:   Wed Mar 11 10:47:00 2015 +0100

    linux-yocto-rt: removed duplicated line

    Seemed that the recipe contained redundant information.

    Signed-off-by: Alexandru.Vaduva <Alexandru.Vaduva@enea.com>

diff --git a/meta/recipes-kernel/linux/linux-yocto-rt_3.14.bb
b/meta/recipes-kernel/linux/linux-yocto-rt_3.14.bb
index 7dbf82c..bcfd754 100644
--- a/meta/recipes-kernel/linux/linux-yocto-rt_3.14.bb
+++ b/meta/recipes-kernel/linux/linux-yocto-rt_3.14.bb
@@ -23,5 +23,4 @@ COMPATIBLE_MACHINE = "(qemux86|qemux86-
64|qemuarm|qemuppc|qemumips)"
 KERNEL_EXTRA_FEATURES ?= "features/netfilter/netfilter.scc
features/taskstats/taskstats.scc"
 KERNEL_FEATURES_append = " ${KERNEL_EXTRA_FEATURES}"
 KERNEL_FEATURES_append_qemux86=" cfg/sound.scc
cfg/paravirt_kvm.scc"
-KERNEL_FEATURES_append_qemux86=" cfg/sound.scc
cfg/paravirt_kvm.scc"
 KERNEL_FEATURES_append_qemux86-64=" cfg/sound.scc"
```

The preceding recipe is very similar to the base one. Here, I am referring to `linux-yocto_3.14.bb`; they are the recipes on which the PREEMPT_RT patches have been applied. The difference between them is that each one is taken from its specific branch, and until now, none of the Linux kernel versions with the PREEMPT_RT patches have provided support for the `qemumips64` compatible machine.

Disadvantages of the PREEMPT_RT patches

Linux, a general purpose operating system that is optimized for throughput, is the exact opposite of what a real-time operating system is all about. Of course it offers a high throughput by using a large, multilayered cache, which is a nightmare for a hard real-time operating process.

In order to have a real-time Linux, there are two available options:

- The first one involves the use of the PREEMPT_RT patches, which offer preemption by minimizing the latency and executing all activities in a thread context.
- The second solution involves the use of real-time extensions that act as layers between Linux and the hardware used for the management of real-time tasks. This second solution includes the previously mentioned RTLinux, RTAI, and XENOMAI solutions, as well as other commercial solutions and variations that involve moving the layer and also separating it in multiple components.

The variations of the second option imply various solution from the isolation of the cores for real-time activities to the assignation of one for such tasks. There are also a lot of solutions that involve the usage of a hypervisor or a hook below the Linux kernel to serve a number of interrupts to the RTOS. The existence of these alternatives have been made available to the reader not only with other options, but also due to the fact that the PREEMPT_RT patch has its disadvantages.

One notable disadvantage is that the reduction of latency was done by forcing the kernel to preempt a task when a higher priority one appeared. This, of course, reduces the throughput for the system because it not only adds a number of context switches in the process but also makes the lower priority tasks wait longer than they would do the normal Linux kernel.

Another disadvantage of the `preempt-rt` patches is that they need to be ported from one kernel version to another and adapted from one architecture or software vendor to another. This only implies that knowledge of the Linux kernel should be available in-house for a particular vendor and it should adapt the solution for each of its available kernels. This fact alone has made it less likeable for BSP or Linux operating system providers.

> One interesting presentation regarding the Linux pre-emption is available in the following link. It can be consulted for more information regarding a Linux real-time solution, and is available at `http://www.slideshare.net/jserv/realtime-linux`.

Linux real-time applications

Having a real-time operating system may not always be enough for everyone. Some people would also require real-time optimized applications running over the operating system. To make sure an rt-application can be designed and interacted with, the required determinism is necessary on the operating system and hardware. With regard to the hardware configuration, the requirements involve a low-latency interrupt handling. The mechanisms causing the ISR latencies should register values around tens of microseconds.

Regarding the kernel configuration required by real-time applications, the following configurations are necessary:

- **On-demand CPU scaling**: Using this configuration helps with the creation of long-latency events when the CPU is in a low-power consumption mode.
- **NOHZ**: This configurations disables the timer interrupt received by CPUs. With this option enabled, the latency spent on a CPU wake up is diminished.

To write an application, there are some things that need to be taken care of, such as making sure that the use of swap is disabled to diminish latencies caused by page faults. The use of global variables or arrays should be kept to a minimum. The 99 priority number is not configured to run an application, and other spin locks are not implemented instead, it uses priority inheritance futexes. Also avoid input/output operations and data sharing between applications.

For a device driver, the advice is a bit different. Previously, we mentioned that the interrupt handling for a real-time kernel is done in a thread context, but the hardware interrupt context can still play a role here. To recognize the hardware interrupt context from the interrupt handler, the `IRQF_NODELAY` flag can be used. If you use the `IRQF_NODELAY` context, make sure you avoid functions such as `wake_up()`, `up()`, or `complete()`.

Benchmarking

The Linux operating system was for a very long time seen as a GPOS, but in the last couple of years, some projects tried to change this by modifying the Linux kernel into a RTOS. One such project is the PREEMPT_RT patch, which was mentioned previously.

In this section of the chapter, I will discuss a series of tests that could be executed for both versions of the Linux OS with or without applying the PREEMPT_RT patches. I should mention that for those of you who are interested in some actual results, there are a number of papers available that try to investigate the latency effect of the PREEMPT_RT or its advantages or disadvantages. One such example is available at `http://www.versalogic.com/downloads/whitepapers/real-time_linux_benchmark.pdf`.

Before continuing further, I believe it is my duty to define a number of technical terms that are necessary to properly understand some information:

- **Interrupt latency**: This indicates the time that has elapsed since an interrupt was generated and until the execution has been started in the interrupt handler.
- **Scheduling latency**: This represents the time between the wake up signal of an event and a scheduler that has the opportunity to schedule a thread for it. It is also called a **dispatch latency**.
- **Worst-case latency**: This indicates the time that has passed since a demand was issued and until the response to that demand was received.
- **Context-switch**: This represents the switching of the CPU from one process or thread to another. It only occurs in the kernel mode.

The **LPPTest** is included in the PREEMPT_RT patch and it contains a Linux driver that only changes a bit value on a parallel port to identify the response time. Another driver responds to the change in a bit value and a user space application that measures the results. The files to look for are `drivers/char/lpptest.c` and `scripts/testlpp.c`. To perform this test, two machines are required: one to send the signal and the other one to receive and send the response. This requirement is stringent since the use of a loopback cable can mess with the measurements.

RealFeel is a test for interrupt processing. The program uses `/dev/rtc` to fire a periodic interrupt, measures the duration between one interrupt to another, and compares it with the expected value. At the end, it prints the variation from the expected value indefinitely so that the variations can be exported in a log file to process later.

Linux Real-Time Benchmarking Framework (**LRTB**) represents a set of scripts and drivers that are used to evaluate various performance counters for the Linux kernel with a real-time addition. It measures the load imposed by real-time patches and their ability to obtain a more deterministic response to interrupts.

For the benchmarking phase, programs such as `hackbench`, `lmbench`, or even the `Ingo Molnar dohell` script can be used. There are, of course, a number of other tools that can be used for both testing (`cyclictest`, `hourglass`, and so on) or benchmarking (`unixbench`, `cache-calibrator`, or any other stress test that takes real-time performances to their limit), but I will let the user test them and apply the ones that suit their needs best.

The PREEMPT_RT patch improves the preemptiveness of the Linux kernel, but this does not mean it is the best solution to use. The usefulness of PREEMPT_RT patch can differ if various aspects of the application domain changes. With regard to the PREEMPT_RT patch, it is ready to be used in a hard real-time system. One conclusion cannot be made, but I must admit that it can be considered hard real-time material if it is used in life sustaining or mission-critical systems. This is a decision for everybody to make, and for this testing is required. One opinion that supports this is from Steven Rostedt, a Linux kernel developer who is the maintainer of the stable version of the real-time Linux kernel patch for Red Hat. It is available at `http://www.linux.com/news/featured-blogs/200-libby-clark/710319-intro-to-real-time-linux-for-embedded-developers`.

> Some interesting information on this matter can be accessed at `http://elinux.org/Realtime_Testing_Best_Practices`.

Meta-realtime

The `meta-realtime` layer is an initiative maintained by Bruce Ashfield from WindRiver, which planned to create a place where real-time activities related to the Linux kernel or system development. It was created as the placeholder for PREEMPT_RT, SCHED_DEADLINE, POSIX real-time, and alternative paring of general purpose operating systems and real-time operating systems, whether this involved a user space RTOS, a hypervisor, or an AMP solution. Also, this is where system partitioning, CPU isolation, and other related applications s reside. Of course, none of this would be considered complete without some performance profiling and benchmarking applications available for the whole Linux operating system.

Although this layer description sounds really exciting at first, its content is really poor. It is only able to incorporate a number of testing tools, more accurately, two of them: `schedtool-dl` and `rt-app`, as well as extra scripts that try to remotely run `rt-app` on the target machine and gather the resulting data.

The first `schedtool-dl` application is a scheduler testing tool used for deadline scheduling. It appears from the need to change or make queries of the CPU-scheduling policies and even processes levels available under Linux. It can also be used to lock processes on various CPUs for SMP/NUMA systems, to avoid skipping in audio/video applications, and in general, to maintain a high level of interaction and responsiveness even under high loads.

> More information about the `schedtool-dl` application can be found at `https://github.com/jlelli/schedtool-dl`.

The next and last available application is `rt-app`, which is used as a test application for the simulation of real-time loads on a system. It does this by starting multiple threads at given periods of time. It offers support for SCHED_FIFO, SCHED_OTHER, SCHED_RR, SCHED_DEADLINE, as well as the **Adaptive Quality of Service Architecture** (**AQuoSA**) framework, which is an open source project that tries to offer adaptive **Quality of Service** (**QoS**) for the Linux kernel.

> More information about the `rt-app` application and the AQuoSa framework can be found at `https://github.com/scheduler-tools/rt-app` and `http://aquosa.sourceforge.net/`.

Besides the included packages, the layer also contains an image that incorporates them, but this is not nearly enough to make this layer one that contains substantial content. Although it does not contain a vast amount of information inside it, this layer has been presented in this chapter because it contains the starting point and offers a development point of view of all the information presented until now. Of course, a number of applications that should reside in this layer are already spread across multiple other layers, such as the `idlestat` package that is available in `meta-linaro`. However, this does not constitute the central point of this explanation. I only wanted to point out the most suitable place that can contain any real-time relate activities, and in my opinion, `meta-realtime` is this place.

Summary

In this chapter, you were given a short introduction to PREEMPT_RT and other alternative solutions for real-time problems of the Linux kernel. We also explored a number of tools and applications that can be used for related real-time activities. However, this presentation would not be complete without references made to the Yocto Project with regards not only to the recipes of the PREEMPT_RT Linux kernel, but also to `meta-realtime` layer applications. Developing an application suitable for a new context was also a concern, so this problem was tackled in the *Linux real-time applications* section. In the end, I hope that I was able to present a complete picture of this subject through links that were provided throughout the chapter to stir the curiosity of the reader.

In the next chapter, a short explanation of `meta-security` and `meta-selinux` layers will be given and a broader picture of the security requirements of the Linux ecosystem in general and the Yocto Project in particular, will be provided. Information regarding a number of tools and applications that try to secure our Linux systems will also be presented, but this is not all. Take a look at the next chapter; I am sure you will enjoy it.

11
Security

In this chapter, you will be presented with various security enhancements tools. Our first stop is the Linux kernel and here, there are two tools, SELinux and grsecurity, both of which are really interesting as well as necessary. Next, the Yocto Project's security-specific layers will also be explained. These include the meta-security and meta-selinux that contain an impressive number of tools and can be used to secure or audit various components of the Linux system. Since this subject is vast, I will also let you inspect various other solutions, both implemented in the Linux kernel but also externally. I hope you enjoy this chapter and that you find this information interesting and useful.

In any operating system, security is a really important concern both for the users and developers. It did not pass much time and developers have started to address these security problems in various methods. This resulted in a number of security methodologies and improvements for available operating systems. In this chapter, a number of security enhancement tools will be introduced along with some policies and verification routines that are defined to ensure that various components, such as the Linux kernel or the Yocto Project, are secure enough to be used. We will also take a look at how various threats or problems are handled as they appear during the course of this chapter.

SELinux and grsecurity are two noticeable security improvements made to the Linux kernel that try to enforce Linux. SELinux is a **Mandatory Access Control** (**MAC**) mechanism that provides identity and role-based access control as well as domain-type enforcement. The second option, grsecurity, is more similar to ACLs and is, in fact, more suitable for web servers and other systems that support remote connections. With regard to how security is implemented for Linux and how the Yocto Project handles this domain, these aspects will be presented in the next section. One thing I must admit is that security handling inside the Yocto Project is still a young project at the time of writing this chapter, but I am waiting with enthusiasm to see how the number of iterations will increase over time.

Security in Linux

At the core of every Linux system is the Linux kernel. Any malicious code that is able to damage or take control of a system also has repercussions that affect the Linux kernel. So, it only makes clear to users that having a secure kernel is also an important part of the equation. Fortunately, the Linux kernel is secure and has a number of security features and programs. The man behind all this is James Morris, the maintainer of the Linux kernel security subsystem. There is even a separate Linux repository for this that can be accessed at `http://git.kernel.org/?p=linux/kernel/git/jmorris/linux-security.git;a=summary`. Also, by inspecting `http://kernsec.org/wiki/index.php/Main_Page`, which is the main page of the Linux kernel security subsystem, you can see the exact projects that are managed inside this subsystem and maybe lend a hand to them if you're interested.

There is also a workgroup that provides security enhancements and verifications to the Linux kernel to make sure that it is secure and also to maintain a certain level of trust in the security of the Linux ecosystem. Their activities include, but of course, are not limited to verification and testing of critical subsystems for various vulnerabilities or the development of tools to assist in the security Linux kernel. The workgroup also consists of guidance and maintenance of security subsystems or security improvements added to various projects or build tools.

All the other Linux software components have their own security teams. Of course, there are some that do not have these teams well defined, or have some internal rules related to this subject, but they are still aware of security threats that occur around their components and try to repair these vulnerabilities. The Yocto Project tries to help with these problems and in some ways unifies these software components. I hope that some improvements are made over the years in this area.

SELinux

SELinux is a security enhancement for the Linux kernel, and is developed by the National Security Agency's office of Information Assurance. It has a policy-based architecture and is one of the Linux security modules that is built on the interface of **Linux Security Modules** (**LSM**) that aims at military-level security.

Currently, it is shipped with a large number of distributions, including the most well known and often used ones, such as Debian, SuSe, Fedora, Red Hat, and Gentoo. It is based on MAC on which administrators can control all interactions with the user space components of a system. It uses the concept of least privileges: here, by default, a user and application have no rights to access the system resources since all of them are granted by an administrator entity. This makes up the part of the system security policies and its emphasis is shown in the following figure:

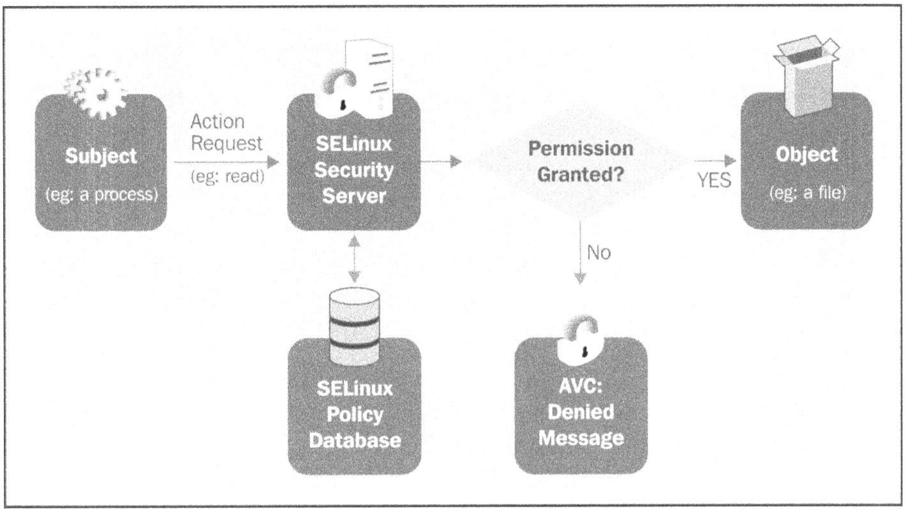

The basic functionalities inside SELinux are sandboxed with the help of the implementation of MAC. Inside the sandbox, each application is allowed to perform only the task it was designed to execute as defined in the security policies. Of course, standard Linux permissions are still available for the system and they will be consulted before the policies when access attempts are required. If no permissions are available, SELinux will not be able to influence the system in any way. However, if the permission rights allow access, then the SELinux policies should be consulted to offer the final verdict on whether access is permitted or denied.

In the context of SELinux, access decisions are made based on the security context of the subject. This may very well be a process associated with a specific user context that is compared with the actual attempted action (such as a file read action), and the security context of the available object, which can be a file.

Before moving on, we will see how the SELinux support can be enabled on a Ubuntu machine. I will first present some basic concepts related to SELinux:

- **Users**: In the SELinux context, the user is not the same as the one available in the UNIX context. The major difference between them is that, in the SELinux context, the user does not change during a user session and there is a possibility for more UNIX users to operate in the same SELinux user context. However, there is also a possibility of operating in a 1:1 user mapping, such as the Linux root user and the SELinux root user. Generally, the SELinux users have the `_u` suffix added to their naming.
- **Roles**: A SELinux user can have one or multiple roles. The meaning of a role is defined in the policies. An object usually has the `object_r` role and the role is generally suffixed with the `_r` string.

- **Types**: It's the primary method applied to take authorization decisions. It can also be referred to as a domain and is generally suffixed with `_t`.
- **Contexts**: Each process and object has its context. It is, in fact, an attribute that determines whether access should be allowed between an object and process. A SELinux context is expressed as three required fields and as an optional one as well, such as `user:role:type:range`. The first three fields represent the SELinux user, role, and the type. The last one represents the range of MLS and it will be presented shortly. More information about MLS can be gathered at `http://web.mit.edu/rhel-doc/5/RHEL-5-manual/Deployment_Guide-en-US/sec-mls-ov.html`.
- **Object Classes**: An SELinux object class represents the category of objects available. Categories, such as `dir` for directories and `file` for files, also have a set of permissions associated with them.
- **Rules**: These are the security mechanisms of SELinux. They are used as a type of enforcement and are specified using the type of the object and process. The rules usually state if a type is allowed to perform various actions.

As mentioned already, the SELinux is so well known and appreciated that it was included in most of the available Linux distributions. Its success is also demonstrated through the fact that a huge number of books were written on this subject. For more information regarding it, refer to `http://www.amazon.com/s/ref=nb_ss_gw/102-2417346-0244921?url=search-alias%3Daps&field-keywords=SELinux&Go.x=12&Go.y=8&Go=Go`. Having said this, let's take a look at the steps required to install SELinux on a Ubuntu host machine. The first step refers to the SELinux package installation:

```
sudo apt-get install selinux
```

With the package installed, the SELinux mode needs to be changed from disabled (the mode in which the SELinux policy is not enforced or logged) to one of the other two available options:

- `Enforcing`: This is most useful in a production system:

  ```
  sudo sed -i 's/SELINUX=.*/SELINUX=enforcing/' /etc/selinux/config
  ```

- `Permissive`: In this mode, policies are not enforced. However, any denials are logged and it is mostly used in debugging activities and when new policies are developed:

  ```
  sudo sed -i 's/SELINUX=.*/SELINUX=permissive/' /etc/selinux/config
  ```

With the configuration implemented, the system needs to reboot, to make sure that the system files are labeled accordingly.

More information about SELinux is also available in the Yocto Project. There is an entire layer dedicated to SELinux support. Also, for more information regarding this tool, you are encouraged to read one of the books dedicated to this matter. If you dislike this method, then there are alternative manuals with information related to SELinux, available inside various distributions, such as Fedora (`https://docs.fedoraproject.org/en-US/Fedora/19/html/Security_Guide/ch09.html`), Red Hat (`https://access.redhat.com/documentation/en-US/Red_Hat_Enterprise_Linux/4/html/SELinux_Guide/index.html`), and so on.

Grsecurity

Grsecurity is a suite of patches released under the GNU General Public License, available for the Linux kernel and will help with the security enhancements for Linux. This suite of patches offers four main benefits:

- Configuration-free operations
- Protection against a large variety of address space change bugs
- It includes an access control list system and a number of auditing systems that are quite comprehensive to meet all sorts of demands
- It is able to interact with multiple operating systems and processor architectures

The grsecurity software is free and its development began in 2001, by first porting a number of security enhancing patches from the Openwall Project. It was first released for the 2.4.1 Linux kernel version and since then, development has continued. Over time, it included a PaX bundle of patches that offered the possibility of protecting memory pages. This is done by using a least-privilege approach, which implies that for the execution of a program, no more than the necessary actions should be taken with the help of extra or fewer steps.

> If you're in interested in finding more about PaX, you can access `http://en.wikipedia.org/wiki/PaX` and `https://pax.grsecurity.net/`.

Grsecurity has a number of features that are suitable mostly for web servers or servers that accept shell access from untrusted users. One of the major feature is the **Role-based Access Control** (**RBAC**), which is the alternative to the already available UNIX **Discretionary Access Control** (**DAC**), or even the latter, mandatory access control (MAC) that is offered by Smack or SELinux. The aim of RBAC is to offer a least privilege system in which the processes and users only have the minimum required privileges needed for archiving their tasks. One other feature that grsecurity has is related to the hardening of the `chroot()` system call to make sure that privilege escalation is eliminated. In addition to this, there are a number of miscellaneous features, such as auditing and `/proc` restrictions.

I took the liberty of keeping the features of the grsecurity defined in groups, as presented on the grsecurity website. They have been presented in the chapter because I think that knowing its features will help users and developers make the right decision when a security solution is required for their activities. A list with all the grsecurity features is mentioned as follows:

- Memory corruption defences:
    - Automatic response to brute force exploits
    - Hardened BPF JIT against spray attacks
    - Hardened userland memory permission
    - Random padding between thread stacks
    - Preventing direct userland access by a kernel
    - Industry leading ASLR
    - Bound checking kernel copies to/from a userland
- Filesystem Hardening:
    - Chroot hardening
    - Eliminating side-channel attacks against admin terminals
    - Preventing users from tricking Apache into accessing other user files
    - Hiding the processes of other users from unprivileged users
    - Providing trusted path execution
- Miscellaneous protections:
    - Preventing process snooping based on ptrace
    - Preventing the dumping of unreadable binaries

  - Preventing attackers from autoloading vulnerable kernel modules
  - Denying access to overly permissive IPC objects
  - Enforcing consistent multithreaded privileges

- RBAC:
  - Intuitive design
  - Automatic full system policy learning
  - Automated policy analysis
  - Human-readable policies and logs
  - Stackable with LSM
  - Unconventional features

- GCC plugins:
  - Preventing integer overflows in size arguments
  - Preventing the leakage of stack data from previous syscalls
  - Adding entropy during early boot and runtime
  - Randomizing kernel structure layout
  - Making read-only sensitive kernel structures
  - Ensuring all kernel function pointers point to the kernel

Keeping the features of grsecurity in mind, we can now move towards the installation phase of grsecurity and its administrator called `gradm`.

The first thing that needs to be done is to get the corresponding packages and patches. As shown in the following command lines, the kernel version for which grsecurity is enabled is `3.14.19`:

```
wget https://www.kernel.org/pub/linux/kernel/v3.x/linux-3.14.19.tar.gz
wget https://www.kernel.org/pub/linux/kernel/v3.x/linux-3.14.19.tar.sign
wget http://grsecurity.net/stable/gradm-3.1-201502222102.tar.gz
wget http://grsecurity.net/stable/gradm-3.1-201502222102.tar.gz.sig
wget http://grsecurity.net/stable/grsecurity-3.1-3.14.36-201503182218.
patch
wget http://grsecurity.net/stable/grsecurity-3.1-3.14.36-201503182218.
patch.sig
```

After the packages are available, their signature needs to be checked. The signature check process for the Linux kernel is big and different from other systems, as follows:

```
wget http://grsecurity.net/spender-gpg-key.asc
sudo gpg --import spender-gpg-key.asc
sudo gpg --verify gradm-3.1-201502222102.tar.gz.sig
sudo gpg --verify grsecurity-3.1-3.14.35-201503092203.patch.sig
gzip -d linux-3.14.19.tar.gz
sudo gpg --verify linux-3.14.19.tar.sign
```

The first time this command is called, the signature is not verified, but the ID field is made available for later use. It is used to identify the public key from the PGP keyserver:

```
gpg: Signature made Mi 17 sep 2014 20:20:53 +0300 EEST using RSA key ID
6092693E
sudo gpg --keyserver hkp://keys.gnupg.net --recv-keys 6092693E
sudo gpg --verify linux-3.14.19.tar.sign
```

After all the packages are available and properly verified, we can now move to the kernel configuration phase. The first step is the patching process, which is done with the grsecurity patch, but this requires access to the Linux kernel source code first:

```
tar xf linux-3.14.19.tar
cd linux-3.14.19/
patch -p1 < ../grsecurity-3.1-3.14.35-201503092203.patch
```

In the patching process, `include/linux/compiler-gcc5.h` is missing from the source code, so this part of the patch requires skipping. However, after this, the patching process is finished without problems. With this step completed, the configuration phase can continue. There are generic configurations that should work without any extra modifications, but for each distribution there would always be some specific configuration available. To go through them and make sure that each one of them matches with your hardware, the following command can be used:

```
make menuconfig
```

If you are calling it for the first time, the preceding command has a warning message that will prompt you with the following:

```
HOSTCC  scripts/basic/fixdep
HOSTCC  scripts/kconfig/conf.o
 *** Unable to find the ncurses libraries or the
 *** required header files.
```

```
 *** 'make menuconfig' requires the ncurses libraries.
 ***
 *** Install ncurses (ncurses-devel) and try again.
 ***
make[1]: *** [scripts/kconfig/dochecklxdialog] Error 1
make: *** [menuconfig] Error 2
```

It can be solved by installing the `libncurses5-dev` package, using the following command:

```
sudo apt-get install libncurses5-dev
```

With these problems fixed, the configuration process can continue. The `grsecurity` option is available inside the security option subsection, as depicted in the following screenshot:

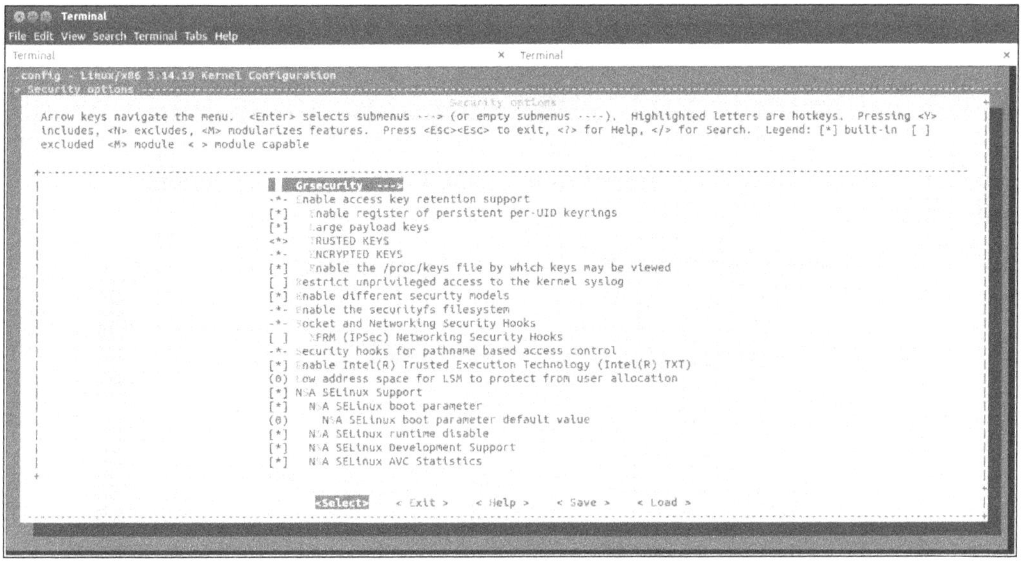

Inside the `grsecurity` option, there are two more submenu options. More details about this can be seen in the following screenshot:

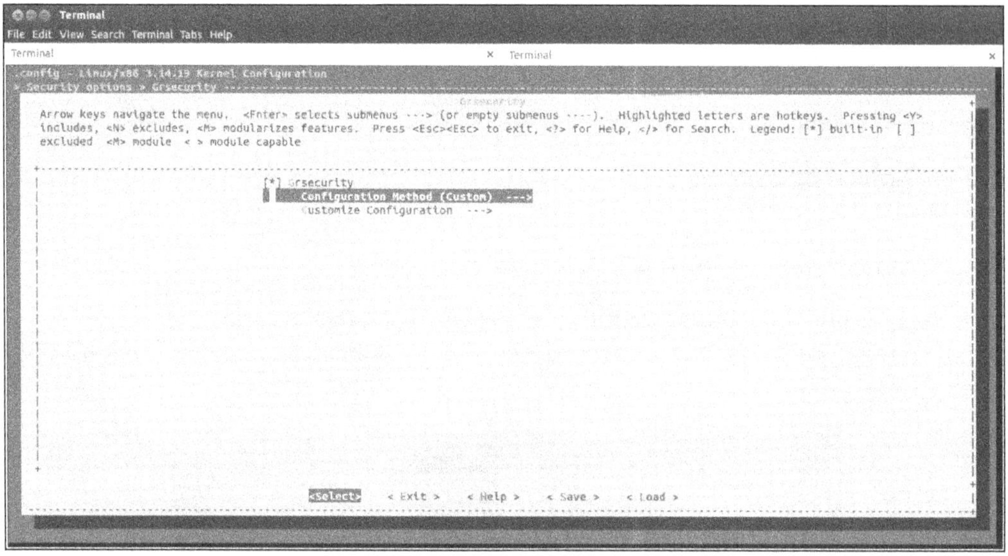

The first option refers to the configuration method, which can be **Custom** or **Automatic**:

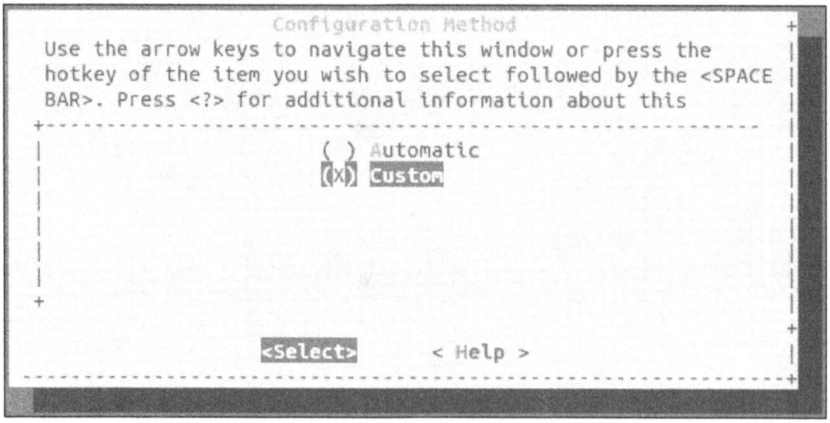

The second option refers to the actual available configuration options:

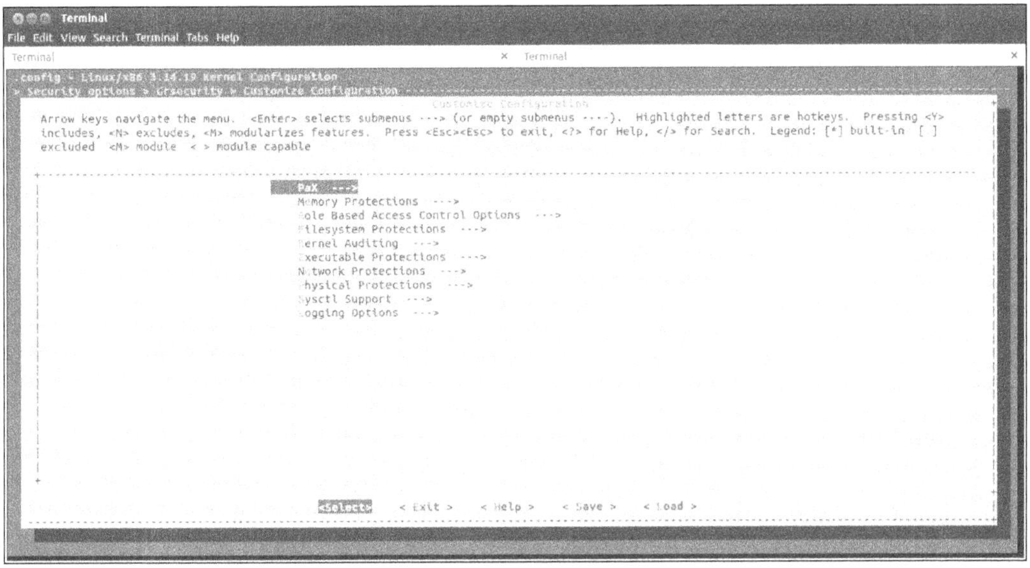

> More information about Grsecurity and the PaX configuration options can be found at `http://en.wikibooks.org/wiki/Grsecurity/Appendix/Grsecurity_and_PaX_Configuration_Options`.

One piece of advice I would like to offer is that first enable the **Automatic** configuration method and then proceed with the Custom configuration to fine tune the Grsecurity and PaX settings if necessary. Another tip would be to enable the **Grsecurity | Customize Configuration | Sysctl Support** option because it offers the possibility of changing the grsecurity options without compiling the kernel again. Of course, if the **Automatic** configuration method is selected, this option is enabled by default. The auditing option produces a big number of logs, so to prevent log flooding, make sure that **Grsecurity | Customize Configuration | Logging Options** is also enabled.

The next tool from the grsecurity family is the `gradm` administrator, which is a powerful parser for ACLs and also optimizes them. To make sure that this utility can be installed, the installation process requires that the host operating machine for `gradm` offers grsecurity support or else the compilation process will fail. There are also a number of other packages that are required before installing `gradm`: `lex`, `flex`, `byacc`, `bison`, and even `pam`, if necessary.

Once all the dependencies are met, the installation process can start. One last bit of information I'd like to give you is that if the distribution that you use comes with a kernel that has support for grsecurity patches, then you may first want to check it because the patches can also come with the `gradm` utility pre-installed.

> More information about the Grsecurity administration can be found at the folllowing links:
>
> `http://en.wikibooks.org/wiki/Grsecurity/The_Administration_Utility`
>
> `http://en.wikibooks.org/wiki/Grsecurity/Additional_Utilities`
>
> `http://en.wikibooks.org/wiki/Grsecurity/Runtime_Configuration`

Inside the Yocto layers, there is support for the `gradm` recipe that is inside the `meta-oe` layer. It is available at `recipes-support/gradm/gradm_3.0.bb` on the master branch. Also, a grsecurity kernel configuration is available on the master branch for the `meta-accel` layer; the exact location for the configuration fragment is `recipes-kernel/linux/linux-yocto-iio/grsec.cfg`. For anyone interested in learning about the concrete grsecurity support provided in Yocto, I believe the road is clear for you to start working on such a thing. One piece of advice, though, you should first ask the Yocto Project community whether anyone has started doing this already.

Security for the Yocto Project

In the Yocto Project, the security question is is still young. Since this project was announced less than five years ago, it is only normal that discussions about security started in the last year or so. There is, of course, a specialized mailing list for the security team and it includes a large number of individuals from various companies, but their working procedure is not quite finished since it's currently in state of work in progress.

The activities that are mainly realized by the members of the security team consist of being aware of the latest and most dangerous security threats and making sure that they find the fixes, even if it includes fixing themselves and applying the changes inside Yocto's available layers.

For the time being, the most time consuming of the security activity revolves around the Poky reference system, but there are also initiatives taken by various companies to try to push a series of patches toward various BSP maintainer layers or other third-party layers. For those of you interested, the mailing list of security-related discussions is `yocto-security@yoctoproject.org`. Also, until the group is formed, they can be found in the `#yocto` IRC available at `http://webchat.freenode.net/?channels=#yocto`, or even at the Yocto technical team meeting that takes place once every two weeks.

> More information about the security team can be found on their Wiki page. I encourage everyone interested in this subject to visit it at least once at `https://wiki.yoctoproject.org/wiki/Security`.

Meta-security and meta-selinux

In this section, the layer initiatives related to the security tools of Linux are presented. In this chapter, two layers that provide both security and hardening tools are available for the Linux kernel and its libraries. Their purpose is to simplify mode embedded devices, make sure that they're secure, and maybe offer the security level similar to a desktop.

Since embedded devices have become increasingly competent and powerful, concerns related to security can only be natural. The Yocto Project's initiative layers, here, I am referring to meta-security and meta-selinux, take another step in simplifying the process to ensure secure, hardened, and protected Linux systems. Together, with the detect and fix vulnerability system, they are implemented inside the security team, and help with the ideal of having the same level of security on embedded devices as desktops, along with taking this idea a step further. Having said this, let's proceed to the actual explanation of layers.

Meta-security

Inside the meta-security layer, there are tools that are used to secure, harden, and protect embedded devices that may offer exterior access to various entities. If the device is connected to the Internet or is susceptible to any form of attack or hijacking, then the meta-security layer may be the first stop for you. With this layer and the meta-selinux layer, the Yocto Project tries to provide security levels that are suitable for most of the community or embedded user devices. Of course, enhancing the support for various tools or adding new ones is not forbidden, so do not hesitate and add your contribution for enhancing tools if you feel the need or urge to do so. Any new commit or committer is welcome - our community is really friendly.

As you're already used to, the tools provided are open source packages that are suitable for embedded devices. Inside the meta-security layer a number of them are available, each one trying to offer not only system hardening, but also security checking, security, port scanning, and other useful features that target various levels of security. The following packages are included:

- Bastille
- Redhat-security
- Pax-utils
- Buck-security
- Libseccomp
- Ckecksecurity
- Nikto
- Nmap
- Clamav
- Isic
- Samhain
- Suricata
- Tripwire

Besides these packages, there are a number of libraries and also **TOMOYO**, a kernel security module for a MAC implementation, which is also very useful as a system analysis tool. It was first released in March 2003, and was sponsored by NTT Data Corporation, Japan, until March 2012.

TOMOYO's main focus is the system behavior. For this, every process involved in the creation of the system declares its behavior and the required resources necessary to achieve a purpose. It consists of two components: one kernel component, linux-ccs, and a user space one, ccs-tools; both are required for proper functionality. TOMOYO tries to provide a MAC implementation that is both practical and easy to use. Finally, it likes to let a system be usable for a majority of users, being perfect for average users and system administrators. It is different from SELinux because it has an automatic policy configuration mechanism offered by the **LEARNING mode**; also, its policy language is very easy to grasp.

After protection is enabled, TOMOYO Linux acts as a watchdog that restricts the processes from using more than what they had declared initially. Its main features include the following:

- System analysis
- Tools that offer aid in the process of policy generation
- Simple to use and understand syntax
- Easy to use
- Increased security of the system through the MAC implementation
- Contains a small number of dependencies (the embedded GNU C library, libncurses, and GNU readline library)
- No modification of the already available binaries inside the root filesystem
- Since the version 2.6.30, the Linux kernel merged with the TOMOYO kernel module, making only the enabling of the module in the configuration phase necessary. It started as a patch that provided MAC support, and the porting inside a mainline kernel required a redesign using hooks into the **LSM** (**Linux Security Modules**), which also includes SELinux, AppArmor, and SMACK. However, since more hooks would be necessary for the integration of the remaining MAC functionalities, there are two other parallel development lines for the project, as follows:
- **TOMOYO Linux 1.x**: This is the original code version:
    - It uses nonstandard specific hooks
    - It offers all the MAC features
    - It is released as a patch for the kernel since it does not depend on LSM
    - Its latest version is 1.7.1

- **TOMOYO Linux 2.x**: This is the mainline source code version:
    - It uses standard LSM hooks
    - It contains a fewer subset of features
    - It is an integral component of the 2.6.30 Linux kernel version
    - The latest version is 2.5.0 and offers support for Linux kernel version 3.2
- **AKARI and TOMOYO 1.x fork version**:
    - It also uses standard LSM hooks
    - It is characterized by having a fewer set of features compared to TOMOYO 1.x but not with TOMOYO 2.x
    - It is released as LSM; no recompilation of the kernel is necessary

> For those of you interested in a comparison between the three versions, refer to `http://akari.sourceforge.jp/comparison.html.en`.

The next package is `samhain`, a system integrity monitoring and reporting tool used by system administrators that suspect changes or activities on their systems. Its operation is based on a client/server environment and is able to monitor multiple hosts while providing a centralized maintenance and logging system. Besides the already advertised functionalities, it is also able to provide port monitoring, detection of rogue SUID, rootkit detection, and also hidden processes that add to the fact that it offers support for multiple platforms; it is a really interesting tool to have.

The next element here falls in the same category as `samhain` and it is called `tripwire`. It is another integrity tool, but this one tries to detect changes for filesystem objects and works as a host intrusion detection system. Information is stored in a database after each file scan and the results are compared with the already available results. Any changes that are made are reported back to the user.

Bastille is a hardening program used to secure the environment and system for a Unix host. It uses rules to accomplish its goals and does this by first calling the `bastille -c` command that makes you pass through a long list of questions. After they are answered, a configuration file is created and executed and this symbolizes the fact that your operating system is now hardened according to your needs. If a configuration file is already available on the system by calling `bastille -b`, it can be set up for system hardening.

The next tool is `redhat-security`, which is a collection of scripts used for various problems related to security scanning. The following are a collection of the tools needed to run a `redhat-security` script to simply invoke one script in the terminal:

- `find-chroot.sh`: This tool scans the whole system for ELF files that call `chroot` and also include a call to `chdir`. The programs that fail this test do not contain `cwd` inside `chroot` and they are not protected and safe to use.
- `find-chroot-py.sh`: This tool is similar to the preceding point, but only tests Python scripts.
- `rpm-chksec.sh`: This tool takes an rpm file and checks its content for its compiling flags. It does this for security reasons. If the results are green, then everything is OK, yellow means passable, and red requires the user's attention.
- `find-nodrop-groups.sh`: This tool scans the whole system for programs that change the UID or GID without calling the `setgroups` and `initgroups` calls.
- `rpm-drop-groups.sh`: This tool scans the whole system similar to the preceding tool, but this one uses the available RPM files.
- `find-execstack.sh`: This tool scans the whole system for ELF files that mark the stack as executable. It is used to identify programs that are susceptible to stack buffer overflow.
- `find-sh4errors.sh`: This tool scans the whole system for shell scripts and checks their correctness by using the `sh -n` command.
- `find-hidden-exec.sh`: This tool scans the system for hidden executables and reports the results back to the user for investigation.
- `selinux-ls-unconfined.sh`: This tool is used to scan all the running processes and look for the `initrc_t` label or `inetd` on them (this means that they are daemons that are running unconfined). The problems should be reported as SELinux policy problems.
- `selinux-check-devides.sh`: This tool checks all the available devices too see if they are correctly labelled. It is also marked as a SELinux policy problem that should be solved.
- `find-elf4tmp.sh`: This tool scans the whole system and checks whether the used `tmp` files are well known, are created with `mktemp`, or have some obscure format.

- `find-sh3tm.sh`: This tool also scans the filesystem, although only inside `/tmp` and looks for ELF files there. When it finds them, it checks if any of the random name generators function was called on them by investigating the symbol table. If the result is affirmative, it will output the string value.
- `lib-bin-check.sh`: This tool checks the packages of libraries and their the package they contain. It is based on the idea that the fewer binaries available on a system, the more secure it is.

Another tool that is included is `pax-utils`. It also includes a number of scripts that scan ELF binaries mostly for consistency, but this is not all. Take a look at some of them:

- `scanelf`: This tool is used to find pre-information about the ELF structure of the binary
- `dumpelf`: This tool is a user space utility used to dump the internal ELF structure in equivalent C structures for debugging or reference purposes
- `pspax`: This tool is used to scan `/proc` and list the various ELF types available and their corresponding PaX flags, attributes, and filenames

Now, the next tool that will be presented is a security scanner that is different from the already presented bastille. Similar to the `redhat-security` command, this one also executes a number of scripts and can be configured to confirm the user's needs. It is suitable for Debian and Ubuntu users, and before calling the buck-security executable, there are a few configurations that need to be done. Use `export GPG_TTY=`tty`` to make sure that all the functionalities of the buck-security are enabled and before executing the tool, check inside the `conf/buck-security.conf` configuration file to check that your needs are fulfilled.

Suricata is a high-performance IDS/IPS and Security Monitoring engine for the network. It is owned and maintained by **OISF** (**Open Information Security Foundation**) and its supporters. It uses the **HTP** library that is a very powerful HTTP parser and normalizer and offers some nice features, such as protocol identification, MD5 checksum, file identification, and even extraction.

ISIC, on the other hand, is what its name suggests, an IP Stack Integrity Checker. It is, in fact, a suite of utilities for IP Stack ad other stacks, such as TCP, ICMP, UDP, and others that test either the firewall, or the protocol itself.

For any web server, **nikto** is the tool to execute on your device. It is a scanner used to run a suite of tests that identifies dangerous CGI1s or other files. It also presents an outdated version for more than 1250 servers and various lists of vulnerabilities for each version.

Next on the list is the **libseccomp** library that provides an easy-to-use abstract interface to the Linux kernel, `syscall`, filtering a mechanism called `seccomp`. It does this by abstracting the BPF `syscall` filter language and presenting it a more user-friendly format for application developers in general.

Checksecurity is the next package on the line which uses a collection of shell scripts and other plugins for testing various changes to `setuid` programs. Using the filter defined in `/etc/checksecurity.conf`, it scans the mounted filesystems and compares the already available list of `setuid` programs to the newly scanned ones and prints the changes for the user to see. It also offers information about these filesystems that were mounted unsecure.

ClamAV is an antivirus for Unix that operates from the command line. It is a very good engine for tracking trojans, malware, viruses, and detection of other malicious threats. It can do a large variety of things from e-mail scanning to web scanning and end-point security. It also has a very versatile and scalable daemon, command-line scanner, and database interaction tool.

The last on the list is **Network Mapper** (**nmap**). It is the most well known and is used for security auditing as well as a network discovery tool by network and system administrators. It is used to manage service upgrade schedules, network inventory, monitoring various services, or even host uptime.

These are the tools supported and offered inside the meta-security layer. I took the liberty of presenting most of them in a succinct manner with the purpose of making them available to you in an easy fashion. It is my opinion that for security problems, one should not overcomplicate things and only keep the solutions that fit your needs best. By presenting a large palette of tools and software components, I tried to do two things: make a larger number of tools available for the general public and also help you make a decision with regard to the tools that might help you in your quest to offer and even maintain a secure system. Of course, curiosity is encouraged, so make sure that you check out any other tools that might help you on your quest to find out more about security, and why they should not be integrated inside the meta-security layer.

Meta-selinux

The other available security layer is represented by the meta-selinux layer. This one is different from meta-security because it only offers support for one tool, but as mentioned in the preceding tool, it is so big and vast that it spreads its wings across the whole system.

The layer's purpose is to enable the support for SELinux and offer it through Poky to anyone in the Yocto Project community for use if required. As mentioned previously, since it influences the whole Linux system, most of the work on this layer is done inside the bbappend files. I hope you enjoy working with the functionalities available inside this layer and maybe even contribute to it if you see fit.

This layer not only contains a number of impressive bbappend files, but also offers a list of packages that could be used not only as SELinux extensions. These packages can be used also for other self-contained purposes too. The available packages inside the meta-selinx layer are as follows:

- audit
- libcap-ng
- setools
- swig
- ustr

I will start the introduction of this layer with the **audit** userspace tool, which as the name suggests, is a tool that can be used for auditing, more specifically for kernel auditing. It uses a number of utilities and libraries to search and store recorded data. The data is generated through an audit subsystem available inside the Linux kernel. It is designed to work as a standalone component, but it cannot offer **Common Criteria** (CC) or **FIPS 140-2** functionalities without a second security component being available.

The next element on the list is **libcap-ng**, an alternative library with simplified POSIX capabilities that can be compared to the traditional libcap solution. It offers utilities that analyze running applications and print out their capabilities, or if they have an open ended bounding set. For an open bounding set that lacks the `securebit`, `NOROOT` flag will permit only by using an `execve()` call to retain full capabilities for applications that retain the `0` UID. By using the libcap-ng libraries, these applications that have the most privileges, are very easy to spot and deal with tools. The interaction and their detection is done with other tools, such as **netcap**, **pscap**, or **filecap**.

SETools is a policy analysis tool. It is in fact, an extension of SELinux and contains a collection of libraries, graphical tools, and command-lines that try simply analyze the the SELinux policies. The primary tools that this open source project are as follows:

- `apol`: This is a tool used to analyze SELinux policies
- `sediff`: This acts as a semantic differentiator between SELinux policies
- `seaudit`: This is a tool used to analyze audit messages for SELinux
- `seaudit-report`: This is used to generate a highly customizable audit report based on available audit logs
- `sechecker`: This is a command-line tool that is engaged in modular checks of SELinux policies
- `secmds`: This is another command-line tool that is used to reach and analyze SELinux policies

Next is **SWIG** (**Simplified Wrapper and Interface Generator**), a software development tool used with a variety of target languages to create a high-level programming environment, user interfacing, and anything else that is necessary. It is usually used for fast testing or prototyping because it generates the glue that a target language can call inside the C or C++ code.

The last component to be presented is a micro string API for a C language called **ustr**, which has the benefit of how overheads compared to available APIs. It is very easy to use in the C code as it only includes a header file and is ready for usage. Its overhead over `strdup()` for strings varies from 85.45 for 1-9 byte strings to 23.85 for 1-198 byte strings. For a simpler example, if an 8 byte storage ustr uses 2 bytes, the `strdup()` function uses 3 bytes.

This is where other tools and libraries are available alongside the SELinux functionality, although some of them can be used as separate components or in tandem with other available software components that were presented here. This would add more value to the SELinux product, so it only seems fair to find them in the same place.

For those of you interested in obtaining a SELinux enhance distribution, you could choose to use one of the two available images in the meta-selinux layer: `core-image-selinux-minimal.bb` or `core-image-selinux.bb`. The alternative would be to incorporate one of the available SELinux-specific defined package groups, `packagegroup-selinux-minimal` or `packagegroup-core-selinux`, into a newly defined image according to the needs of a developer. After this choice is made and the configuration is done accordingly, the only thing remaining would be to call `bitbake` for the chosen image and at the end of the build process, a custom Linux distribution will reveal itself with SELinux support enabled and can be tweaked some more if necessary.

Summary

In this chapter, you were presented with information about both kernel-specific security projects as well as external projects. Most of these were presented in a bad manner. You were also given information related to how various security subsystems and subgroups are keeping pace with various security threats and security project implementations.

In the next chapter, we will move on to another interesting subject. Here, I am referring to the virtualization area. You will find more about the meta-virtualization aspect later along with various virtualization implementations, such as KVM, which has gathered a huge track over the last few years and has established itself as a standard. I will let the other elements, which will be presented in the next chapter, be a secret. Let's now further explore the content of this book.

12
Virtualization

In this chapter, you will be presented with information about various concepts that appeared in the Linux virtualization section. As some of you might know, this subject is quite vast and selecting only a few components to be explained is also a challenge. I hope my decision would please most of you interested in this area. The information available in this chapter might not fit everyone's need. For this purpose, I have attached multiple links for more detailed descriptions and documentation. As always, I encourage you to start reading and finding out more, if necessary. I am aware that I cannot put all the necessary information in only a few words.

In any Linux environment today, Linux virtualization is not a new thing. It has been available for more than ten years and has advanced in a really quick and interesting manner. The question now does not revolve around virtualization as a solution for me, but more about what virtualization solutions to deploy and what to virtualize.

There are, of course, scenarios in which virtualization is not a solution. In embedded Linux, there are a large category of domains for which virtualization does not apply, mostly because some workloads are a better fit on top of hardware. However, for others that do not have these kind of requirements, there are quite a few advantages to using virtualization. More information about the various virtualization strategies, cloud computing, and other related topics will be discussed in this chapter, so let's have a look.

Linux virtualization

The first benefit everyone sees when looking at virtualization is the increase in server utilization and the decrease in energy costs. Using virtualization, the workloads available on a server are maximized, which is very different from scenarios where hardware uses only a fraction of the computing power. It can reduce the complexity of interaction with various environments and it also offers an easier-to-use management system. Today, working with a large number of virtual machines is not as complicated as interaction with a few of them because of the scalability most tools offer. Also, the time of deployment has really decreased. In a matter of minutes, you can deconfigure and deploy an operating system template or create a virtual environment for a virtual appliance deploy.

One other benefit virtualization brings is flexibility. When a workload is just too big for allocated resources, it can be easily duplicated or moved on another environment that suit its needs better on the same hardware or on a more potent server. For a cloud-based solution regarding this problem, the sky is the limit here. The limit may be imposed by the cloud type on the basis of whether there are tools available for a host operating system.

Over time, Linux was able to provide a number of great choices for every need and organization. Whether your task involves server consolidation in an enterprise data centre, or improving a small nonprofit infrastructure, Linux should have a virtualization platform for your needs. You simply need to figure out where and which project you should chose.

Virtualization is extensive, mainly because it contains a broad range of technologies, and also since large portions of the terms are not well defined. In this chapter, you will be presented with only components related to the Yocto Project and also to a new initiative that I personally am interested in. This initiative tries to make **Network Function Virtualization** (**NFV**) and **Software-Defined Networking** (**SDN**) a reality and is called **Open Platform for NFV** (**OPNFV**). It will be explained here briefly.

SDN and NFV

I have decided to start with this topic because I believe it is really important that all the research done in this area is starting to get traction with a number of open source initiatives from all sorts of areas and industries. Those two concepts are not new. They have been around for 20 years since they were first described, but the last few years have made possible it for them to resurface as real and very possible implementations. The focus of this section will be on the *NFV* section since it has received the most amount of attention, and also contains various implementation proposals.

NFV

NFV is a network architecture concept used to virtualize entire categories of network node functions into blocks that can be interconnected to create communication services. It is different from known virtualization techniques. It uses **Virtual Network Functions** (**VNF**) that can be contained in one or more virtual machines, which execute different processes and software components available on servers, switches, or even a cloud infrastructure. A couple of examples include virtualized load balancers, intrusion detected devices, firewalls, and so on.

The development product cycles in the telecommunication industry were very rigorous and long due to the fact that the various standards and protocols took a long time until adherence and quality meetings. This made it possible for fast moving organizations to become competitors and made them change their approach.

In 2013, an industry specification group published a white paper on software-defined networks and OpenFlow. The group was part of **European Telecommunications Standards Institute** (**ETSI**) and was called Network Functions Virtualisation. After this white paper was published, more in-depth research papers were published, explaining things ranging from terminology definitions to various use cases with references to vendors that could consider using NFV implementations.

ETSI NFV

The ETSI NFV workgroup has appeared useful for the telecommunication industry to create more agile cycles of development and also make it able to respond in time to any demands from dynamic and fast changing environments. SDN and NFV are two complementary concepts that are key enabling technologies in this regard and also contain the main ingredients of the technology that are developed by both telecom and IT industries.

The NFV framework consist of six components:

- **NFV Infrastructure** (**NFVI**): It is required to offer support to a variety of use cases and applications. It comprises of the totality of software and hardware components that create the environment for which VNF is deployed. It is a multitenant infrastructure that is responsible for the leveraging of multiple standard virtualization technologies use cases at the same time. It is described in the following **NFV Industry Specification Groups** (**NFV ISG**) documents:
    - NFV Infrastructure Overview
    - NFV Compute

- NFV Hypervisor Domain
- NFV Infrastructure Network Domain

The following image presents a visual graph of various use cases and fields of application for the NFV Infrastructure.

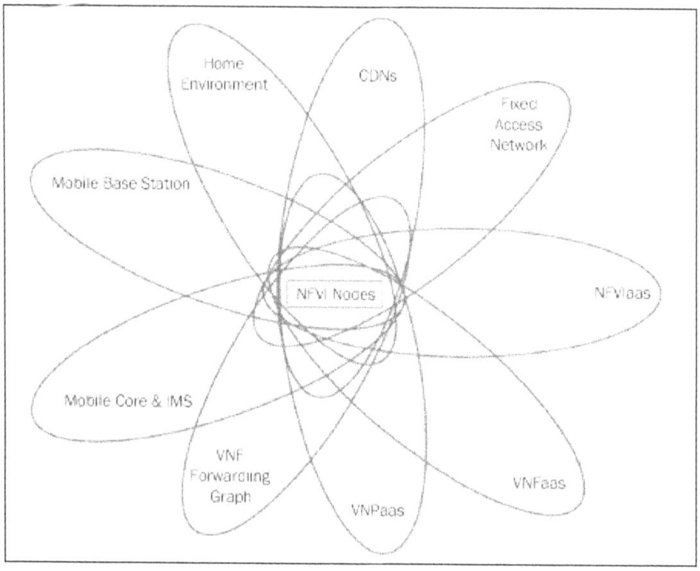

- **NFV Management and Orchestration (MANO)**: It is the component responsible for the decoupling of the compute, networking, and storing components from the software implementation with the help of a virtualization layer. It requires the management of new elements and the orchestration of new dependencies between them, which require certain standards of interoperability and a certain mapping.
- **NFV Software Architecture**: It is related to the virtualization of the already implemented network functions, such as proprietary hardware appliances. It implies the understanding and transition from a hardware implementation into a software one. The transition is based on various defined patterns that can be used in a process.
- **NFV Reliability and Availability**: These are real challenges and the work involved in these components started from the definition of various problems, use cases, requirements, and principles, and it has proposed itself to offer the same level of availability as legacy systems. It relates to the reliability component and the documentation only sets the stage for future work. It only identifies various problems and indicates the best practices used in designing resilient NFV systems.

- **NFV Performance and Portability**: The purpose of NFV, in general, is to transform the way it works with networks of future. For this purpose, it needs to prove itself as wordy solution for industry standards. This section explains how to apply the best practices related to performance and portability in a general VNF deployment.
- **NFV Security**: Since it is a large component of the industry, it is concerned about and also dependent on the security of networking and cloud computing, which makes it critical for NFV to assure security. The Security Expert Group focuses on those concerns.

An architectural of these components is presented here:

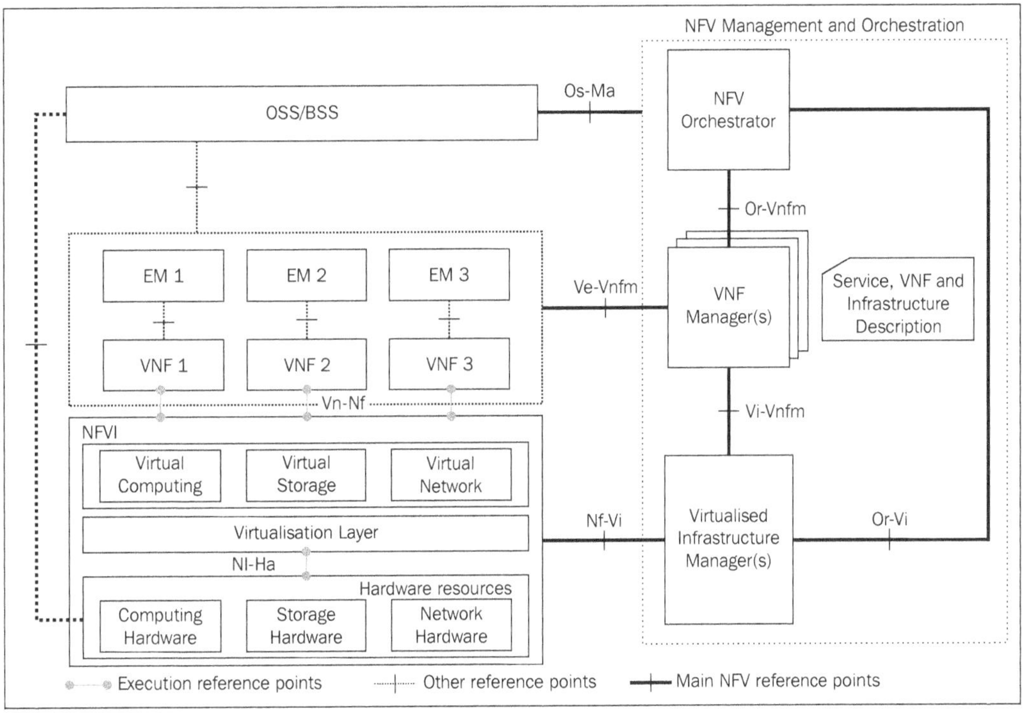

After all the documentation is in place, a number of proof of concepts need to be executed in order to test the limitation of these components and accordingly adjust the theoretical components. They have also appeared to encourage the development of the NFV ecosystem.

> For more information about the available roof of concepts and specifications for NFV, refer to these links: `http://www.etsi.org/technologies-clusters/technologies/nfv/nfv-poc?tab=2` and `http://www.etsi.org/technologies-clusters/technologies/nfv`.

SDN

Software-Defined Networking (**SDN**) is an approach to networking that offers the possibility to manage various services using the abstraction of available functionalities to administrators. This is realized by decoupling the system into a control plane and data plane and making decisions based on the network traffic that is sent; this represents the control plane realm, and where the traffic is forwarded is represented by the data plane. Of course, some method of communication between the control and data plane is required, so the OpenFlow mechanism entered into the equation at first; however other components could as well take its place.

The intention of SDN was to offer an architecture that was manageable, cost-effective, adaptable, and dynamic, as well as suitable for the dynamic and high-bandwidth scenarios that are available today. The OpenFlow component was the foundation of the SDN solution. The SDN architecture permitted the following:

- **Direct programming**: The control plane is directly programmable because it is completely decoupled by the data plane.
- **Programmatically configuration**: SDN permitted management, configuration, and optimization of resources though programs. These programs could also be written by anyone because they were not dependent on any proprietary components.
- **Agility**: The abstraction between two components permitted the adjustment of network flows according to the needs of a developer.
- **Central management**: Logical components could be centered on the control plane, which offered a viewpoint of a network to other applications, engines, and so on.

- **Opens standards and vendor neutrality**: It is implemented using open standards that have simplified the SDN design and operations because of the number of instructions provided to controllers. This is smaller compared to other scenarios in which multiple vendor-specific protocols and devices should be handled.

Also, meeting market requirements with traditional solutions would have been impossible, taking into account newly emerging markets of mobile device communication, Internet of Things (IoT), Machine to Machine (M2M), Industry 4.0, and others, all require networking support. Taking into consideration the available budgets for further development in various IT departments, were all faced to make a decision. It seems that the mobile device communication market all decided to move toward open source in the hope that this investment would prove its real capabilities, and would also lead to a brighter future.

OPNFV

The Open Platform for the NFV Project tries to offer an open source reference platform that is carrier-graded and tightly integrated in order to facilitate industry peers to help improve and move the NFV concept forward. Its purpose is to offer consistency, interoperability, and performance among numerous blocks and projects that already exist. This platform will also try to work closely with a variety of open source projects and continuously help with integration, and at the same time, fill development gaps left by any of them.

This project is expected to lead to an increase in performance, reliability, serviceability, availability, and power efficiency, but at the same time, also deliver an extensive platform for instrumentation. It will start with the development of an NFV infrastructure and a virtualized infrastructure management system where it will combine a number of already available projects. Its reference system architecture is represented by the x86 architecture.

The project's initial focus point and proposed implementation can be consulted in the following image. From this image, it can be easily seen that the project, although very young since it was started in November 2014, has had an accelerated start and already has a few implementation propositions. There are already a number of large companies and organizations that have started working on their specific demos. OPNFV has not waited for them to finish and is already discussing a number of proposed project and initiatives. These are intended both to meet the needs of their members as well as assure them of the reliability various components, such as continuous integration, fault management, test-bed infrastructure, and others. The following figure describes the structure of OPNFV:

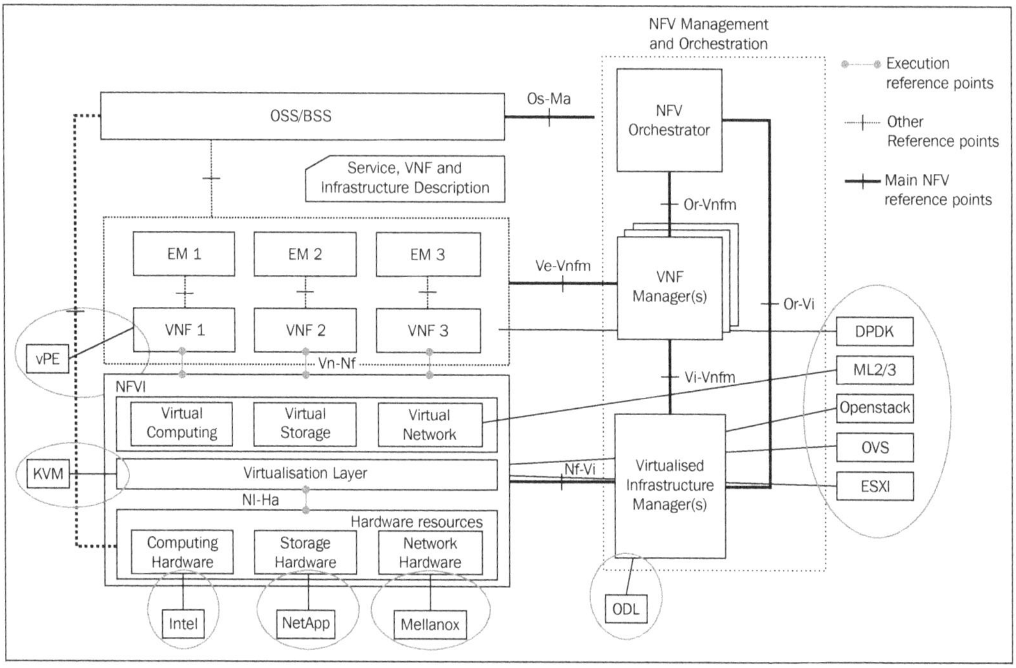

The project has been leveraging as many open source projects as possible. All the adaptations made to these project can be done in two places. Firstly, they can be made inside the project, if it does not require substantial functionality changes that could cause divergence from its purpose and roadmap. The second option complements the first and is necessary for changes that do not fall in the first category; they should be included somewhere in the OPNFV project's codebase. None of the changes that have been made should be up streamed without proper testing within the development cycle of OPNFV.

Another important element that needs to be mentioned is that OPNFV does not use any specific or additional hardware. It only uses available hardware resources as long the VI-Ha reference point is supported. In the preceding image, it can be seen that this is already done by having providers, such as Intel for the computing hardware, NetApp for storage hardware, and Mellanox for network hardware components.

The OPNFV board and technical steering committee have a quite large palette of open source projects. They vary from **Infrastructure as a Service** (**IaaS**) and hypervisor to the SDN controller and the list continues. This only offers the possibility for a large number of contributors to try some of the skills that maybe did not have the time to work on, or wanted to learn but did not have the opportunity to. Also, a more diversified community offers a broader view of the same subject.

There are a large variety of appliances for the OPNFV project. The virtual network functions are diverse for mobile deployments where mobile gateways (such as Serving Gateway (SGW), Packet Data Network Gateway (PGW), and so on) and related functions (Mobility Management Entity (MME) and gateways), firewalls or application-level gateways and filters (web and e-mail traffic filters) are used to test diagnostic equipment (Service-Level Agreement (SLA) monitoring). These VNF deployments need to be easy to operate, scale, and evolve independently from the type of VNF that is deployed. OPNFV sets out to create a platform that has to support a set of qualities and use-cases as follows:

- A common mechanism is needed for the life-cycle management of VNFs, which include deployment, instantiation, configuration, start and stop, upgrade/downgrade, and final decommissioning
- A consistent mechanism is used to specify and interconnect VNFs, VNFCs, and PNFs; these are independant of the physical network infrastructure, network overlays, and so on, that is, a virtual link
- A common mechanism is used to dynamically instantiate new VNF instances or decommission sufficient ones to meet the current performance, scale, and network bandwidth needs
- A mechanism is used to detect faults and failure in the NFVI, VIM, and other components of an infrastructure as well as recover from these failures
- A mechanism is used to source/sink traffic from/to a physical network function to/from a virtual network function
- NFVI as a Service is used to host different VNF instances from different vendors on the same infrastructure

There are some notable and easy-to-grasp use case examples that should be mentioned here. They are organized into four categories. Let's start with the first category: the Residential/Access category. It can be used to virtualize the home environment but it also provides fixed access to NFV. The next one is data center: it has the virtualization of CDN and provides use cases that deal with it. The mobile category consists of the virtualization of mobile core networks and IMS as well as the virtualization of mobile base stations. Lastly, there are cloud categories that include NFVIaaS, VNFaaS, the VNF forwarding graph (Service Chains), and the use cases of VNPaaS.

> More information about this project and various implementation components is available at `https://www.opnfv.org/`. For the definitions of missing terminologies, please consult `http://www.etsi.org/deliver/etsi_gs/NFV/001_099/003/01.02.01_60/gs_NFV003v010201p.pdf`.

Virtualization support for the Yocto Project

The `meta-virtualization` layer tries to create a long and medium term production-ready layer specifically for an embedded virtualization. This roles that this has are:

- Simplifying the way collaborative benchmarking and researching is done with tools, such as KVM/LxC virtualization, combined with advance core isolation and other techniques
- Integrating and contributing with projects, such as OpenFlow, OpenvSwitch, LxC, dmtcp, CRIU and others, which can be used with other components, such as OpenStack or Carrier Graded Linux.

To summarize this in one sentence, this layer tries to provide support while constructing OpenEmbedded and Yocto Project-based virtualized solutions.

The packages that are available in this layer, which I will briefly talk about are as follows:

- `CRIU`
- `Docker`
- `LXC`
- `Irqbalance`

- `Libvirt`
- `Xen`
- `Open vSwitch`

This layer can be used in conjunction with the `meta-cloud-services` layer that offer cloud agents and API support for various cloud-based solutions. In this section, I am referring to both these layers because I think it is fit to present these two components together. Inside the `meta-cloud-services` layer, there are also a couple of packages that will be discussed and briefly presented, as follows:

- `openLDAP`
- `SPICE`
- `Qpid`
- `RabbitMQ`
- `Tempest`
- `Cyrus-SASL`
- `Puppet`
- `oVirt`
- `OpenStack`

Having mentioned these components, I will now move on with the explanation of each of these tools. Let's start with the content of the meta-virtualization layer, more exactly with `CRIU` package, a project that implements **Checkpoint/Restore In Userspace** for Linux. It can be used to freeze an already running application and checkpoint it to a hard drive as a collection of files. These checkpoints can be used to restore and execute the application from that point. It can be used as part of a number of use cases, as follows:

- **Live migration of containers**: It is the primary use case for a project. The container is check pointed and the resulting image is moved into another box and restored there, making the whole experience almost unnoticeable by the user.
- **Upgrading seamless kernels**: The kernel replacement activity can be done without stopping activities. It can be check pointed, replaced by calling kexec, and all the services can be restored afterwards.
- **Speeding up slow boot services**: It is a service that has a slow boot procedure, can be check pointed after the first start up is finished, and for consecutive starts, can be restored from that point.

- **Load balancing of networks**: It is a part of the `TCP_REPAIR` socket option and switches the socket in a special state. The socket is actually put into the state expected from it at the end of the operation. For example, if `connect()` is called, the socket will be put in an `ESTABLISHED` state as requested without checking for acknowledgment of communication from the other end, so offloading could be at the application level.
- **Desktop environment suspend/resume**: It is based on the fact that the suspend/restore action for a screen session or an `X` application is by far faster than the close/open operation.
- **High performance and computing issues**: It can be used for both load balancing of tasks over a cluster and the saving of cluster node states in case a crash occurs. Having a number of snapshots for application doesn't hurt anybody.
- **Duplication of processes**: It is similar to the remote `fork()` operation.
- **Snapshots for applications**: A series of application states can be saved and reversed back if necessary. It can be used both as a redo for the desired state of an application as well as for debugging purposes.
- **Save ability in applications that do not have this option**: An example of such an application could be games in which after reaching a certain level, the establishment of a checkpoint is the thing you need.
- **Migrate a forgotten application onto the screen**: If you have forgotten to include an application onto the screen and you are already there, CRIU can help with the migration process.
- **Debugging of applications that have hung**: For services that are stuck because of `git` and need a quick restart, a copy of the services can be used to restore. A dump process can also be used and through debugging, the cause of the problem can be found.
- **Application behavior analysis on a different machine**: For those applications that could behave differently from one machine to another, a snapshot of the application in question can be used and transferred into the other. Here, the debugging process can also be an option.
- **Dry running updates**: Before a system or kernel update on a system is done, its services and critical applications could be duplicated onto a virtual machine and after the system update and all the test cases pass, the real update can be done.
- **Fault-tolerant systems**: It can be used successfully for process duplication on other machines.

The next element is `irqbalance`, a distributed hardware interrupt system that is available across multiple processors and multiprocessor systems. It is, in fact, a daemon used to balance interrupts across multiple CPUs, and its purpose is to offer better performances as well as better IO operation balance on SMP systems. It has alternatives, such as `smp_affinity`, which could achieve maximum performance in theory, but lacks the same flexibility that `irqbalance` provides.

The `libvirt` toolkit can be used to connect with the virtualization capabilities available in the recent Linux kernel versions that have been licensed under the GNU Lesser General Public License. It offers support for a large number of packages, as follows:

- KVM/QEMU Linux supervisor
- Xen supervisor
- LXC Linux container system
- OpenVZ Linux container system
- Open Mode Linux a paravirtualized kernel
- Hypervisors that include VirtualBox, VMware ESX, GSX, Workstation and player, IBM PowerVM, Microsoft Hyper-V, Parallels, and Bhyve

Besides these packages, it also offers support for storage on a large variety of filesystems, such as IDE, SCSI or USB disks, FiberChannel, LVM, and iSCSI or NFS, as well as support for virtual networks. It is the building block for other higher-level applications and tools that focus on the virtualization of a node and it does this in a secure way. It also offers the possibility of a remote connection.

> For more information about `libvirt`, take a look at its project goals and terminologies at `http://libvirt.org/goals.html`.

The next is `Open vSwitch`, a production-quality implementation of a multilayer virtual switch. This software component is licensed under Apache 2.0 and is designed to enable massive network automations through various programmatic extensions. The `Open vSwitch` package, also abbreviated as **OVS**, provides a two stack layer for hardware virtualizations and also supports a large number of the standards and protocols available in a computer network, such as sFlow, NetFlow, SPAN, CLI, RSPAN, 802.1ag, LACP, and so on.

Xen is a hypervisor with a microkernel design that provides services offering multiple computer operating systems to be executed on the same architecture. It was first developed at the Cambridge University in 2003, and was developed under GNU General Public License version 2. This piece of software runs on a more privileged state and is available for ARM, IA-32, and x86-64 instruction sets.

A hypervisor is a piece of software that is concerned with the CPU scheduling and memory management of various domains. It does this from the **domain 0 (dom0)**, which controls all the other unprivileged domains called **domU**; Xen boots from a bootloader and usually loads into the dom0 host domain, a paravirtualized operating system. A brief look at the Xen project architecture is available here:

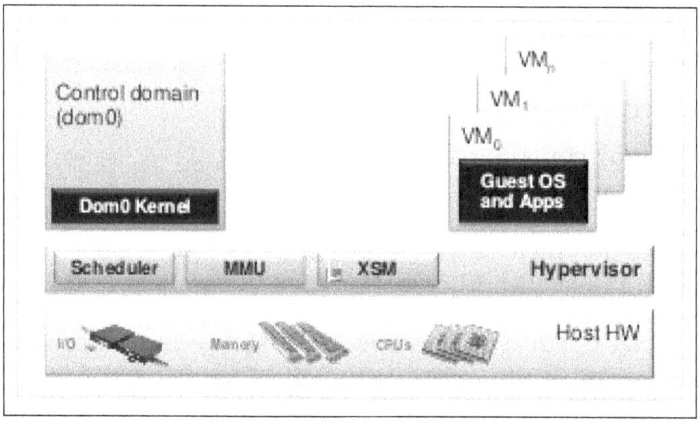

Linux Containers (**LXC**) is the next element available in the meta-virtualization layer. It is a well-known set of tools and libraries that offer virtualization at the operating system level by offering isolated containers on a Linux control host machine. It combines the functionalities of kernel **control groups** (**cgroups**) with the support for isolated namespaces to provide an isolated environment. It has received a fair amount of attention mostly due to Docker, which will be briefly mentioned a bit later. Also, it is considered a lightweight alternative to full machine virtualization.

Both of these options, containers and machine virtualization, have a fair amount of advantages and disadvantages. If the first option, containers offer low overheads by sharing certain components, and it may turn out that it does not have a good isolation. Machine virtualization is exactly the opposite of this and offers a great solution to isolation at the cost of a bigger overhead. These two solutions could also be seen as complementary, but this is only my personal view of the two. In reality, each of them has its particular set of advantages and disadvantages that could sometimes be uncomplementary as well.

[More information about Linux containers is available at https://linuxcontainers.org/.]

The last component of the `meta-virtualization` layer that will be discussed is **Docker**, an open source piece of software that tries to automate the method of deploying applications inside Linux containers. It does this by offering an abstraction layer over LXC. Its architecture is better described in this image:

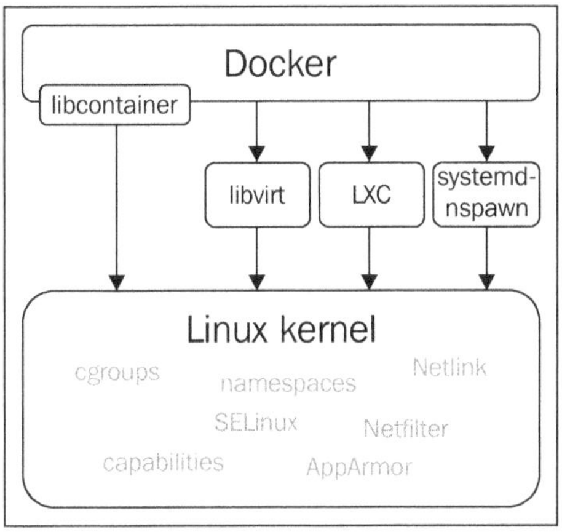

As you can see in the preceding diagram, this software package is able to use the resources of the operating system. Here, I am referring to the functionalities of the Linux kernel and have isolated other applications from the operating system. It can do this either through LXC or other alternatives, such as `libvirt` and `systemd-nspawn`, which are seen as indirect implementations. It can also do this directly through the `libcontainer` library, which has been around since the 0.9 version of Docker.

Docker is a great component if you want to obtain automation for distributed systems, such as large-scale web deployments, service-oriented architectures, continuous deployment systems, database clusters, private PaaS, and so on. More information about its use cases is available at `https://www.docker.com/resources/usecases/`. Make sure you take a look at this website; interesting information is often here.

> More information about the Docker project is available on their website. Check out the **What is Docker?** section at `https://www.docker.com/whatisdocker/`.

After finishing with the `meta-virtualization` layer, I will move next to the `meta-cloud-services` layer that contains various elements. I will start with **Simple Protocol for Independent Computing Environments** (**Spice**). This can be translated into a remote-display system for virtualized desktop devices.

It initially started as a closed source software, and in two years it was decided to make it open source. It then became an open standard to interaction with devices, regardless of whether they are virtualized one not. It is built on a client-server architecture, making it able to deal with both physical and virtualized devices. The interaction between backend and frontend is realized through **VD-Interfaces** (**VDI**), and as shown in the following diagram, its current focus is the remote access to QEMU/KVM virtual machines:

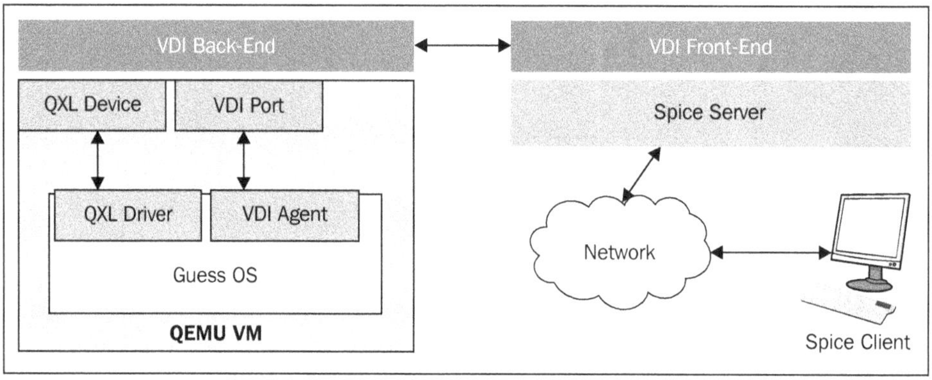

Next on the list is **oVirt**, a virtualization platform that offers a web interface. It is easy to use and helps in the management of virtual machines, virtualized networks, and storages. Its architecture consists of an oVirt Engine and multiple nodes. The engine is the component that comes equipped with a user-friendly interface to manage logical and physical resources. It also runs the virtual machines that could be either oVirt nodes, Fedora, or CentOS hosts. The only downfall of using oVirt is that it only offers support for a limited number of hosts, as follows:

- Fedora 20
- CentOS 6.6, 7.0
- Red Hat Enterprise Linux 6.6, 7.0
- Scientific Linux 6.6, 7.0

As a tool, it is really powerful. It offers integration with `libvirt` for **Virtual Desktops and Servers Manager** (**VDSM**) communications with virtual machines and also support for SPICE communication protocols that enable remote desktop sharing. It is a solution that was started and is mainly maintained by Red Hat. It is the base element of their **Red Hat Enterprise Virtualization** (**RHEV**), but one thing is interesting and should be watched out for is that Red Hat now is not only a supporter of projects, such as oVirt and Aeolus, but has also been a platinum member of the OpenStack foundation since 2012.

> For more information on projects, such as oVirt, Aeolus, and RHEV, the following links can be useful to you: `http://www.redhat.com/promo/rhev3/?sc_cid=70160000000Ty5wAAC&offer_id=70160000000Ty5NAAS` `http://www.aeolusproject.org/`, and `http://www.ovirt.org/Home`.

I will move on to a different component now. Here, I am referring to the open source implementation of the Lightweight Directory Access Protocol, simply called **OpenLDAP**. Although it has a somewhat controverted license called **OpenLDAP Public License**, which is similar in essence to the BSD license, it is not recorded at opensource.org, making it uncertified by **Open Source Initiative** (**OSI**).

This software component comes as a suite of elements, as follows:

- A standalone LDAP daemon that plays the role of a server called **slapd**
- A number of libraries that implement the LDAP protocol
- Last but not the least, a series of tools and utilities that also have a couple of clients samples between them

There are also a number of additions that should be mentioned, such as ldapc++ and libraries written in C++, JLDAP and the libraries written in Java; LMDB, a memory mapped database library; Fortress, a role-based identity management; SDK, also written in Java; and a JDBC-LDAP Bridge driver that is written in Java and called **JDBC-LDAP**.

Cyrus SASL is a generic client-server library implementation for **Simple Authentication and Security Layer** (**SASL**) authentication. It is a method used for adding authentication support for connection-based protocols. A connection-based protocol adds a command that identifies and authenticates a user to the requested server and if negotiation is required, an additional security layer is added between the protocol and the connection for security purposes. More information about SASL is available in the RFC 2222, available at **http://www.ietf.org/rfc/rfc2222.txt**.

> For a more detailed description of Cyrus SASL, refer to `http://www.sendmail.org/~ca/email/cyrus/sysadmin.html`.

Qpid is a messaging tool developed by Apache, which understands **Advanced Message Queueing Protocol** (**AMQP**) and has support for various languages and platforms. AMQP is an open source protocol designed for high-performance messaging over a network in a reliable fashion. More information about AMQP is available at `http://www.amqp.org/specification/1.0/amqp-org-download`. Here, you can find more information about the protocol specifications as well as about the project in general.

Qpid projects push the development of AMQP ecosystems and this is done by offering message brokers and APIs that can be used in any developer application that intends to use AMQP messaging part of their product. To do this, the following can be done:

- Letting the source code open source.
- Making AMQP available for a large variety of computing environments and programming languages.
- Offering the necessary tools to simplify the development process of an application.
- Creating a messaging infrastructure to make sure that other services can integrate well with the AMQP network.
- Creating a messaging product that makes integration with AMQP trivial for any programming language or computing environment. Make sure that you take a look at Qpid Proton at `http://qpid.apache.org/proton/overview.html` for this.

> More information about the the preceding functionalities can be found at `http://qpid.apache.org/components/index.html#messaging-apis`.

RabbitMQ is another message broker software component that implements AMQP, which is also available as open source. It has a number of components, as follows:

- The RabbitMQ exchange server
- Gateways for HTTP, **Streaming Text Oriented Message Protocol** (**STOMP**) and **Message Queue Telemetry Transport** (**MQTT**)

- AMQP client libraries for a variety of programming languages, most notably Java, Erlang, and .Net Framework
- A plugin platform for a number of custom components that also offer a collection of predefined one:
    - **Shovel**: It is a plugin that executes the copy/move operation for messages between brokers
    - **Management**: It enables the control and monitoring of brokers and clusters of brokers
    - **Federation**: It enables sharing at the exchange level of messages between brokers

> You can find out more information regarding RabbitMQ by referring to the RabbitMQ documentation section at `http://www.rabbitmq.com/documentation.html`.

Comparing the two, Qpid and RabbitMQ, it can be concluded that RabbitMQ is better and also that it has a fantastic documentation. This makes it the first choice for the OpenStack Foundation as well as for readers interested in benchmarking information for more than these frameworks. It is also available at `http://blog.x-aeon.com/2013/04/10/a-quick-message-queue-benchmark-activemq-rabbitmq-hornetq-qpid-apollo/`. One such result is also available in this image for comparison purposes:

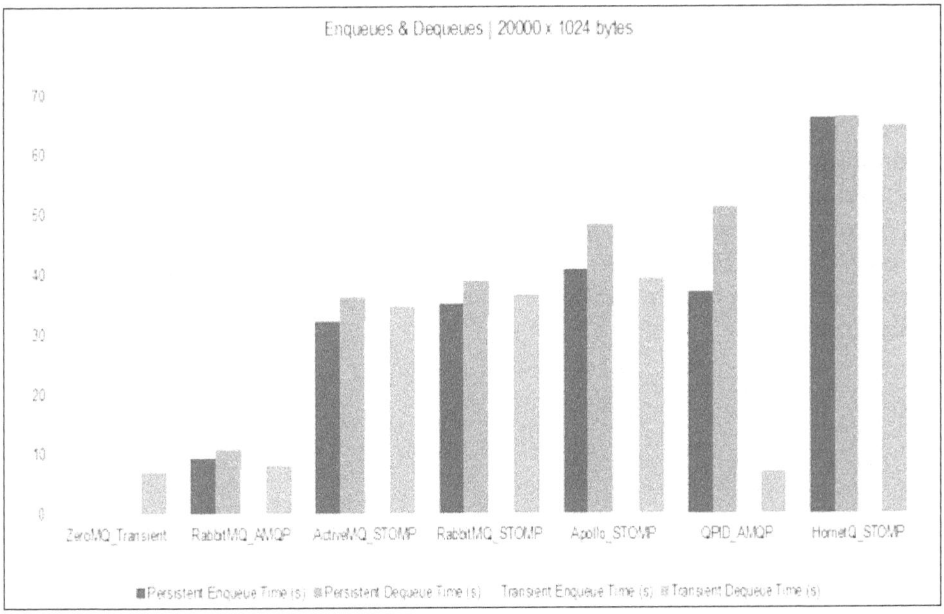

The next element is **puppet**, an open source configuration management system that allows IT infrastructure to have certain states defined and also enforce these states. By doing this, it offers a great automation system for system administrators. This project is developed by the Puppet Labs and was released under GNU General Public License until version 2.7.0. After this, it moved to the Apache License 2.0 and is now available in two flavors:

- **The open source puppet version**: It is mostly similar to the preceding tool and is capable of configuration management solutions that permit for definition and automation of states. It is available for both Linux and UNIX as well as Max OS X and Windows.
- **The puppet enterprise edition**: It is a commercial version that goes beyond the capabilities of the open source puppet and permits the automation of the configuration and management process.

It is a tool that defines a declarative language for later use for system configuration. It can be applied directly on the system or even compiled as a catalogue and deployed on a target using a client-server paradigm, which is usually the REST API. Another component is an agent that enforces the resources available in the manifest. The resource abstraction is, of course, done through an abstraction layer that defines the configuration through higher lever terms that are very different from the operating system-specific commands.

> If you visit `http://docs.puppetlabs.com/`, you will find more documentation related to Puppet and other Puppet Lab tools.

With all this in place, I believe it is time to present the main component of the meta-cloud-services layer, called **OpenStack**. It is a cloud operating system that is based on controlling a large number of components and together it offers pools of compute, storage, and networking resources. All of them are managed through a dashboard that is, of course, offered by another component and offers administrators control. It offers users the possibility of providing resources from the same web interface. Here is an image depicting the Open Source Cloud operating System, which is actually OpenStack:

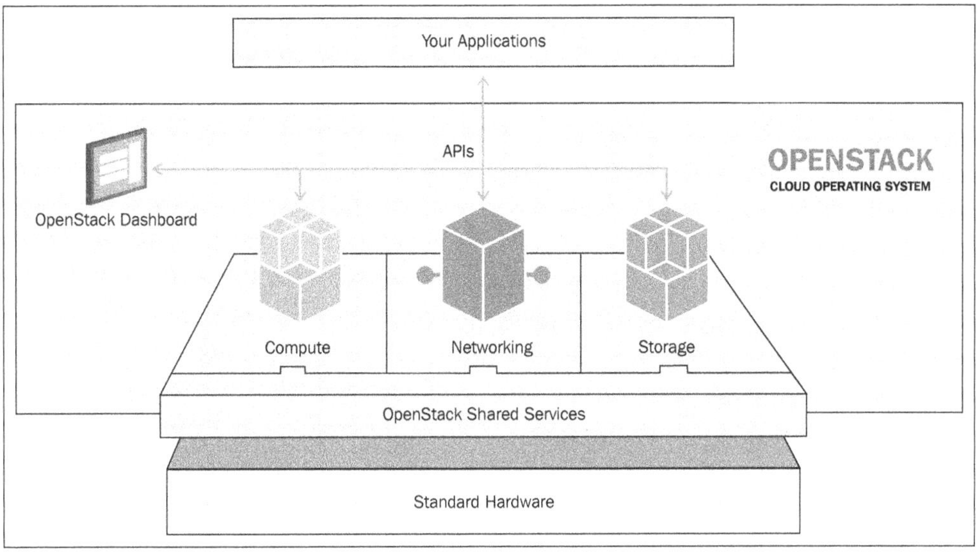

It is primarily used as an IaaS solution, its components are maintained by the OpenStack Foundation, and is available under Apache License version 2. In the Foundation, today, there are more than 200 companies that contribute to the source code and general development and maintenance of the software. At the heart of it, all are staying its components Also, each component has a Python module used for simple interaction and automation possibilities:

- **Compute (Nova)**: It is used for the hosting and management of cloud computing systems. It manages the life cycles of the compute instances of an environment. It is responsible for the spawning, decommissioning, and scheduling of various virtual machines on demand. With regard to hypervisors, KVM is the preferred option but other options such as Xen and VMware are also viable.
- **Object Storage (Swift)**: It is used for storage and data structure retrieval via RESTful and the HTTP API. It is a scalable and fault-tolerant system that permits data replication with objects and files available on multiple disk drives. It is developed mainly by an object storage software company called **SwiftStack**.

- **Block Storage (Cinder)**: It provides persistent block storage for OpenStack instances. It manages the creation and attach and detach actions for block devices. In a cloud, a user manages its own devices, so a vast majority of storage platforms and scenarios should be supported. For this purpose, it offers a pluggable architecture that facilitates the process.
- **Networking (Neutron)**: It is the component responsible for network-related services, also known as **Network Connectivity as a Service**. It provides an API for network management and also makes sure that certain limitations are prevented. It also has an architecture based on pluggable modules to ensure that as many networking vendors and technologies as possible are supported.
- **Dashboard (Horizon)**: It provides web-based administrators and user graphical interfaces for interaction with the other resources made available by all the other components. It is also designed keeping extensibility in mind because it is able to interact with other components responsible for monitoring and billing as well as with additional management tools. It also offers the possibility of rebranding according to the needs of commercial vendors.
- **Identity Service (Keystone)**: It is an authentication and authorization service It offers support for multiple forms of authentication and also existing backend directory services such as LDAP. It provides a catalogue for users and the resources they can access.
- **Image Service (Glance)**: It is used for the discovery, storage, registration, and retrieval of images of virtual machines. A number of already stored images can be used as templates. OpenStack also provides an operating system image for testing purposes. Glance is the only module capable of adding, deleting, duplicating, and sharing OpenStack images between various servers and virtual machines. All the other modules interact with the images using the available APIs of Glance.
- **Telemetry (Ceilometer)**: It is a module that provides billing, benchmarking, and statistical results across all current and future components of OpenStack with the help of numerous counters that permit extensibility. This makes it a very scalable module.

- **Orchestrator (Heat)**: It is a service that manages multiple composite cloud applications with the help of various template formats, such as Heat Orchestration Templates (HOT) or AWS CloudFormation. The communication is done both on a CloudFormation compatible Query API and an Open Stack REST API.
- **Database (Trove)**: It provides Cloud Database as service functionalities that are both reliable and scalable. It uses relational and nonrelational database engines.
- **Bare Metal Provisioning (Ironic)**: It is a components that provides virtual machine support instead of bare metal machines support. It started as a fork of the Nova Baremetal driver and grew to become the best solution for a bare-metal hypervisor. It also offers a set of plugins for interaction with various bare-metal hypervisors. It is used by default with PXE and IPMI, but of course, with the help of the available plugins it can offer extended support for various vendor-specific functionalities.
- **Multiple Tenant Cloud Messaging (Zaqar)**: It is, as the name suggests, a multitenant cloud messaging service for the web developers who are interested in **Software as a Service** (**SaaS**). It can be used by them to send messages between various components by using a number of communication patterns. However, it can also be used with other components for surfacing events to end users as well as communication in the over-cloud layer. Its former name was **Marconi** and it also provides the possibility of scalable and secure messaging.
- **Elastic Map Reduce (Sahara)**: It is a module that tries to automate the method of providing the functionalities of Hadoop clusters. It only requires the defines for various fields, such as Hadoop versions, various topology nodes, hardware details, and so on. After this, in a few minutes, a Hadoop cluster is deployed and ready for interaction. It also offers the possibility of various configurations after deployment.

Having mentioned all this, maybe you would not mind if a conceptual architecture is presented in the following image to present to you with ways in which the above preceding components are interacted with. To automate the deployment of such an environment in a production environment, automation tools, such as the previously mentioned Puppet tool, can be used. Take a look at this diagram:

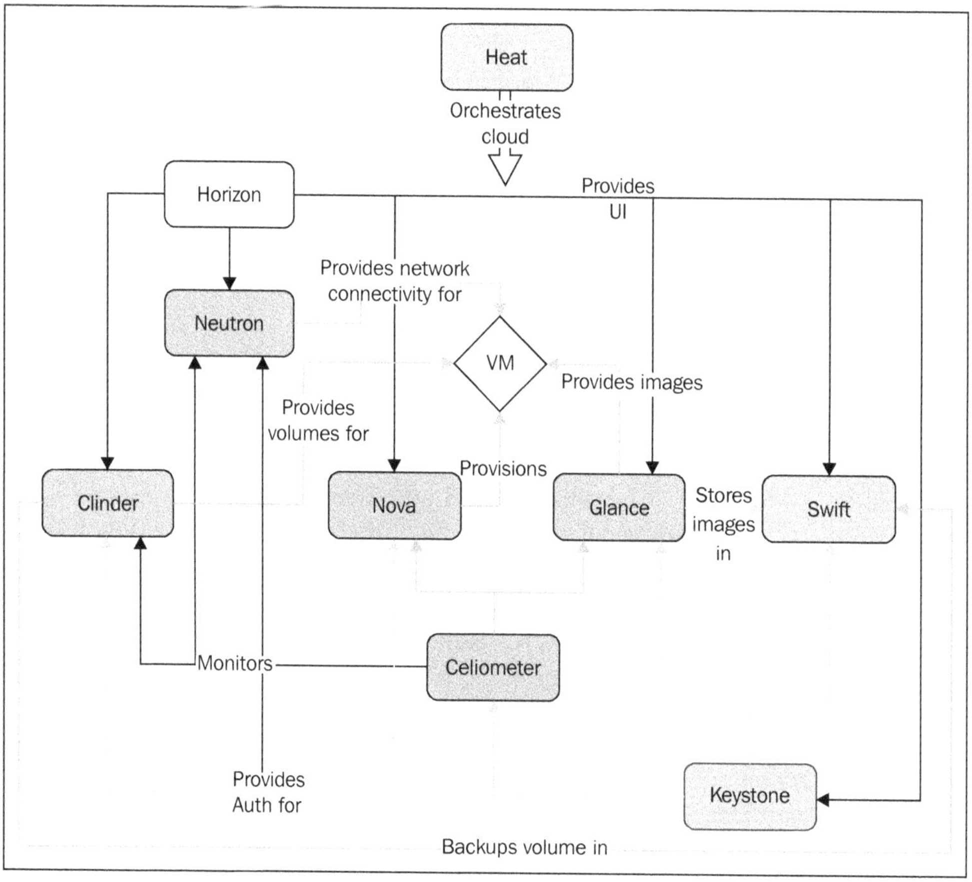

Now, let's move on and see how such a system can be deployed using the functionalities of the Yocto Project. For this activity to start, all the required metadata layers should be put together. Besides the already available Poky repository, other ones are also required and they are defined in the layer index on OpenEmbedded's website because this time, the `README` file is incomplete:

```
git clone -b dizzy git://git.openembedded.org/meta-openembedded
git clone -b dizzy git://git.yoctoproject.org/meta-virtualization
git clone -b icehouse git://git.yoctoproject.org/meta-cloud-
services
source oe-init-build-env ../build-controller
```

After the appropriate controller build is created, it needs to be configured. Inside the `conf/layer.conf` file, add the corresponding machine configuration, such as qemux86-64, and inside the `conf/bblayers.conf` file, the `BBLAYERS` variable should be defined accordingly. There are extra metadata layers, besides the ones that are already available. The ones that should be defined in this variable are:

- `meta-cloud-services`
- `meta-cloud-services/meta-openstack-controller-deploy`
- `meta-cloud-services/meta-openstack`
- `meta-cloud-services/meta-openstack-qemu`
- `meta-openembedded/meta-oe`
- `meta-openembedded/meta-networking`
- `meta-openembedded/meta-python`
- `meta-openembedded/meta-filesystem`
- `meta-openembedded/meta-webserver`
- `meta-openembedded/meta-ruby`

After the configuration is done using the `bitbake openstack-image-controller` command, the controller image is built. The controller can be started using the `runqemu qemux86-64 openstack-image-controller kvm nographic qemuparams="-m 4096"` command. After finishing this activity, the deployment of the compute can be started in this way:

```
source oe-init-build-env ../build-compute
```

With the new build directory created and also since most of the work of the build process has already been done with the controller, build directories such as `downloads` and `sstate-cache`, can be shared between them. This information should be indicated through `DL_DIR` and `SSTATE_DIR`. The difference between the two `conf/bblayers.conf` files is that the second one for the `build-compute` build directory replaces `meta-cloud-services/meta-openstack-controller-deploy with meta-cloud-services/meta-openstack-compute-deploy`.

This time the build is done with `bitbake openstack-image-compute` and should be finished faster. Having completed the build, the compute node can also be booted using the `runqemu qemux86-64 openstack-image-compute kvm nographic qemuparams="-m 4096 -smp 4"` command. This step implies the image loading for OpenStack Cirros as follows:

```
wget download.cirros-cloud.net/0.3.2/cirros-0.3.2-x86_64-disk.img
scp cirros-0.3.2-x86_64-disk.img  root@<compute_ip_address>:~
```

```
ssh root@<compute_ip_address>

./etc/nova/openrc

glance image-create -name "TestImage" -is=public true -container-
format bare -disk-format qcow2 -file /home/root/cirros-0.3.2-x86_64-
disk.img
```

Having done all of this, the user is free to access the Horizon web browser using http://<compute_ip_address>:8080/ The login information is admin and the password is password. Here, you can play and create new instances, interact with them, and, in general, do whatever crosses your mind. Do not worry if you've done something wrong to an instance; you can delete it and start again.

The last element from the meta-cloud-services layer is the **Tempest integration test suite** for OpenStack. It is represented through a set of tests that are executed on the OpenStack trunk to make sure everything is working as it should. It is very useful for any OpenStack deployments.

> More information about Tempest is available at https://github.com/openstack/tempest.

Summary

In this chapter, you were not only presented with information about a number of virtualization concepts, such as NFV, SDN, VNF, and so on, but also a number of open source components that contribute to everyday virtualization solutions. I offered you examples and even a small exercise to make sure that the information remains with you even after reading this book. I hope I made some of you curious about certain things. I also hope that some of you documented on projects that were not presented here, such as the **OpenDaylight** (**ODL**) initiative, that has only been mentioned in an image as an implementation suggestion. If this is the case, I can say I fulfilled my goal. If not, maybe this summary will make you go through the previous pages again.

In the next chapter, we will visit a new and real carrier graded one. It will be the last chapter of this book and I will conclude it with a topic that is very important to me personally. I will discuss the Yocto shy initiative called **meta-cgl** and its purpose. I will present the various specifications and changes for the **Carrier Graded Linux** (**CGL**), and the requirements of **Linux Standard Base** (**LSB**). I hope you enjoy reading it as much as I have enjoyed writing it.

13
CGL and LSB

In this chapter, you will be presented with information about the last topic of the book, the **Carrier Grade Linux** (**CGL**) and **Linux Standard Base** (**LSB**) initiative and of course, a parallel with what there is integrated and supported related to those two standards into the Yocto Project. This will also be mentioned here and you will not only be able to find a little bit about these standards and their specifications, but also about the level of support that Yocto offers for them. I will also present some of the initiatives adjacent to CGL, such as **Automotive Grade Linux** and **Carrier Grade Virtualization**. They also constitute viable solutions that are available in a wide palette of applications.

In any Linux environment today, there is necessity for a common language for available Linux distributions. This common language would have not been achieved without defining actual specifications. A part of these specifications is also represented by the carrier grade alternative. It coexists with other specifications that are already presented in this book or in other similar books. Taking a look at the available specifications and standardizations only shows us how much the Linux ecosystem has evolved over time.

The latest report published by the guys working at the Linux Foundation shows how the development of the Linux kernel is actually done nowadays, what it's like to work on it, who is sponsoring it, what changes are being made to it, and how fast things are moving. The report is available at `https://www.linuxfoundation.org/publications/linux-foundation/who-writes-linux-2015`.

As depicted in the report, less than 20 percent of development on the kernel is done by individual developers. Most of the development is realized by companies, such as Intel, Red Hat, Linaro, Samsung, and others. This means that over 80 percent of the developers working at Linux kernel development are paid for their job. The fact that Linaro and Samsung are some of the companies with the most number of commits, only presents a favorable perception of the ARM processors in general, and Android in particular.

Another interesting piece of information is that more than half of the Linux kernel developers are at their first commit. This means that a really small number of developers are doing the vast majority of work. This dysfunction in the development of the Linux kernel process is being tried to be reduced by the Linux Foundation by offering various programs for students to make them more involved in the development process. Whether this is a success, only time will tell, but it is my opinion that they are doing the right thing and are moving in the right direction.

All of this information has been explained with regard to the Linux kernel, but parts of it are applicable for other open source components. The thing that I want to emphasize here is that the ARM support in Linux is much more mature than in architectures such as PowerPC or MIPS. This has started to not only be obvious, but is also an indication of the approach that the Intel x86 stage has taken. Until now, this approach was simply not disturbed by anyone.

Linux Standard Base

LSB appeared to lower the costs of support offered by Linux platforms by reducing the differences between various available Linux distributions. It also helps with costs for porting applications. Every time a developer writes an application, they need to make sure that the source code produced on one Linux distribution will also be able to be executed on other distributions as well. They would also like to make sure that this remains possible over the years.

The LSB workgroup is a Linux Foundation project that tries to address these exact problems. For this purpose, LSB workgroup started working on a standard that could describe a set of APIs that a Linux distribution should support. With the standards defined, the workgroup also moved a few steps further and developed a set of tools and tests to measure the support levels. With this done, they were able to define certain sets of compliance and also detect the certain differences between various distributions.

The LSB was the first effort to be made in this direction by the Linux Foundation and became an umbrella for all the workgroups that have tried to provide standardization to various areas of the Linux platform. All these workgroups have the same roadmap and they deliver their corresponding set of specifications, software components, such as conformance tests, developments tools, and other available samples and implementations.

Every software component developed by one of the workgroups that is available inside the Linux Standard Base is defined as a `lsb` module. All of these modules have a common format to facilitate easier integration between them. There are modules that are required and optional. The required ones are the ones that meet the acceptance criteria for LSB. The optional ones are still a work in progress and are, at the moment of specifications defining, not written in the acceptance criteria, but will be included in future versions of the LSB standard.

There are, of course, workgroups that do not produce `lsb` modules. They have not worked on the standard either but instead, they have integrated various patches in projects, such as the Linux kernel or other packages and even documentation. These are not the workgroups that this section is referring to. This section only takes LSB-related workgroups into account.

From time to time, whenever a new specification document is released, a testing kit is also made available to vendors to test the kit's compliance to a particular version. The vendors could test their product compliance, which can be in the form of an application or a Linux distribution. The result of the testing kit is a certification that indicates that their product is LSB certified. For an application we, of course, have an **LSB Application Testkit**. There is also a similar one for a Linux distribution as well as others that are available for a variety of distributions.

For vendors who are interested in optional modules, these are not only available to help vendors prepare their future LSB compliance certification, but also to expose them to optional modules in order to get more vocal reviews and contributions from them. Also, the vendor's vote is related to the existence of these modules in future LSB specification documentations whose release is also important. The vendors could establish whether one optional module is eligible for future inclusions or not.

The LSB workgroup is governed by the Steering Committee and is led by a Chairperson who is elected. These two entities represent the interests of the workgroup. The workgroup operates on a rough consensus model. This indicates the solution of the group regarding a particular problem, that is, a solution that is determined by the elected Chairperson. If the contributor does not consider their decision and does not meet the criteria required to reach a rough consensus, then the Steering committee is appealed.

All business that is specific to the LSB workgroup is carried out inside an open forum. It can include a mailing list, conference, wiki page, or even a face-to-face meeting; the activities are not closed for members of workgroups. Also, membership is not restricted and decisions are clearly documented because there is always a possibility of having a further discussion on a particular subject at a later time.

There are clearly defined roles in workgroups:

- **Contributor**: This refers to actively involved individuals. They always have list with them available for the Chairperson, but any individual may request inclusion to the Contributors list.
- **Chairperson**: This refers to the representative Project leader. A person is elected to this position by Contributors and approved by the Steering Committee and the Linux Foundation board. Once elected, they are able to hold this position for two years. There is no limit to the number of times someone can be elected. Removal from this position can occur in case of a lack of confidence on behalf of the Steering Committee or the Linux Foundation board. After the position is vacant, a new election is carried out. During the vacancy period, the Steering Committee will assign an acting Chairperson.
- **Election Committee**: This refers to a committee of Contributors that are established by the Steering Committee for Chairperson election. It is responsible for selecting candidates for the position of Chairperson within at least 30 days before the Chairperson's term expires or 10 days after the Chairperson's position is vacant. It is responsible for conducting elections, which is done through electronic ballots. There is only one vote accepted from an individual; the votes are secret and only done by eligible members. The voting period is one week, and then the results are presented to the Steering Committee, which approves the votes and declares the winner.
- **Steering Committee**: It consists of representative workgroup stakeholders. They may be distribution vendors, OEMs, ISVs, upstream developers, and the Chairpersons of the LSB sub workgroups that come under the LSB charter. The committee is appointed by the Chairperson and depending on their involvement in workgroup activities, they can keep the position indefinitely. One member can be removed from the Steering Committee by three entities: the Chairperson, the other Steering Committee members, or by the Linux Foundation board.

Here is an image depicting a more detailed structure of the LSB workgroup:

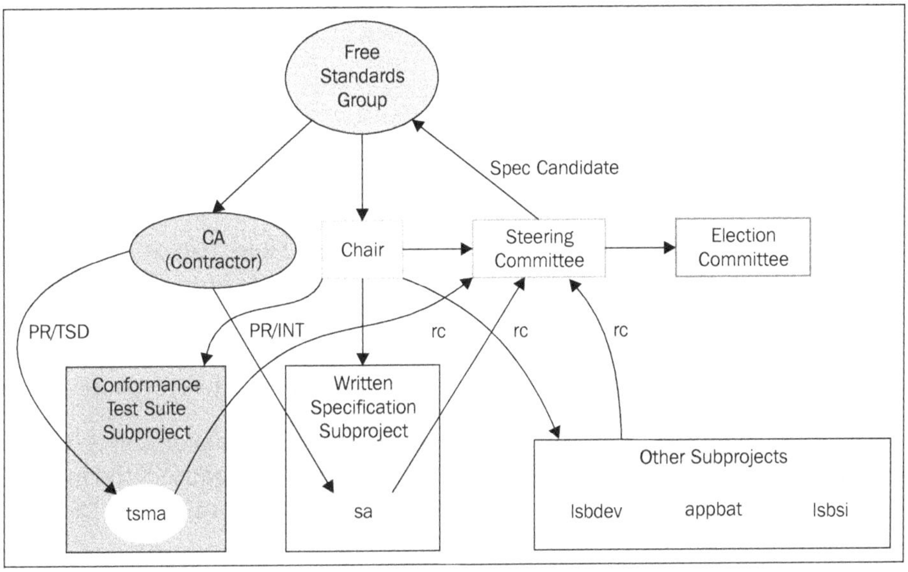

The LSB is a fairly complex structure, as depicted in the preceding image, so more roles can be defined in a workgroup if necessary. The main focus of the workgroup remains its mission; for this to be achievable, new workgroups need to be promoted and nurtured. They require a certain level of independence, but also be accountable for the activities done in the LSB Chairperson. This mainly involves making sure that certain deadlines are met and that the project sticks to its roadmap.

The first step in the interaction process with the LSB deliverables should be establishing the exact LSB requirements that need to be met by a target system. The specifications are available as two components: architecture-dependent and architecture-independent, or as it is also called, a generic component. The architecture-dependent components contain three modules:

- Core
- C++
- Desktop

Architecture independent components contain five modules:

- Core
- C++
- Desktop
- Printing
- Languages

There is, of course, another structure used to order them. Here, I am referring to the fact that some of these are mandatory and others are in a state of trial and testing. The first category is in order to have a distribution that is compliant with LSB standards, while the second category is not a strict requirement for having a compliant distribution that could represent future candidates for the next few versions of LSB.

The following image represents the key deliverable components of LSB. I hope it guides you through the components of this project as well as gathers the information that you need for future interaction with the various components of the LSB workgroup.

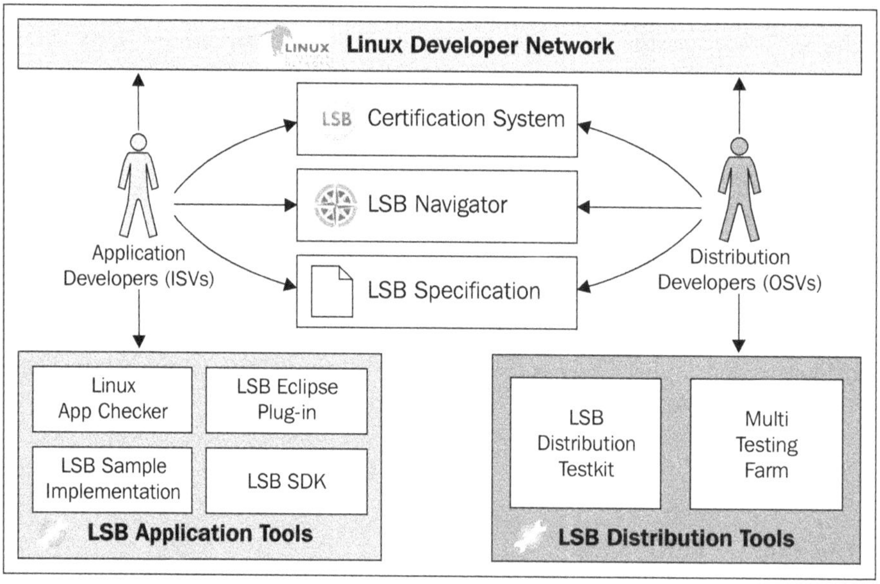

Depending on the interest of users, they can chose to either interact with the distribution development or the development of the components of an application. As clearly depicted in the preceding image, each of the two roads has its tools for the job. Before starting a job, make sure that you take a look at the website of the LSB Navigator and gather the required information. For users who are interested in a demonstration of LSB navigator, there is one available in the following link that also involves the interaction of Yocto. Make sure that you check it out and interact with it to get an idea of how it works.

> The LSB Navigator can be accessed at `http://www.linuxbase.org/navigator/commons/welcome.php`.

Let's assume that the interaction is already done and you are now interested in collaborating with this project. Of course, there are multiple methods to do this. Whether you are a developer or a software vendor, your feedback is always helpful for any project. Also, for developers who would like to contribute with code, there are multiple components and tools that could benefit from your help. That is not all. There are a lot of testing frameworks and testing infrastructures that always require improvements, so someone can contribute not only with code but also bug fixing and development or the testing of tools. Also, remember that your feedback is always appreciated.

Before moving to the next section, I want to introduce one more thing. As depicted in the previous diagram, any activity that is executed by a developer, with regard to the components of the LSB workgroup, should be done after the LSB specifications are inspected and the appropriate version is selected. For example, in the CGL Specifications, there is an explicit requirement of at least LSB 3.0, as well as the required modules, that are indicated in the same requirement description. For developers who want more information about the required specification and its components, refer to `http://refspecs.linuxfoundation.org/lsb.shtml`. Make sure that you also inspect the progress made on the newly available LSB 5 specifications, which passed the beta stage and, at the moment, is in its RC1 state. More information about this is available at `https://www.linuxfoundation.org/collaborate/workgroups/lsb/lsb-50-rc1`.

[More information about the LSB is available at `http://www.linuxfoundation.org/collaborate/workgroups/lsb`.]

Carrier grade options

Multiple options will be discussed in this section, and we'll start by defining the term *carrier grade*. This seems like the perfect start. So, what does this term mean in a telecommunications environment? It refers to a system, software, and even hardware components that are really reliable. Here, I am not referring only to the five-nines or six-nines that CGL provides because not all industries and scenarios require this kind of reliability. We are only going to refer to something that can be defined as reliable in the scope of a project. For a system, software, or hardware component to be defined as carrier grade, it should also prove itself as well tested along with all sorts of functionalities, such as high availability, fault tolerance, and so on.

These five-nines and six-nines refer to the fact that a product is available 99.999 or 99.9999 percent of the time. This translates per year in a downtime of around 5 minutes for five-nines and 30 seconds for six-nines requirements. Having explained this, I will move on and present the available options of carrier grade.

Carrier Grade Linux

It is the first and oldest option available. It appeared as a necessity for the telecommunication industry in order to define a set of specifications, which in turn defined a set of standards for Linux-based operating systems. After implementations, this would make the system carrier grade capable.

The motivation behind the CGL is to present an open architecture as a possible solution or an alternative to the already available proprietary and closed source available solutions that were already available in telecommunication systems. The open architecture alternative is the best not only because it avoids a monolithically form, is not hard to maintain, scale, and develop, but also it offers the advantage of speed. It is faster and cheaper to have a system that is decoupled and makes its components accessible to a larger number of software or hardware engineers. All of these components would be able to serve the same purpose in the end.

The workgroup was initially started by the **Open Source Development Lab** (**OSDL**), which after its merger with Free Standards Group formed The Linux Foundation. Now all the work moved there together with the workgroup. The latest available release for CGL is 5.0 and it includes registered Linux distributions, such as Wind River, MontaVista, and Red Flag.

The OSDL CGL workgroup has three categories of applications that CGL could fit into:

- **Signalling server applications**: This includes products that provide control services for calls and services, such as routing, session control, and status. These products usually handle a large number of connections, around 10000 or 100000 simultaneous ones, and also because that they have real-time requirements that require obtaining results from processes under a millisecond.
- **Gateway applications**: These provide the bridging of technology and administrative domains. Besides the characteristics that have been mentioned already, these handle a large number of connections in a real-time environment over a not very large number of interfaces. These are also required to not lose frames or packages in the communication process.
- **Management applications**: These usually provide billing operations, network management, and other traditional services. They does not have the same strong requirements for real-time operations, but instead, concentrate on fast database operations and other communication-oriented requests.

To make sure that it is able to satisfy the preceding categories, the CGL workgroup focuses on two main activities. The first one involves communicating with all the preceding categories, the identification of their requirements, and the writing specifications that should be implemented by distribution vendors. The second one involves gathering and helping projects that meet the requirements defined in the specifications. As a conclusion to what I mentioned previously, CGL tries to represent not only the telecommunication industry representatives and Linux distributions, but also end users and service providers; it also provides carrier grade options for each one of these categories.

Each distribution vendor who wants to get the CGL certification offers its implementation as a template. It is filled with versions of packages, names, and other extra information. However, it does this without disclosing too much information about the implementation process; these packages have the possibility of being proprietary software. Also, the disclosed information is owned and maintained by the vendor. The CGL workgroup only displays the link offered by the vendor.

The specification document is now at version 5.0 and contains both requirements that are, in fact, mandatory for applications or optional and are related to the implementations made in the Linux distribution for a carrier grade certification. The mandatory ones are described by the P1 priority level and the optional ones are marked as P2. The other elements are related to the gap aspect that represents a functionality, which is not implemented since an open source implementation is not available for it. The requirements are presented in the specification document to motivate distribution developers contribute to them.

As depicted in the following image and as emphasized in the information contained in the specification document, the CGL system should provide a large number of functionalities:

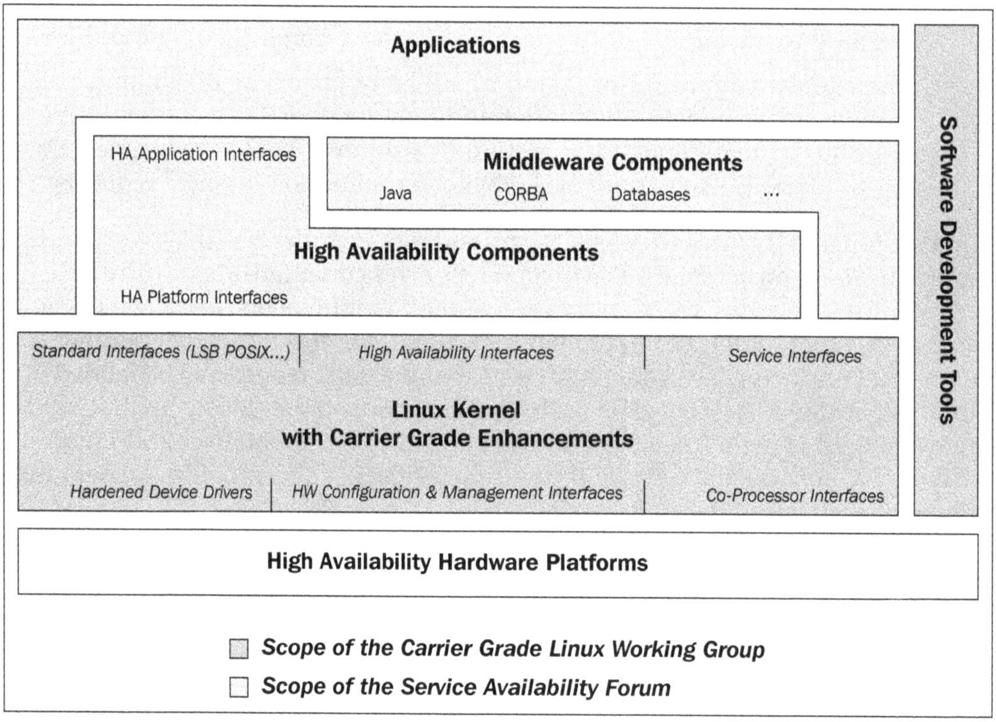

Since the requirement for number of functionalities is big, the workgroup decided to group them into various categories as follows:

- **Availability**: It is relevant for single node availability and recovery.
- **Clustering**: It describes components that are useful in building a cluster from individual systems. The key target behind this is the high availability of the system and load balancing that could also bring some performance improvements.

- **Serviceability**: It covers the maintenance and servicing features of the system.
- **Performance**: It describes features, such as real-time requirements and others, that could help the system attain better performance.
- **Standards**: These are provided as references to various APIs, standards, and specifications.
- **Hardware**: It presents various hardware-specific support that is necessary for a carrier grade operating system. Much of it comes from hardware vendors who are themselves involved in this process and the requirements from this section has been highly diminished in the latest CGL specification release.
- **Security**: It represents the relevant features needed to build a secure system.

> For more information on CGL requirements, refer to `https://www.linuxfoundation.org/sites/main/files/CGL_5.0_Specification.pdf`. You can also refer to the CGL workgroup at `https://www.linuxfoundation.org/collaborate/workgroups/cgl`.

Automotive Grade Linux

Automotive Grade Linux is also a Linux Foundation workgroup. It is newly formed and tries to offer an open source solution that has automotive applications. Its primary focus is the In-Vehicle-Infotainment sector, but it includes telematics systems and instrument clusters. It efforts are based on open source components that are already available. These are suitable for its purposes and try to also enable rapid development, which is much needed in this industry.

The goals of the workgroup are:

- A transparent, collaborative, and open environment for involved elements.
- A Linux operating system stack that is focused on automotives and uses the open source community represented by exponents, such as developers, academic components, and companies as back support.
- A collective voice for interaction in the open source community released this time in the reverse form, from the AGL to the community.
- An embedded Linux distribution used for fast prototyping.

By using projects, such as Tizen, as the reference distribution and having projects, such as Jaguar, Nissan, Land Rover, or Toyoto, this project is interesting enough to be followed closely. It has just been developed but has potential for improvements. For those of you interested in it, refer to `https://www.linuxfoundation.org/collaborate/workgroups/automotive-grade-linux`. The project's wiki page is an interesting resource and can be consulted at `https://wiki.automotivelinux.org/`.

Carrier Grade Virtualization

The recent development of CGL made virtualization an interesting option for the carrier grade field because it involved a reduction in costs as well as transparency in leveraging multicore equipment that runs single-core designed applications. Virtualization options also needed to meet the same expectations as the other carrier grade systems.

Carrier Grade Virtualization has tried to become a vital component to be integrated in carrier grade platforms that are already available. This is done to preserve the attributes and performance of the system. It also tries to extend the appliance target and permits **Original Equipment Manufacturer** (**OEM**) to derive the benefits from the same support as the CGL. These benefits are in the form of well established targets.

Virtualization's application is more widespread, which can be seen ranging from the x86 architecture to ARM and DSP-based processors as well as a variety of domains. The examination of virtualization from a carrier grade point of view is the focus of this solution because, in this way, you can get a clearer perspective of the areas that require improvements. In this way, these can be identified and enhancements can also be applied as required. Unfortunately, this initiative has not been as exposed as some other ones, but is still a very good source of documentation and is available from virtualLogix at `http://www.linuxpundit.com/documents/CGV_WP_Final_FN.pdf`. I hope you enjoy its content.

Specific support for the Yocto Project

In the Poky reference system, support is provided for the development of LSB and LSB compatible applications. Inside Poky, there is a special `poky-lsb.conf` distribution policy configuration that is defined in case a distribution is interested in developing applications that are LSB-compliant. This holds true when generating a Linux distribution that is LSB-compliant or at least prepares to take the LSB certification. The build steps required for a Linux distribution that prepares for an LSB certification will be presented here. In case you are interested in developing LSB-compliant applications, the process is simpler and will also be briefly presented here; however, it is in contrast to the former.

The first step is simple: it only requires cloning the poky repository and the `meta-qt3` dependency layer because of the requirements of the LSB modules:

```
git clone git://git.yoctoproject.org/poky.git
git clone git://git.yoctoproject.org/meta-qt3
```

Next, the build directory needs to be created:

```
source oe-init-build-env -b ../build_lsb
```

Inside the `conf/bblayers.conf` file, only the `meta-qt3` layer needs to be added. Inside the `conf/local.conf` file, the corresponding machine should be selected. I would suggest a capable platform, but using an emulated architecture, such as `qemuppc`, ought to be enough for such a demo if enough CPU power and memory is offered to it. Also, make sure that you change the `DISTRO` variable to `poky-lsb`. Having all these in place, the build process can start. The command necessary for this is is:

```
bitbake core-image-lsb
```

After the resulting binaries are generated and booted on the selected machine, the user is able to either run all the tests using the `LSB_Test.sh` script, which also sets the LSB test framework environment, or run specific test suites:

```
/usr/bin/LSB_Test.sh
```

You can also use the following command:

```
cd /opt/lsb/test/manager/utils
./dist-checker.pl -update
./dist-checker.pl -D -s 'LSB 4.1' <test_suite>
```

If various tests are not passing, the system needs to be reconfigured to ensure the required compatibility level. Inside `meta/recipes-extended/images`, besides the core-`image-lsb.bb` recipes, there are also two similar recipes:

- `core-image-lsb-sdk.bb`: It includes a `meta-toolchain` and the necessary libraries and development headers that are needed to generate an SDK for application development
- `core-image-lsb-dev.bb`: It is suitable for development work on targets since it includes `dev-pkgs`, which exposes the necessary headers and libraries for image-specific packages

Inside the Yocto Project, is a layer defined as `meta-cgl`, which intends to be the stepping stone for the CGL initiative. It aggregates all the available and required packages defined by the CGL workgroup. This layer's format tries to set the stage for the next implementations that will be made to support CGL on various machines. Inside the `meta-cgl` layer, there are two subdirectories:

- `meta-cgl-common`: It is the focus place of the activity and the subdirectory that offers support for machines available inside poky, such as `qemuarm`, `qemuppc`, and so on.
- `meta-cgl-fsl-ppc`: It is a subdirectory that defines BSP-specific support. Such layers should be made available if the support for other machines is required.

As I've already mentioned, the `meta-cgl` layer is responsible for the CGL support. As mentioned previously, one of the requirements of CGL is to have LSB support and this support is available inside Poky. It is integrated inside this layer as a specific requirement. Another recommendation for the `meta-cgl` layer is to group all the available packages into package groups that define various categories. The available package groups are very generic, but all the available ones are integrated in a core one called `packagegroup-cgl.bb`.

The layer also exposes a CGL-compliant operating system image. This image tries to include various CGL-specific requirements for starters, and intends to grow by including all the requirements defined in the CGL specification document. Besides the resultant Linux operating system that will be compliant with the CGL requirements and is ready for the CGL certification, the layer also tries to define a CGL-specific testing framework. The task may seem similar to the one required for the LSB checking compliance, but I assure you it is not. It not only requires a CGL-specific language definition that has to be made according to the defined specifications, but also a number of tests definitions that should be in sync with what the language defines. Also, there are requirements that could be met with one package or the functionality of a package and these things should be gathered together and combined. There are various other scenarios that can be interpreted and answered correctly; this is a condition that makes the testing of CGL a hard task to accomplish.

Inside the `meta-cgl` layer, there are recipes for the following packages:

- `cluster-glue`
- `cluster-resource-agents`
- `corosync`
- `heartbeat`
- `lksctp-tools`
- `monit`
- `ocfs2-tools`
- `openais`
- `pacemaker`
- `openipmi`

Besides these recipes, there are also other ones that are necessary for various CGL requirements. The fact that the `meta-cgl` initiative is shown in the support it offers as described in the previous sections. It is not complete but it will be in time. It will also contain these packages:

- `evlog`
- `mipv6-daemon-umip`
- `makedumpfile`

All of these are necessary to offer a Linux-based operating system that has LSB support and CGL compliance. This will be carried out in time, and maybe by the time this book reaches your hands, the layer will be in its final format and be the standard for CGL compliance.

I will now start to explain a couple of packages that you might come across in the CGL environment. I will first start with the Heartbeat daemon, which provides communication and membership for cluster services. Having it in place will enable clients to determine the present state of the processes available on other machines and establish communication with them.

To make sure that the Heartbeat daemon is useful, it needs to be put together with a **Cluster Resource Manager** (**CRM**), which is the component responsible for starting and stopping various services to obtain a highly available Linux system. This CRM was called **Pacemaker** and it was unable to detect resource-level fails and was only able to interact with two nodes. In time, it evolved, and it now has better support and additional user interfaces available. Some of these services are as follows:

- **crm shell**: It is a command-line interface realized by Dejan Muhamedagic to hide the XML configuration and help with interactions.
- **The high availability web console**: It is an AJAX frontend
- **Heartbeat GUI**: It is an advanced XML editor that offers a lot of relevant information
- **Linux Cluster Management Console (LCMC)**: It started as **DRBD-Management Console** (**DRBD-MC**) and is a Java platform that is used for the management purposes of Pacemaker.

Pacemaker accepts three types of resource agents (a resource agent represents a standard interface between the cluster resources). The Resource Agents is a project that is also managed by Linux-HA. It is available and maintained by the guys at ClusterLabs. Depending on the type that is selected, it is able to perform operation, such as start/stop for a given resource, monitor, validation, and so on. The Resource Agents that are supported are:

- LSB Resource Agents
- OCF Resource Agents
- The legacy Heartbeat Resource Agent

Cluster Glue is a set of libraries, utilities, and tools used in conjuncture with Pacemaker/Heartbeat. It is the glue that basically puts everything together between the cluster resource manager (I am referring to Pacemaker) and the messaging layer (which could be Heartbeat). It is now managed as a separate component by the Linux-HA subproject, although it started as a component of Heartbeat. It has a number of interesting components:

- **Local Resource Manager (LRM)**: It acts as an interface between Pacemaker and the Resource Agent and is not cluster-aware. Its tasks include the processing of commands received from the CRM, passing them to the resource agent, and reporting these activities.
- **Shoot The Other Node In The Head (STONITH)**: It is a mechanism used for the purpose of node fencing by making a node that is considered dead by a cluster so that it can be removed from it and prevent any interaction risks.
- **hb_report**: It is an error reporting utility often used for bug fixing and isolation problems.
- **Cluster Plumbing Library**: It is a low-level intercluster communication library.

> For more information related to Linux-HA the following link could be of help: `http://www.linux-ha.org/doc/users-guide/users-guide.html`

The next element is the Corosync cluster engine. It is a project derived from OpenAIS, which will be presented shortly. It is a Group Communication System with a set of features and implementations that try to offer high-availability support and is licensed under BSD. Its features include the following:

- An availability manager for the restarting of an application in case of failure.
- A quorum system that notifies about the state of a quorum and whether it's been achieved or not.
- A closed process group communication model with support for synchronization to replicate state machines.
- A configuration and statistics database that resides in the memory. It provides the ability to receive, retrieve, set, and change various notifications.

Next, we'll take a look at OpenAIS. It is the open implementation for **Application Interface Specification** (**AIS**) provided by **Service Availability Forum** (**SA** or **SA Forum** as it is also called). It represents an interface that provides high-availability support. The source code available in OpenAIS was refactored over time in OpenAIS and only remained SA Forum-specific APIs and in Corosync. It was also placed in all the core infrastructure components. OpenAIS is very similar to Heartbeat; it is, in fact, an alternative to it, which is industry standard-specific. It is also supported by Pacemaker.

> More information about AIS can be found by referring to its Wikipedia page and the SA Forum web site at `http://www.saforum.org/page/16627~217404/Service-Availability-Forum-Application-Interface-Specification`.

Next is the `ocfs2-tools` package. It is a collection of utilities that enable the work to be done with the OCFS2 filesystem in the form of creating, debugging, repairing, or managing it. It includes tools that are very similar to the ones a Linux user is accustomed to, such as `mkfs.ocfs2`, `mount.ocfs2 fsck.ocfs2`, `tunefs.ocfs2`, and `debugfs.ocfs2`.

Oracle Cluster File System (**OCFS**) was the first shared disk filesystem developed by Oracle and was released under GNU General Public License. It was not a POSIX compliant filesystem, but this changed when OCFS2 appeared and was integrated into the Linux kernel. In time, it became a distributed lock manager capable of providing both high availability and high performance. It is now used in a variety of places, such as virtualization, database clusters, and middleware, and appliances. These are some of its most notable features:

- Optimized allocations
- REFLINKs
- Metadata checksums
- Indexed directories
- Extended attributes per inode
- User and group quotas
- Advanced security, such as SELinux and POSIX ACLs support
- Cluster-aware tools such as the ones mentioned previously and include mkfs, tunefs, fsck, mount, and debugfs
- In-built Clusterstack with a Distributed Lock Manager
- Journaling

- Variable block and cluster size
- Buffered, memory mapped, splice, direct, asynchronous I/Os
- Architecture and endian neutral

The `lksctp-tools` package is a Linux user space utility that includes a library and appropriate C language headers for the purpose of interaction with the SCTP interface. The Linux kernel has had support for SCTP since the 2.6 release, so the existence of the user space compatibility tools is no surprise for anyone. Lksctp offers access to the SCTP socket-based API. The implementation is made according to the IETF Internet draft available at `http://tools.ietf.org/html/draft-ietf-tsvwg-sctpsocket-15`. It provides a flexible and consistent method of developing socket-based applications that takes advantage of **Stream Control Transmission Protocol (SCTP)**.

SCTP is a message-oriented transport protocol. As a transport layer protocol, it runs over IPv4 or Ipv6 implementations and besides the functionality of TCP, it also provides support for these features:

- Multistreaming
- Message framing
- Multihoming
- Ordered and unordered message delivery
- Security and authentication

These special features are necessary for industry carrier graded systems and are used in fields such as telephony signaling.

> More information about SCTP is available at `http://www.ietf.org/rfc/rfc2960.txt` and `http://www.ietf.org/rfc/rfc3286.txt`

Now, I will change the pace a bit and explain **monit**, a very small yet powerful utility to monitor and manage the system. It is very useful in automatic maintenance and repairing Unix systems, such as BSD distribution, various Linux distributions, and other platforms that can include OS X. It can be used for a large variety of tasks ranging from file monitoring, changes in filesystems, and interaction with event processes if various thresholds were passed.

It is easy to configure and control monit since all the configurations are based on a token-oriented syntax that is easy to grasp. Also, it offers a variety of logs and notifications about its activities. It also provides a web browser interface for easier access. So, having a general system resource manager, which is also easy to interact with, makes monit an option for a carrier graded Linux system. If you are interested in finding more about it, access the project's website at `http://mmonit.com/monit/`.

OpenIPMI is an implementation of **Intelligent Platform Management Interface (IPMI)** that tries to offers access to all the functionalities of IPMI and also offers abstractions for easier usage. It is comprised of two components:

- A kernel driver insertable in the Linux kernel
- A library that offers the abstraction functionality of IPMI and also provides access to various services used by an operating system

IPMI represents a set of computer interface specifications that try to reduce the total cost of ownership by offering an intelligent and autonomous system that is able to monitor and manage the capabilities of the host system. Here, we are referring to only about an operating system but also the firmware and CPU itself. The development of this intelligent interface was led by Intel and is now supported by an impressive number of companies.

> More information about IPMI, OpenIMPI, and other supported IPMI drivers and functionality are available at `http://openipmi.sourceforge.net/` and `http://www.intel.com/content/www/us/en/servers/ipmi/ipmi-home.html`.

There are some of packages that also should be present in the `meta-cgl` layer, but at the time of writing this chapter, they were still not available there. I will start with `mipv6-daemon-umip`, which tries to provide data distribution for **Mobile Internet Protocol version 6 (MIPv6)** daemons. **UMIP** is an open source Mobile IPv6 stack for Linux based on MIPL2 and maintains the latest kernel versions. The packages is a set of patches for MIPL2 by the **UniverSAl playGround for Ipv6 (USAGI)** Project, which tries to offers industry ready quality for IPsec (for both IPv6 and IPv4 options) and IPv6 protocol stack implementations for the Linux system.

> More information about UMIP is available at `http://umip.linux-ipv6.org/index.php?n=Main.Documentation`.

Makedumfile is a tool that offers the possibility of compressing the size of dump files and can also exclude memory pages that are not required for analysis. For some of the Linux distributions, it comes along with a package called `kexec-tools` that can be installed in your distribution using RPM, the package manager supported by the carrier graded specifications. It is quite similar to commands, such as `gzip` or `split`. The fact that it receives input only from files an ELF format, makes it the first choice for `kdumps`.

Another interesting project is `evlog`, a **Linux Event Logging system** for Enterprise-class systems. It also is compliant with POSIX standards and provides logging for a variety of forms that range from `printk` to `syslog` as well as other kernel and user space functions. The output events are available in a POSIX-compliant format. It also offers support while selecting logs that match certain defined filters or even register a special event format. These can only be notified about when the registered event filter is met. Its features certainly make this package interesting and are available at `http://evlog.sourceforge.net/`.

There are a number of other packages that could be included into the `meta-cgl` layer. Taking a look at the registered CGL distribution could help you understand the complexity of such a project. For easier access to this list, refer to `http://www.linuxfoundation.org/collaborate/workgroups/cgl/registered-distributions` in order to simplify the search procedure.

To interact with the `meta-cgl` layer, the first necessary step would be to make sure that all the interdependent layers are available. The latest information about how to build a carrier graded compatible Linux image is always available in the attached `README` file. I've also given you an example here for purpose of demonstrating it:

```
git clone git://git.yoctoproject.org/poky.git
cd ./poky
git clone git://git.yoctoproject.org /meta-openembedded.git
git clone git://git.enea.com/linux/meta-cgl.git
git clone git://git.yoctoproject.org/meta-qt3
git clone git://git.yoctoproject.org/meta-virtualization
git clone git://git.yoctoproject.org/meta-selinux
git clone git://git.yoctoproject.org/meta-cloud-services
git clone git://git.yoctoproject.org/meta-security
git clone https://github.com/joaohf/meta-openclovis.git
```

Next, the build directory needs to be created and configured:

```
source oe-init-build-env -b ../build_cgl
```

Inside the `conf/bblayers.conf` file, these are the layers that need to be added:

```
meta-cgl/meta-cgl-common
meta-qt3
meta-openembedded/meta-networking
meta-openembedded/meta-filesystems
meta-openembedded/meta-oe
meta-openembedded/meta-perl
meta-virtualization
meta-openclovis
meta-selinux
meta-security
meta-cloud-services/meta-openstack
```

Inside the `conf/local.conf` file, the corresponding machine should be selected. I would suggest `qemuppc`, as well as the `DISTRO` variable that can be changed to `poky-cgl.` `BBMASK` should be made available due to duplication of recipes:

```
BBMASK = "meta-openembedded/meta-oe/recipes-support/multipath-
tools"
```

Having all these place, the build process can start. The necessary command for this is:

```
bitbake core-image-cgl
```

Make sure that you have time to spend on this because the build could take a while, depending on the configuration of your host system.

Summary

In this chapter, you were presented with information about the specifications required for the Carrier Grade Linux and Linux Standard Base. Other options, such as Automotive Grade and Carrier Grade Virtualization, were also explained and in the end, support for the Yocto Project and a couple of demonstrations were shown to you to complete this learning process.

This is the last chapter of this book and I hope you've enjoyed the journey. Also, I hope I was able to pass on some of the information I have acquired on to you. Since we're at the end of this book, I must admit that I have also learned and gathered new information in the process of writing the book. I hope that you catch the Yocto bug as well and are also able to add your contributions to the Yocto Project and the open source community in general. I am confident that from now on, the embedded world holds fewer secrets for you. Make sure you shed some light about this topic on others too!

Index

Symbol

A

B

C

D

E

F

G

H

I

M

N

Q

R

S

V

W

X

Y

Thank you for buying
Learning Embedded Linux Using the Yocto Project

About Packt Publishing

Packt, pronounced 'packed', published its first book, *Mastering phpMyAdmin for Effective MySQL Management*, in April 2004, and subsequently continued to specialize in publishing highly focused books on specific technologies and solutions.

Our books and publications share the experiences of your fellow IT professionals in adapting and customizing today's systems, applications, and frameworks. Our solution-based books give you the knowledge and power to customize the software and technologies you're using to get the job done. Packt books are more specific and less general than the IT books you have seen in the past. Our unique business model allows us to bring you more focused information, giving you more of what you need to know, and less of what you don't.

Packt is a modern yet unique publishing company that focuses on producing quality, cutting-edge books for communities of developers, administrators, and newbies alike. For more information, please visit our website at `www.packtpub.com`.

About Packt Open Source

In 2010, Packt launched two new brands, Packt Open Source and Packt Enterprise, in order to continue its focus on specialization. This book is part of the Packt Open Source brand, home to books published on software built around open source licenses, and offering information to anybody from advanced developers to budding web designers. The Open Source brand also runs Packt's Open Source Royalty Scheme, by which Packt gives a royalty to each open source project about whose software a book is sold.

Writing for Packt

We welcome all inquiries from people who are interested in authoring. Book proposals should be sent to `author@packtpub.com`. If your book idea is still at an early stage and you would like to discuss it first before writing a formal book proposal, then please contact us; one of our commissioning editors will get in touch with you.

We're not just looking for published authors; if you have strong technical skills but no writing experience, our experienced editors can help you develop a writing career, or simply get some additional reward for your expertise.

[PACKT] open source
community experience distilled
PUBLISHING

Linux Shell Scripting Cookbook

Second Edition

ISBN: 978-1-78216-274-2 Paperback: 384 pages

Over 110 practical recipes to solve real-world shell problems, guaranteed to make you wonder how you ever lived without them

1. Master the art of crafting one-liner command sequence to perform text processing, digging data from files, backups to sysadmin tools, and a lot more.
2. And if powerful text processing isn't enough, see how to make your scripts interact with the web-services like Twitter, Gmail.
3. Explores the possibilities with the shell in a simple and elegant way - you will see how to effectively solve problems in your day to day life.

Linux Shell Scripting Cookbook

ISBN: 978-1-84951-376-0 Paperback: 360 pages

Solve real-world shell scripting problems with over 110 simple but incredibly effective recipes

1. Master the art of crafting one-liner command sequence to perform tasks such as text processing, digging data from files, and lot more.
2. Practical problem solving techniques adherent to the latest Linux platform.
3. Packed with easy-to-follow examples to exercise all the features of the Linux shell scripting language.

Please check **www.PacktPub.com** for information on our titles

www.ingramcontent.com/pod-product-compliance
Lightning Source LLC
Chambersburg PA
CBHW080928060326
40690CB00042B/3166
* 9 7 8 1 7 8 4 3 9 7 3 9 5 *